READING TRAUMA NARRATIVES

Reading Trauma Narratives

The Contemporary Novel & the Psychology of Oppression

LAURIE VICKROY

University of Virginia Press Charlottesville and London

University of Virginia Press
© 2015 by the Rector and Visitors of the University of Virginia
All rights reserved
Printed in the United States of America on acid-free paper

First published 2015

9 8 7 6 5 4 3 2

Library of Congress Cataloging-in-Publication Data
Vickroy, Laurie, 1954–
    Reading trauma narratives / Laurie Vickroy.
        pages   cm
    Includes bibliographical references and index.
    ISBN 978-0-8139-3737-3 (cloth : acid-free paper) — ISBN 978-0-8139-3738-0 (pbk. : acid-free paper) — ISBN 978-0-8139-3739-7 (e-book)
    1. American fiction—20th century—History and criticism. 2. Psychic trauma in literature. 3. Narration (Rhetoric) 4. Psychology in literature. 5. Modernism (Literature) 6. English fiction—20th century—History and criticism. 7. Canadian fiction—20th century—History and criticism. I. Title.
    PS374.P69V53 2015
    813'.509353—dc23

2015016448

For Tony and the dispossessed

Contents

Preface ix

INTRODUCTION
Ways of Reading Trauma in Literary Narratives 1

ONE
Re-creating the Split Self in Margaret Atwood's
The Blind Assassin and *Alias Grace* 33

TWO
Fear and Commodification in the Shaping of America
in Toni Morrison's *Paradise* and *A Mercy* 66

THREE
Obsessions and Possessions in William Faulkner's
Absalom, Absalom! 100

FOUR
The Traumas of Love and Death in Jeanette Winterson's
Written on the Body 132

FIVE
Trauma, Gender, and Commodification in Chuck Palahniuk's
Fight Club and *Invisible Monsters* 154

CONCLUSION
Trauma as a Critical Juncture of Society, Culture,
and Human Psychology 179

Notes 185
Bibliography 187
Index 195

Preface

You write in order to change the world, knowing perfectly well that you probably can't, but also knowing that literature is indispensable to the world. . . . The world changes according to the way people see it, and if you alter, even by a millimeter, the way . . . people look at reality, then you can change it.
—JAMES BALDWIN

Psychological trauma remains a compelling and vital human phenomenon and subject of inquiry. Traumatic reactions are indicators of how people face extreme circumstances that are often human-made. Many possible situations of trauma, of violence, social neglect, and commodification, endure in a world of increasing inequity. Further investigations of these contexts and their effects may help raise questions about these situations, help avoid them in the future, and mitigate the propensity to blame victims. Though severe, traumatic experience also provides insight into more common defensive human responses to stress.

In the past twenty years the abundance of artistic and scholarly work published on the causes and effects of trauma testifies to the many permutations and complexities of the experience of trauma and questions raised by traumatic experiences. Influential contemporary humanist monographs in trauma studies include J. Brooks Bouson's *Quiet As It's Kept: Shame, Trauma, and Race in the Novels of Toni Morrison* (2000); Cathy Caruth's *Unclaimed Experience: Trauma, Narrative, and History* (1996); Shoshana Felman and Dori Laub's *Testimony: Crises of Witnessing in Literature, Psychoanalysis, and History* (1991); Suzette Henke's *Shattered Subjects: Trauma and Testimony in Women's Life-Writing* (1998); and Kali Tal's *Worlds of Hurt: Reading the Literatures of Trauma* (1996). Some more recent contributions include Michelle

Balaev's *Contemporary Approaches to Trauma Theory* (2014); Jennifer L. Griffiths's *Traumatic Possessions: The Body and Memory in African American Women's Writing and Performance* (2009); Jill L. Matus's *Shock, Memory and the Unconscious in Victorian Fiction* (2009); and E. Ann Kaplan's *Trauma Culture: The Politics of Terror and Loss in Media and Literature* (2005). This study also joins an emerging branch of trauma studies that considers the ethical dimensions of trauma, such as how it is created, but also raises questions about not only the treatment of the traumatized but also how they in turn treat others. This last issue, trauma victims' treatment of others, can make an ethical evaluation of victims challenging, so keys to understanding trauma victims' behavior are indispensable.

My theoretical approach is multidisciplinary, so as to address a broad range of possible contexts and the extensive ramifications of trauma. I focus on psychological research because it considers the interrelationship of cultural, cognitive, and physiological contributions to the production and evaluation of emotions. Also, some psychologists suggest it is not fair to separate survivors' defensive behaviors from the social contexts creating them (see discussions of Root and Brown in chapter 1). Psychoanalysis, the framework for many humanist trauma studies, offers a relevant but narrower focus on original traumas and their repression and repetition, but this does not tell the whole story. Psychological frameworks share with trauma fiction an investigation of the situational and social variables shaping the experience of trauma survivors. They help reveal the many emotional, social, and cognitive implications of trauma. Narrative theory and its cognitive studies of readers support my analysis in enabling me to pinpoint the relationship of cognition and emotion in textual representations of characters and in the reading process. Narrative theorists have located storytelling methods that make aspects of fictional characters' minds available to readers, through their thought reports, social aspects of mind, focalizations, and the like (see chapter 1). These narrative strategies draw readers in and help them develop mental models of the characters and ascribe mental states and lived experience to the characters. Further, they stimulate readers' perceptual and ethical frameworks, and suggest ways to assess characters' behaviors in relation to these frameworks and to authors' rhetorical frameworks.

The writers whose work I examine in this book have made important contributions to the vast conversation about trauma by going beyond the most severe contexts of trauma—war, the Holocaust, rape—into realms of sexual, class, and racial traumas consequent on objectification under aggressively normalizing ideologies and the social mechanisms attached to those ideologies, which attempt to shape the individual into a psychically death-dealing functionality. Effective trauma fiction seems able to suggest connections and similar mechanisms affecting the individual and broader cultural pathologies. The psychological and experiential investigative framework that narrative theories provide makes these connections easier to see.

Trauma fiction provides scenarios that confront readers with subjective endurance in the face of crisis and conflict, representing how defensive responses are created out of many types of wounding. This fiction also provides a contemplative and experiential link to traumatic processes (Vickroy, *Trauma and Survival* 24), effectively charting the remnants of characters' traumas and fear-producing associations, as well as the fixed ideas that help them cope. These texts involve readers in the worlds that traumatized individuals try to construct for themselves, where they build psychological defenses against threats. Moreover, the books' narratives mimic aspects of traumatic experiences, such as fragmented thoughts or a dissociated outlook.

I have chosen to investigate novels by Margaret Atwood, Toni Morrison, William Faulkner, Jeanette Winterson, and Chuck Palahniuk that recognize trauma as an indicator of social injustice or oppression, and as the ultimate cost of destructive sociocultural institutions. Examining the details of traumatic experience in their own unique ways, these writers each uncover the powerful effects of social forces on individuals that warp or immobilize characters emotionally and perpetuate legacies of fear and destruction. I want readers to appreciate the ethical importance and psychic nuance of trauma fiction, in the ways such narratives depict the defenses and acting out that become part of the personalities of victims and illustrate the afflicted characters' difficulties in social and personal relational contexts. This study focuses in particular on the traumatic circumstances of objectification and its devastating effects on individual personality. However, on a more optimistic note, the works I consider also highlight individuals' struggles to maintain their humanity and resist forces of control and homogenization.

This study endeavors to assist scholarly and classroom communities in disentangling the complexities of these texts. It does so by employing theories of trauma, narrative, and cognition to analyze the ways in which these texts engage readers cognitively and ethically in a reading process that immerses them in, while providing perspective on, the flawed thinking and behavior of the traumatized, and by exploring how the psychology of fear drives individuals and society. By explaining these texts' gestures toward readers, I hope to help readers discover that these writers want readers to understand their own role in systems of power and how they have internalized systems' ideologies. The goal is to create public awareness in the hope that it might reduce people's complicity in these ideologies.

The introduction outlines the theoretical framework of this study in the course of defining and articulating the benefits of a trauma studies approach. The introduction articulates the problems revealed by trauma, establishes the capacity of literary narrative to express traumatic experience, and elucidates the methods I have developed from trauma and narrative theory and ethical studies to examine my chosen literary texts.

Chapter 1, "Re-creating the Split Self in Margaret Atwood's *The Blind Assassin* and *Alias Grace*," demonstrates that Atwood's works are particularly effective in examining the effects of trauma on human personality. This is explored through characters' split selves and focalization, dissociations, constricted emotions, distrust of others, and reduced capacity to love. Atwood wants to counteract the general public's impulse to blame victims and decontextualize victims' situations as a way to protect itself from feeling vulnerable. The large historical canvases of the two novels I discuss use the haunting pasts of the protagonists to reflect on societal problems and issues of justice and ethics.

Chapter 2, "Fear and Commodification in the Shaping of America in Toni Morrison's *Paradise* and *A Mercy*," shows how, by plunging readers into the survival modes of thinking that compromise "the individual's perceptual, decisional, and relational processes" (Root 247), Morrison establishes a framework whereby readers are better able to cognitively and emotionally reconstruct the psychological and environmental complexities that create and perpetuate trauma. Like Atwood, Morrison examines the exercise of power and how the damage to personality makes people replicate power relations in their personal lives. She engages readers with a simultaneously immersive and distanced perspective on traumatized individuals' flawed thinking. Such thinking is driven by wounding and fear, and perpetuates the characters' difficulties. Again like Atwood, Morrison wants readers to understand their own internalizations and the continuance of destructive social ideologies.

Chapter 3, "Obsessions and Possessions in William Faulkner's *Absalom, Absalom!*," examines Faulkner's representation of individuals as objectified and commodified in racialized capitalist and class systems that are themselves elaborate defenses against the recognition of their effects. Faulkner's novel unveils the traumatic origins of the elaborate illusions of Southern manhood, illustrated in the protagonist Thomas Sutpen's dream of success as a form of avoidance and denial. The narrative immerses readers in the fears and obsessions that powerfully motivate human belief and actions, and in the persistent repetitions and stasis Faulkner witnesses in Southern thought and behaviors. The novel calls our attention to trauma-induced silences around the effects of patriarchy, slavery, and miscegenation, effects that are elaborately unacknowledged, forbidden, and camouflaged to avoid the tragic consequences of rigidly drawn color lines.

Chapter 4, "The Traumas of Love and Death in Jeanette Winterson's *Written on the Body*," investigates Winterson's exploration of the emotional lives of adults neglected and abandoned as children in her novel, *Written on the Body*. This analysis demonstrates that such neglect prompts survivors' traumas, which characters act out in seeking and destroying attempts at love that deny them the love and recognition necessary to feel alive and needed. Their failures at love leave them empty, inducing a kind of emotional death. Winterson takes on nothing less than the traumas of love and death. Love, its pursuit and loss, is traumatic, particularly as love becomes associated with illness and death, but through the power of art and narrative the lover's imagination transforms and staves off death in the story world Winterson creates. Imagining, for protagonist and author, becomes a coping mechanism, and then a way of deferring death and recovering the beloved.

Chapter 5, "Trauma, Gender, and Commodification in Chuck Palahniuk's *Fight Club* and *Invisible Monsters*," analyzes Palahniuk's satirical—but with serious consequence to his characters—exploration of individuals' traumatic responses to the absence of parental and social regard. Palahniuk links these early disconnections to the objectification of individuals in late capitalist society and to the gender-specific pressures and coping mechanisms survivors adopt. His protagonists suffer failed recognition in their families, making them vulnerable to seeking comfort in their own commodification. As *Fight Club* deals with disrespect experienced by men, *Invisible Monsters* does the same for women, both attempting some redefinition of gender norms and identity.

Palahniuk demystifies contemporary culture in hilarious descriptions of body-torturing clothes that underscore the emptiness of a world that externalizes desire by compelling people to attain their desires by purchasing objects or images. These "purchases" are always soul-destroying and deprive individuals of any kind of internalized identity.

The goal of my study coincides with that of the fiction writers I examine here, and that is to help readers engage in an enhanced reading experience and thoughtful conversations about the complexities of these texts' representations of trauma, and of trauma itself. Like these writers, I hope to change public perceptions of trauma victims and survivors. For this to happen, readers must be brought into the fraught and split nature of this experience. They must also understand the relationship between the social environment and behavior that demonstrates to us how individual personality is reactive rather than a fixed trait. Eliminating this view of human personality as fixed would help promote a greater awareness of, and empathy toward, traumatic experience. It may also counter prejudices against victims and the absolutist thinking about human behavior that prevents us from seeing its true causes.

I am most appreciative of the scholars and writers who paved the way for my own examinations of trauma, whose insights I hope I have sufficiently acknowledged here. I am greatly indebted to the readers of my manuscript, whose meticulous critiques made this study more comprehensive, thoughtful, and accessible. I would also particularly like to thank members of the Contemporary Narrative in English Research Group at the University of Zaragoza, who invited me to speak at their "Ethics and Trauma" conference, particularly Francisco Collado-Rodríguez, Dolores Herrero, and Sonia Baelo-Allué. Their invitation reinvigorated my scholarship, and my collaborations with them inspired portions of the chapters on Morrison and Palahniuk. Portions of chapter 3 appeared in slightly different form in *Between the Urge to Know and the Need to Deny: Trauma and Ethics in Contemporary British and American Literature*, edited by M. Dolores Herrero and Sonia Baelo-Allué. Portions of chapter 6 appeared in slightly different form in *Chuck Palahniuk: Fight Club/Invisible Monsters/Choke*, edited by Francisco Collado-Rodríguez (Bloomsbury Press, 2013). I am also particularly grateful for the opportunities to collaborate with J. Brooks Bouson and appreciative of her work on trauma in the writings of Margaret Atwood and Toni Morrison. Portions of chapter 2 appeared in slightly different form in my chapter

"Sexual Trauma, Ethics, and the Reader in the Works of Margaret Atwood," in *Critical Insights: Margaret Atwood*, edited by J. Brooks Bouson (Salem Press, 2012). This material is used by permission of EBSCO Information Services, Ipswich, Massachusetts. I owe many thanks to colleagues at Bradley University who read and critiqued my work, in particular Tim Conley, Danielle Glassmeyer, and Caitriona Moloney. And to Tony: may the journey continue for a long while.

READING TRAUMA NARRATIVES

INTRODUCTION

Ways of Reading Trauma in Literary Narratives

The study of trauma in the post–World War II period has enlarged our understanding of the relationship between social forces and the individual. Public knowledge of war trauma and post-traumatic stress syndrome (PTSD) has increased since the 1970s, and the disorder is once again at the forefront of U.S. public awareness because of recent wars and the continued use of terror to subjugate populations. Trauma writers rely on this public awareness to elicit the kinds of reader responses they hope for. Concurrent with greater public awareness of trauma, trauma narratives have emerged over the past thirty years largely as personalized responses to the late twentieth century's and early twenty-first century's coalescing awareness of the catastrophic effects on the individual psyche of wars, sexual and physical assaults, poverty, and colonization. Writers of these narratives, fiction or nonfiction, see trauma as an indicator of social injustice or oppression and as the ultimate cost of destructive sociocultural institutions. These literary narratives contextualize trauma for readers by embedding them in scenarios of social and historical significance.

Fiction that helps readers access traumatic experience has assumed an important place among diverse artistic, scholarly, and testimonial representations that illustrate the effects of trauma on memory and identity. In focusing on historical or group traumas, many authors explore the cultural origins of trauma in the contexts of racial, sexual, and class oppressions. In *Trauma and Survival in Contemporary Fiction*, I looked at socially and politically oppressive scenarios, often postcolonial, and relational effects such as mothering. This book revisits some of these contexts but is more oriented toward the human dilemmas that arise in contexts of commodification and aggressive normalization that destroy individual personality and deprive it of recognition. The examples of trauma literature I investigate also demonstrate how thought-provoking fiction challenges readers' thinking about human responses and engages readers in exploring the complexities of the human mind (Comer Kidd and Costano 377). These texts' examinations of the effects of trauma on cognition and sense of self raise important epistemological and ontological questions, such as how the nature of knowledge and existence is compromised when associated with wounding.

My particular interest is in how individuals survive adversity and the difficult adaptations they make to a world seemingly aligned against them. This struggle is chronicled by an impressive array of modernist and contemporary writers using intricate character studies and a broad range of narrative strategies. I have come to see my role as critic and teacher as one of attempting to assist scholarly and classroom communities in unraveling the complexities of these texts by analyzing the social, theoretical, and imaginative frameworks their writers use to help readers grasp the situations of the traumatized. Fiction plays a valuable role by depicting many of the social and psychological challenges facing us; and, aided by theories of trauma, narrative, and cognition, we can analyze the reading process and the ways these texts engage readers cognitively and emotionally.

The fiction writers whose work I explore in this book present an array of possible triggers of trauma, from gender and economic exploitation (Atwood, Palahniuk), to class issues and the aftermath of war (Faulkner), to love (Winterson). Toni Morrison and William Faulkner envision practices of love, race (miscegenation), gender, and class as traumatic, and they rhetorically challenge our conceptions of the power of normative social forces. Examining fictionalized trauma scenarios allows the development of insights into subjective endurance, crisis, and conflict and shows that the defensive responses of trauma link many types and degrees of wounding, informing a common humanity.

Since the eighteenth century, the novel has been a forum for psychological inquiry and an elaboration of the role of the individual in society because complex character studies and discourses grew up around the genre. Trauma narratives provide ways to revisit the psychological novel that move beyond the social programming of realism and complicate the modernist single point of view by highlighting both the singularities of character and the shared features of the experience. For example, in *Paradise,* Toni Morrison portrays some traumatized characters caught in static repetitions and others trying to escape unproductive behavioral patterns. Contemporary writers, informed by postmodernism, more directly link subjects' psyches to societal designations and contexts than do modernists. They provide readers with many looks at the characters' experience through the use of multiple and split narrative strategies and perspectives. Narratives developed along these lines attempt to engage readers ethically by making them interlocutors and interpreters of multiple viewpoints. What kinds of reader stimulus do these views create? They can create conflict and build suspense and interest; readers are urged to compare motives and behaviors. Weighing, as Louise Rosenblatt conceptualizes it, the intricate interrelation of a factual reading approach with the aesthetic or emotional effects presented in texts can help readers shape their ethical judgments (Rosenblatt 11–13). Modernist and contemporary, postwar-period texts share narrative techniques and views of human psychology, though knowledge of trauma and its effects is greater since the 1970s.

Trauma is an ancient human phenomenon, but trauma literature—that is, literature written with a conscious awareness of the concept—has become a kind of contemporary genre. Located at a particular juncture in history with common types of stories, it demonstrates knowledge of psychological processes and includes literary elements and figurative language reflecting the causes and consequences of traumatic reactions. For instance, many narratives incorporate the gaps, uncertainties, dissociations, and visceral details of living through traumatic experiences as a way of immersing readers in the characters' states of mind.

The twentieth-century novel in particular developed a fuller view of inner experience. Trauma narratives add to these depictions through focalization (storytelling through a narrator's or character's perceptual angle) that highlights characters' ability or willingness to love or be intimate, their trains of thought, and their relationships to their bodies. The wounded adopt defended, sometimes provisional identities and survival strategies that disguise shame or assert control, but their suppressed emotions can emerge under stress or in their imaginative or dream lives.

Two of the writers covered in this study, Jeanette Winterson and Chuck Palahniuk, are specifically identified as postmodern. Toni Morrison and Margaret Atwood share Faulkner's modernist depth of character and consciousness but their writing features some postmodern elements as well, such as overt self-consciousness. Because the contemporary writers (all except Faulkner) explore similarities between postmodern and trauma studies sensibilities, it is useful to explore how these are related. Postmodern fiction and trauma fiction bear witness to social and personal fragmentation, though trauma fiction shows the most painful and alienating causes and consequences. These types of narrative share values and properties despite a different tone and mimetic emphasis. Both are skeptical and critical of the uses of power and its attendant discourses, and both employ similar storytelling techniques, such as fragmentation and unstable meanings. Trauma fiction also embraces the postmodernists' sense that tensions between the individual subject and society govern human existence (Varsava 72). Earlier literary conceptualizations sought closure of these tensions: in the bildungsroman and modernist texts, protagonists are depicted respectively as either co-opted by society or alienated from it. In the "alienation novel" the tension between self and other is dissolved through "self-destruction or a retreat from society" (Varsava 71–72). Postmodern fiction refuses such closure, keeping the tensions alive with inconclusive endings or repeating cycles Similarly, in trauma fiction, even if pain is ameliorated, and the individual is in a stronger, more self-aware position, some tensions remain. Trauma texts exhibit a postmodern influence in their rejection of traditional ideologies that retain, in Jerry Varsava's words, "suspicion of unresolvable dialectical thought, i.e., paradox," and posit subjectivity as absolute, along with "the primacy of absolutist, non-situational ethics" (73–74). Trauma texts focus more minutely on psychological and social dilemmas than do postmodern texts, which are generally more cerebral and satirical in their approach; and in so doing they add emotional and ethical stakes to their shared sense of the contingent states of human existence.

In a postmodern context, trauma could be a painful symptom of competing cultural interests. For example, individual identity or rights may collide with forces that demand obedience or silence. Struggles of power and control are key themes of postmodern and trauma fiction. Gerhard Hoffmann concludes that in postmodern fiction, "the psychic state of the self is determined by the lack of balance between self and world, by fundamental uncertainty" (434). Hoffmann adds that "the relations between the self and the world are directionless and do not contribute to a sense of clarity and (self) understanding" in many postmodern texts (435). However, in the trauma texts I analyze in this book, writers depict communities acting on the characters out of their own self-preservation and self-interest. The paradox of postmodernism is that it regards "human ideas, concepts and values [as] . . . fictions of the mind," writes Hoffmann (434), yet postmodern writers like Thomas Pynchon and postmodern trauma writers like Palahniuk depict individuals who become more aware of their predicament even as they endure traumatizing forces. These writers want to affect readers with the emotional consequences of domination, and they pay respect to the desire, though idealistic, for a "socially responsible and self-fulfilling self" (438).

Insofar as much postmodern literature avoids psychological realism, one might be surprised to encounter postmodern trauma fiction. The two types of narrative generally diverge in tone, with postmodernism more parodistic and playful and trauma narratives working to depict psychological extremes honestly. Compared with the psychological depth of modernist characters, postmodern characters are "less cognizant, more opaque to interpretation"; they are not likely to have a relation to their past or their selves, or to "consider moral or philosophical implications" (Hoffmann 433–34). However, such disconnection from the past and from ethics resembles the defensive patterns of trauma victims, and, if provided with enough textual evidence, readers could interpret these as signs of trauma.

Fragmented narrative and subject positions are necessary extensions of postmodernists' and trauma writers' belief in multiple, conflicting environmental influences, which undermine notions of a stable and consistent identity. Postmodern narrative typically conveys a fractured view of self, blown about by forces beyond one's control, living outside chronology, and disconnected from the past. In a trauma narrative fragmentation is psychologically debilitating; painful, humiliating experiences and attempts to cope disconnect individuals from the past, from significant others, and from a strong sense of self. Traumatic fragmentation is punitive in ways that other types of postmodern personality fragmenting are not. One can play several roles in life without dire repercussions, but psychologically, it is difficult for most people to live with the cognitive dissonance brought on by wounding.

Responses to human suffering indicate a strong attraction in our culture to a sense of personal cohesion and agency on one's own behalf. Trauma texts' characters achieve some healing, but not perfect wholeness. Neither, however, do trauma therapies: retelling one's story involves structure and a safe distance from intense emotions, or one learns to manage the emotions, not eliminate them. Trauma fiction reflects the more realistic goal of a relatively more balanced sense of being an individual in the world as one copes with pain and rebuilds assumptions and relationships (Janoff-Bulman 93–95). Agency isn't absolute, it's still contingent.

Following from these writers' depictions, my analysis focuses on contexts of trauma that include the extremes of war and rape, but usually have to do with more typical human traumas. They contemplate key emotional and existential issues by attending to the traumatic experiences that affect most people, such as love and loss, death, and the loss of self consequent on the commodification, objectification, and disrespect that accompany the debilitating enforcement of social norms. These trauma texts offer paradigms for understanding human behavior that eludes our usual understanding and awareness in lived situations; we are typically unable to comprehend the impact of events as they occur, or to immediately identify patterns in our own behavior. Similarly, we are often unaware of how emotional contexts and their limitations guide our behavior, or that the emotions we display often are apparent to others (Damasio 42–43). Although their experience may be more intense, trauma survivors employ defensive reactions that are similar to what people in more commonplace stress situations employ.

How can we as readers learn to understand these depictions? In the remainder of this introduction I will set out my interpretive structure. First, trauma must be defined and contextualized for the purposes of my inquiry. Second, I want to establish the value of interdisciplinary work for explaining trauma and literature. Finally, I want to discuss narrative theories that help establish methods of reading and interpreting that aid our comprehension of traumatized characters' states of mind.

Trauma Defined and Located

Trauma is an individual's response to events that is of such intensity that it impairs emotional or cognitive functioning and can bring lasting psychological disruption. Despite the human propensity to survive and adapt, traumatic experiences can alter people's psychological, biological, and social equilibrium such that they become obsessed with the past, their attention diverted from dealing with new situations (Van der Kolk and McFarlane 4). In the worst such cases, survivors live with fragmented or repressed memory, a tainted and diminished sense of self, and a feeling of alienation from others (J. Herman 42–47). Trauma and its concurrent shame, doubt, or guilt destroy important beliefs, especially belief in one's own safety or competence to act or live in the world and one's view of oneself as decent, strong, and autonomous (Janoff-Bulman 19–22).

Symptoms of trauma include periods of nervous activity, hypervigilance, rages, startle responses to everyday sights, feelings of helplessness, and, especially pertinent to works in this study, the "closing off of the spirit as the mind tries to insulate itself from further harm" (Erikson 457). The intensity of these symptoms varies among survivors according to their situations and ability to cope. For some, the symptoms are debilitating, while others may be able to cope and function but have impaired ability to feel or to trust others. The more complex and interesting characterizations in trauma fiction explore characters' ways of coping, which can range from destructive or dysfunctional to functional and necessarily self-preserving.

The sociologist Kai Erikson has emphasized that causes can be entrenched in daily life as well as embedded in horrific events such as the Shoah or war or rape. Trauma can result "from a continuing pattern of abuse as well as from a single assault, from a period of attenuation and wearing away as well as from a moment of shock" (457). Some trauma theorists advocate extending the boundaries of how we view traumatic experience because among vulnerable populations, PTSD can be a widespread cultural phenomenon that even the therapeutic community has tried to ignore. The psychologist Laura S. Brown asserts that limited (i.e., white, middle-class) therapeutic parameters have tended to minimize the effects of the constant stress and humiliation associated with being a person of low socioeconomic status. She further contends there is a collective will to repress how aspects of our social life, such as violence, poverty, or abuse, allow and even encourage the traumatization of women, people of color, and gays (Brown 102–3).

Recent research indicates that exposure to some traumatic events is fairly common, noted by about 60 percent of men and 50 percent of women in a survey of people ages fifteen to fifty-four. The rates of developing full-blown PTSD were different for the sexes: 10 percent for women, 5 percent for men. Women were less exposed to trauma but also were more likely to develop PTSD, with gender definitions and expectations exacerbating their experience (Keane, Marx, and Sloan 3–4).

Because stress can change physiology, traumatic experiences are processed differently from nontraumatic experience by the central nervous system (Van der Kolk and Van der Hart 442). Traumatic "memories" appear in the repetitive, intrusive forms of visualizations of the trauma scene, nightmares, or associated affects for the most severely wounded (Caruth, *Unclaimed* 11). There is a simultaneous desire to remember (in attempts to replay and resolve the past) and to forget these experiences, which can be quickly reactivated through encounters, touch, "triggers," or associative conditions. A stressful situation will bring current thoughts along the same neural pathways as the earlier traumatic events. Consequently, at their worst, traumatic memories remain overwhelming, frozen in time and little affected by subsequent experience (Van der Kolk and Van der Hart 441–42). This could account for individuals' repetitive behavior and returns to situations of abuse (445). Most victims remember their situations of trauma, though they might try to avoid the sense or the visceral memories returning them to that scene, and their defenses might cause them to structure their lives to avoid such triggers. In some cases memories are inaccessible (as Freud said of childhood trauma), but often they are intrusive and difficult to avoid. Memory studies indicate that very few trauma survivors completely forget what they went through (McNally 190). Recovery necessitates that "trauma [be] relived repeatedly, until a person learns to remember simultaneously the affect and cognition associated with the trauma through access to language" (Van der Kolk and Ducey 271).

Trauma disrupts our notions of fixed personality traits and draws attention to reactive behavior. Often victims separate or dissociate themselves from physical and emotional self-awareness to avoid pain. Splitting off from one's body or awareness can reduce the victim's immediate sense of violation and help the person endure and survive the situation (J. Herman 43, 101–2). However, such self-preservation can worsen the post-traumatic response, says Judith Herman: "The attempt to avoid reliving the trauma too often results in a narrowing of consciousness, a withdrawal from engagement with others, and an impoverished [emotional] life" (42). An unresolved past promotes fixed ideas, which motivate impotent attempts to re-create past events. Novels effectively chart the progress of characters' original and subsequent traumas, the associations that create fears, and the fixed ideas that help individuals cope.

People's actual experiences of trauma are located within a dynamic process of feeling, remembering, assimilating, or recovering from the experience. Clinical practitioners and theorists such as Herman, Erikson, Brown, Maria Root, and Bessel Van der Kolk have examined vulnerable populations and the causes and effects of the trauma those populations experienced. They have done so in part to move the focus away from the internalized isolated psychic elements that are the key points of psychoanalysis and toward the interaction of social and behavioral constructs associated with trauma. Learning theorists explain that trait-driven conceptions of personality are less accurate measures of behavioral causes than an individual's personal history of conditioning, personal constructs, and psychological circumstances. The psychologist Walter Mischel has found that "conditions or 'situational variables' of the psychological environment provide the individual with information . . . thereby affecting cognitive and behavioral activities under those conditions" (376). Thus, environmental contingencies are crucial to behavior.

The social environment, the severity of the event, and the individual's characteristics, sense of control, and experience all determine how a person will cope with trauma (MacCurdy 17; Root 248, 250). The social environment influences the causes and outcomes of traumatic experience in a variety of ways. It forms the circumstances out of which trauma is created, but it can also provide or withhold the support needed for healing. Cultural attitudes about trauma and family responses to trauma may either bring the victim into healing connections or prevent such a conjunction (McFarlane and Van der Kolk 27). These attitudes and practices influence notions of expected behavior, responses, and even symptoms. Life roles and emotional management are "facilitated and ordered" within a culturally prescribed social and community structure where stress, illness, and grief are dealt with on personal and group levels (de Vries 401). Optimum circumstances for healing exist when a "society organizes the process of suffering, rendering it a meaningful mode of action and identity within a larger social framework," Martin W. de Vries writes (401–2). When cultures do not function this way, individuals feel unprotected and are forced to cope in isolation. Further, as victims measure themselves against social or cultural standards, they are made to feel shame and other self-destructive emotions. Trauma writers juxtapose victims with other characters to help readers ascertain normative or desirable behavior under the circumstances. This contrastive juxtaposition also helps clarify the nature of survivors' wounds and their altered capacity for feeling.

In her examination of the effects of trauma on personality, Maria Root extends the range of traumatic experience to those suffering low status because of gender, class, or race (230). Their traumas are "insidious" because they are endemic to underclass situations that are repeated in ways that maintain situations of dominance. Victims' pathologies are too often misunderstood, Root believes, because it is socially normative to view their behavior as separate from the social contexts of their traumas, and this biased view reinforces their victimization. Root embraces psychological learning theory views, focusing on victims' experience of events in trauma-producing environments rather than on the events themselves. She wants to "depathologize" what could be considered normal responses to "horrible experiences" (237). "Factors such as isolation, blame, loss of social status, and effect on ability to take care of one's self and/or family add to the trauma of the original event," she writes (237). Further, she contends, "viewing survival behaviors as a reflection of a healthy capacity for self-defense provides an expanded view of the normative range of human functioning in context" (250). Similarly, Ronnie Janoff-Bulman believes that "we have over-pathologized denial and intrusion as problematic symptoms and have too often failed to recognize their considerable adaptive value" (95). Margaret Atwood expresses a similar approach to victims when in *Alias Grace* she illustrates how the social and political climate of the time creates assumptions of Grace's guilt because Grace is an immigrant servant and seems to have lax morals (in that she does not appear to obey double standards of sexual behavior). Atwood shows us a more complicated and sympathetic picture when Grace tells her life story and names the multiple traumas connected to her lower-class immigrant status. Root's term "insidious" is appropriate because unresolved traumas are passed on when succeeding generations fail to nurture children properly, as illustrated in Atwood's *The Blind Assassin* and with Faulkner's Thomas Sutpen and his children and grandchildren in *Absalom, Absalom!*

As Root also shows, communities perpetuate the isolation felt by trauma survivors because they protect themselves against feeling vulnerable. They want to avoid what survivors have suffered, and thus prevent survivors from sharing their experience with others. Victims must adapt in an unsympathetic environment as best they can: "When the survival state is activated, the individual's perceptual, decisional, and relational processes are transformed; survival consumes and redirects all energy toward defensive strategies that may rapidly alternate. Subsequently, behavioral interactions appear unsocialized" (247). In such a state the victim can no longer empathize with or take the part of others; victims have used up their energy on defenses, with nothing left for relating to others: "no taking the other person's perspective, no considerateness, no generosity, no forgiveness, no humor" (247). Survival characteristics trauma victims adopt can include "egocentrism and self-referencing; quickness to anger (fight); social and emotional withdrawal (flight); perseveration (rumination) and shutting down (dissociation)" (248). Self-referencing entails scanning the environment for potential threats, for self-protection; this trait is present in all the protagonists of my study. Another persistent trait is a narrow focus of attention on the self, "directed toward self-preservation" (249); present in some traumatized fiction characters, it seems immature, regrettable, or even monstrous to other characters. Other common traits Root brings up that are depicted in trauma fiction are perseverating, or persistent ruminating on or reliving past experience such that the past comes to dominate the present (e.g., Rosa in *Absalom, Absalom!*, the men in Morrison's *Paradise*); social and emotional withdrawal; and splitting, or "dichotomizing people as good and bad, [which] reflects a separation of threatening cues from safe cues" (250), evident again with the town leaders of *Paradise*, the protagonist in *Written on the Body*, and Faulkner's Rosa. Two final self-defeating characteristics are difficulty resolving conflict and difficulty reestablishing trust (251).

Root addresses further consequences: the breakdown of *"dimensions of security* by which we come to know ourselves, others, and the world. The destruction of each dimension of security represents a trauma" (251). These dimensions include how physical well-being is destroyed by neglect, abuse, or injury, as portrayed fictionally in the character of Mavis and other outsider women in *Paradise* and Iris in *The Blind Assassin*. The broken psychological dimension of security manifests as a "confrontation with mortality, loss of [a] significant other, isolation and helplessness" (252). This breakage is evident in Atwood's characters Iris, Laura, and Grace; the protagonist of Winterson's *Written on the Body*; and Faulkner's Rosa and Judith. The broken spiritual dimension, Root writes, manifests as a "crushing of spirit [as a result of] emotional abuse, brainwashing, humiliation, perceived lack of meaning in one's life, or a sense of dislocation, a loss of identity, such as in refugee experience" (253). Virtually all the characters I examine experience such a crushed spirit and seek ways out of it. The final security dimension Root describes concerns interpersonal relations, including betrayal, abuse of power, rejection, invisibility, and loss of significant others, all of which impair individuals' sense of trust, control, and self-worth (253). Again, these types of interaction are ubiquitous in the fictional characters' lives and must be confronted.

This deprivation of a sense of self is reiterated and further examined in the ethical philosopher Axel Honneth's work on the denial of recognition and its consequences. This denial of self-respect and the response to it form another critical component of characters' circumstances in the novels covered here. Honneth argues that recognition on personal, moral, and social levels is essential to human self-regard. Individuals construct their sense of self from intersubjective recognition and relations, and failed recognition can be traumatic: "The experience of being disrespected carries with it the danger of an injury that can bring the identity of the person as a whole to the point of collapse" ("Personal Identity" 131–32). Honneth characterizes disregard as a kind of moral injustice affecting one's self-relation and producing a "mental shock" when a person is deprived of one of the "conditions of the subject's own identity. Because it destroys an essential presupposition of the individual's capability to act, every moral injury represents an act of personal harm" ("Recognition" 24). The consequences of disrespect include psychological and social death, and wounds that manifest in emotional reactions of shame, rage, indignation, and other negative emotions.

Similar to Root, Honneth asserts that the necessary bedrocks of self-relation are (1) the fulfillment of physical needs, (2) feeling oneself a morally accountable subject, and (3) having valuable capabilities in a social setting ("Recognition" 26). Injuries to one's physical body are the most destructive form of humiliation and destroy one's trust in oneself ("Personal Identity" 132). Denigration that affects "a person's moral self-respect," such as being "structurally excluded from the possession of certain rights within a society" that are available to others, deprives individuals of moral rights and responsibility (133). The injury from being denied a place in a community and a sense of social significance alienates and stigmatizes the wounded, bringing loss of self-esteem because self-realization often comes with "group solidarity" (134). All three forms of denigration—physical, moral, and social—are relevant to my literary examples, but I focus most on moral denigration because situations of inequality and injustice that deprive people of an ethical life are most representative of what injures and motivates the characters I discuss. The denigration of moral self-respect has the most resonance for considering the ethical dilemmas of trauma presented in the novels, and for readers trying to interpret these works.

The characters' traumas become evident through their responses to nonrecognition, manifested in wounded narcissism and in destructive attempts to reclaim recognition that tend to injure others and further isolate the traumatized. These attempts fail when the wounded do not take the suffering of others into account. Healing is not possible when individuals merely reinflict the wounds they receive, such as the men in *Paradise* who recreate their own racial wounds. Similarly, Sutpen in *Absalom, Absalom!* destroys his family members with the goal of creating a racially perfect family. The men in Chuck Palahniuk's *Fight Club* become as violent as the society they want to destroy. Self-assertion can bring a narcissistic focus and isolation; this self-focus is a defense, brought on by the necessity of existing in a survival mode (Root 247). However, this defense becomes destructive as characters turn away from loved ones and become unable to fulfill duties toward them, as exemplified by Iris betraying her sister in *The Blind Assassin* and the narrator of *Written on the Body* abandoning a lover suffering from cancer. Healing and recapturing recognition are possible only by acknowledging the pains and rights of others, and one's connection to those others.

The authors examined in this study offer a variety of contexts of failed recognition. In *Written on the Body* the narrator-protagonist's history of failure in love leads to feeling unloved, and to doubts about his or her (we are uncertain of the sex of the narrator) ability to devote him- or herself to another. In Atwood's *Alias Grace*, recognition and love are rarely encountered among the underclasses in their struggle for survival. Regularly subjected to physical violence and only recognized as subordinates, they are denied agency and moral accountability, that is, any path of action for the underclasses or any consequences for the hypocritical upper classes that victimize them. In the world of manufactured desires that Palahniuk's characters populate, they are treated as drones, consumers, and pawns, and thereby are denied a self-concept and moral accountability, by corrupt and exploitative systems of work and values sold by corporate media and consumerism. Society no longer provides contexts of close relationship, not even in families. Some individuals try to create contexts of existential meaning in support groups where people unite in their pain and fear of death.

Literary renditions of trauma offer important insights into this phenomenon by allegorizing the therapeutic process of putting traumatic experience into words. They offer readers facsimiles of the misuses of power that create the traumas and defended mentalities of survivors. Finally, they highlight how humanity tries to evade the psychological consequences of objectifying individuals. Literary works provide a contemplative and experiential link to traumatic processes (Vickroy, *Trauma and Survival* 24). Readers are brought into analogies of this fraught, split, sometimes empty, sometimes dramatically overdetermined and disturbing sense of being. The divisions within individuals are particularly compelling, for the individuals exist both inside and outside their experience, wanting simultaneously to remember and to forget. The complex literary characterizations include traits associated with traumatic experience and demonstrate how identities can shift and flow because of circumstances. I have chosen to focus on texts with damaged but somewhat functional characters with altered personalities. They are generally on a path toward some kind of change or healing (with the exception of Faulkner's Sutpen).

Trauma fiction serves many important functions. Effective trauma texts engage readers in a critical process by immersing them in, while providing perspective on, the flawed thinking, feeling, and behavior of the traumatized. This type of text also aims to engage us in what Geoffrey Hartmann suggests is another important role of trauma literature, its examination of conscience and bearing witness to pain. This is demonstrated textually with personal dilemmas reflecting on broader social and collective traumas.

Psychologists and trauma scholars have noted the therapeutic effect of writing for understanding behavior and healing. The psychologists Keith Oatley and Jennifer Jenkins point out that writing helps make our emotions conscious, and that "written narrative literature . . . concentrates on our emotional lives and their problematics—as if story telling and story listening have always been attempts to understand these matters. The activity is satisfying because stories provide possibilities of vicarious action and pieces of solutions to the problems of how to act and how to be a person in the society that is depicted" (368–69). Psychotherapists have found narrative contemplations are helpful in therapeutic situations, taking patients through a process that engages their issues yet distances them aesthetically and emotionally. In *The Writing Cure*, Stephen J. Lepore and Joshua M. Smyth report that "expressive writing can change people's perceptions about their responses to a situation . . . it integrates thoughts with feelings. . . . People writing expressively about traumas subsequently perceived those experiences as more controllable" (110–11). Marian MacCurdy has recreated this process in her writing classes with students, exploring the pairing of emotions and images (92–93). Literary trauma narratives with first-person narrators offer readers an approximate view into this type of experience.

The writers I have chosen to study perform the unique task of literature as keen observers of how social systems and circumstances affect individuals. These authors have made important contributions to the vast conversation about trauma by discussing sexual, class, and racial traumas consequent on the aggressively normalizing ideologies and social mechanisms attached to those ideologies that attempt to shape the individual to a psychically death-dealing functionality. Atwood, Morrison, Faulkner, Winterson, and Palahniuk all demonstrate the effects of these systems and individuals' attempts to break from them.

Interdisciplinarity, Literature, and Theory

Because of its many implications, social, emotional, and intellectual, trauma has inspired an array of disciplinary and interdisciplinary inquiries and perspectives, including psychological and literary studies, as well as sociological, critical theoretical, cultural, racial, and gendered approaches. Each approach offers valuable insights into the processes and representations of trauma. Psychology and sociology reflect on the personal and interpersonal ramifications of traumatic experience and on possible recovery. Cultural and racial approaches have examined the contexts and personal consequences of historical traumas such as wars, slavery, and the Shoah, which are also features of trauma literature. Gender is a significant consideration because of the PTSD statistics showing that women are more greatly affected than men, and because trauma fiction is largely, though not exclusively, written by women, who identify gender as determining the nature of victimization and reflect on the gender-specific effects of trauma on women. Male authors also examine gender-specific traumas and masculine gender-inflected defensive behaviors.

Perhaps unlike many of my humanist, poststructuralist colleagues, I approach psychology and the scientific study of human behavior with more attention and regard. This is because of all the disciplines, psychology has examined the complexities of trauma the most, and its professionals work with real victims. There are many benefits to understanding the mechanisms of emotion and behavior that are part of a social science analysis. Such an analysis can account for the complex interrelationships among physiological, cognitive, and cultural contributions to the production and evaluation of emotion. A multidisciplinary approach supplements and broadens the psychoanalytic perspective, which primarily concerns itself with originary traumas, repression, and repetition (which still remain important concepts). I believe this kind of analysis, particularly in its cognitive psychological aspects, which have been integrated recently into narrative studies, has much to offer for understanding human behavior and is too hastily rejected as mere universalizing.

Moreover, literary narrative offers opportunities for analysis. Of course, characters are not real human beings, but trauma fiction often presents realistic human dilemmas in representations that attempt to meditate on human responses to shock. And the discourses included by authors enable them to construct texts so that readers can consider the social values attached to trauma and its emotional fallout. That narrative creation is used in therapy and to chronicle and shape the ways individuals conceive of their daily lives is well documented (D. Herman, "Stories" 163–65). Narrative can help bring about awareness of emotion. "Emotions emerge when we encounter problems, uncertainties in life, when we do not know how to act. They tell us something is happening to which we should pay attention. Often they demand a creative response. What artists do is to bring these vague feelings, the conflicts with others and within the self, the uncertainties that they represent, into awareness, giving them content and particularity by expressing them as works of art," write Keith Oatley and Jennifer Jenkins (370). The emotions are important to our lives for several reasons: they "point to goals or concerns," they become part of our habits and inner sense of life, and, though emotions seem vague and unconnected, part of the process of self-discovery is noting their expression and making sense of them (362). Writing one's experience can become, according to Suzette Henke, a "therapeutic reenactment" in which "narrative cohesion can reconfigure the individual's obsessive mental processing of embedded traumatic scripts" (*Shattered Subjects* xii, xviii). The psychoanalyst Judith Herman values survivors' reconstructions of their stories more for their witnessing and testimonial value, for remembering in a protected environment, than as thorough documentation, which survivors may not be able to tolerate (181–83).

Research on readers' cognitions while reading indicates that readers become absorbed in texts when they are offered believable facsimiles of human situations and behaviors that are familiar to them, or when they can identify with characters, or at least be induced to care about what happens to them (Keen 68–69). For reader response critics such as Richard Gerrig, readers' psychological reactions are not impediments to interpretation but are part of how the reading experience is constructed and how meaning is formed (20). If prompted well by the literature and given useful theoretical frameworks for analysis, readers can join a meditative process for understanding human responses to shock.

Many critics have legitimately questioned the presumption that readers can or should fully identify or empathize with trauma victims. Some feminist and postcolonial critics reject the concept of empathy, and particularly its assumed basis in "universal human emotions." These critics see culture as the primary determinant of human life and behavior, rather than psychological mechanisms or responses to the environment. Also, to critics who view emotion as culturally constructed, some scientists' focus on neurophysiology, which deemphasizes cognition and cultural differences (Keen 161), seems alienating and "explains a great deal of the resistance to empirical disciplines (such as psychology) in the humanities and in some social sciences" (147). In *Key Concepts of Postcolonial Studies* the authors insist that all universal concepts of human life and experience suggest a hegemonic view of existence because the presumption of sharing experiences, they believe, serves the interests of those in power (Ashcroft, Griffiths, and Tiffin 235, qtd. in Keen 147). For these postcolonial critics, "empathy" becomes yet another example of the Western imagination's imposition of its own values on cultures and peoples that it scarcely knows but presumes to "feel with, in a cultural imperialism of the emotions" (Keen 147–48). No doubt there have been occasions when this was true, but attempts at empathy have also benefited victims, as happens with the work of relief organizations.

Critics who focus on culture at the expense of psychological functions mistake content for process and create an unnecessary binarism. They pit culture against psychology or physiology even though behavioral research demonstrates that all these different dimensions work together and contribute to overall expression and meaning, according to cultural and other psychologists (Strongman 72). As the cultural psychologist Carroll Izard concludes, "The experiential component of emotion is a quality of consciousness or feeling, and at this level the emotion state is invariant across cultures" (qtd. in Levy 223). Psychologists also recognize that cultures alter the forms that govern emotional expressions, but they insist on some underlying basis for emotions. Cultural anthropologists have found similar structures of feeling and thought in common stories and rituals across cultures. Therefore, while there are some measurable psychological and physiological processes, there are also situational factors involved when we look at the complete picture of human experience and learning. Emotional processes or mechanisms can be similar across cultures, but at the same time the expression of emotion (content) is influenced by culture and by individuals' specific situations (Shweder 211–13). For instance, we can ascertain cultural and psychological influences in whether trauma victims are acknowledged or aided, and in how they adopt defenses against an unsympathetic environment, as well as against private, painful memories.

Another counterargument invokes the deep connections between human psychology and culture and holds that humans, despite cultural differences, share many of the same emotions and psychological processes. In *Emotion: A Very Short Introduction*, Dylan Evans suggests that if we read texts from different cultures, we recognize familiar emotions. "If emotions were cultural inventions, changing as swiftly as language, these texts would seem alien and impenetrable." He concludes:

> Our common emotional heritage binds humanity together, then, in a way that transcends cultural difference. In all places, and at all times, human beings have shared the same basic emotional repertoire. Different cultures have elaborated on this repertoire, exalting different emotions, downgrading others, and embellishing the common feelings with cultural nuances, but these differences are more like those between two interpretations of the same musical work, rather than those between different compositions. (8)

Suzanne Keen acknowledges that though fiction can evoke temporary sympathy for victims, it often produces failed empathy, a "delusion" that casual readers can understand the suffering of others from a different culture, gender, race, or class. The literary works I analyze try to avoid sentimental attachment to characters, who are presented not as merely pitiable but as fighting to survive. These texts involve much more than pulling the reader's heartstrings. Trying to understand anyone else, even those close to us, involves a leap of imagination, and it's this kind of leap these texts attempt. What's to be gained by examining traumatic scenarios is insight into possible views of endurance, suffering, crisis, and conflict. The writers I consider offer facsimiles of the dynamic relation between the environment and individuals, and attempt to involve readers in the worlds that traumatized individuals try to construct for themselves: edifices of defenses against threats.

However, psychology emphasizes that emotions and even physiology are affected by the environment and by learning. Learning theory, the basis of Root's comments on personality issues and trauma, has been theorized and elaborated by the eminent psychologist Walter Mischel. Learning theorists hold that trait-driven conceptions of personality are less accurate measures of behavioral causes than the individual's personal history of conditioning, personal constructs, and psychological circumstances. Mischel observes that "conditions or 'situational variables' of the psychological environment provide the individual with information which influences the previously discussed person variables, thereby affecting cognitive and behavioral activities under those conditions" (376). Thus, environmental contingencies are crucial to behavior.

Fictional narrative has a unique capacity to represent the interweaving of the environment and human emotions learned in such environments. Many contemporary writers are able to recreate the living atmospheres in which individual traumas and dysfunction are linked to social oppression, and writers such as Morrison, Atwood, and Jane Smiley have a strong sense of individual psychology and their own social commitments. Smiley, for example, in her novel *A Thousand Acres* locates sexual abuse within the norms of a patriarchal farm community that exploits women and the land (Vickroy, "Voices"). This kind of fiction seems able to suggest connections between and similar mechanisms affecting the individual and broader cultural pathologies that are not as easy to see without the psychological and experiential framework that narrative offers.

It is important not to further exploit victims, but I see the potential of literature to imaginatively place readers into difficult and alienating situations. The degree to which this is possible must be qualified. For instance, Dominick LaCapra believes fiction can reveal the emotional experience of historical phenomena such as slavery (13–14). However, he favors texts that put readers into a position of "empathic unsettlement," that is, that take readers through a process of working through trauma to put readers into a critical as well as an empathic mode of thought, one that nevertheless does not entitle readers to be in the "victim's . . . position" (78). I believe much of the trauma literature I discuss undercuts any uncritical or sentimental views by creating characters who are sympathetic but who problematically complicate their lives, behave unethically, and are unable to bond with others. However, they also encounter their own commodification in unforgiving sociocultural contexts of racial, sexual, and economic dominance. Iris, the protagonist of Margaret Atwood's *The Blind Assassin*, is sacrificed to gender and class requirements that put her in an abusive marriage, destroy her sense of self, and create inner conflicts that make her unable to understand or help her suicidal sister, and eventually make Iris complicit in her death. These examples suggest a broader questioning of normative values that make victims instruments of pathology and destruction.

Attaining a critical understanding of the forces creating trauma and how individuals live with it gives us a clearer sense of how social contexts are connected to psychological life. These contexts shape circumstances and experience, creating emotional and cognitive patterns that in turn shape social attitudes and structures of living. Toni Morrison illustrates this powerfully in *Paradise*, in the construction of a rigidly safe but murderous town life that responds to but also perpetuates, on a smaller scale, the historically race-based traumas of rejection and exile. Morrison and Faulkner both reenact in their fiction the traumas of racial hierarchies and patriarchal power that attempt to control life patterns and plans, and demonstrate how women unwillingly fit into the designs of men's sense of destiny. Their novels investigate the causes of and responses to traumas, which also help readers question how such forces instill a fear that precludes ethical judgment and mutual human obligations.

Methods of Reading Cognition and Emotion

Authors wanting to shape readers' cognitive frameworks regarding victims must signal for readers the effects of trauma. Moreover, they must engage the cognitive and emotional responses of readers that enable readers to attribute mental states to characters. Narratology provides analytical tools to help identify how writers produce textual material that stimulates readers to envision these mental states, and to demonstrate how cognition and emotion are key aspects of both storytelling and reading processes. Narrative theory has produced methods to help readers look at the storytelling features and interpretive possibilities of trauma literature. These methods include showing how characters' cognitions, emotions, and behavior are shaped by wounding; how unrecognized memory and its effects emerge in the narrative; and the evidence of defenses that suggests characters' mental states. Deploying familiar literary elements, trauma fiction creates constructs of the trauma experience through prototypically imagined situations and symptoms, metaphorical dreams, and death imagery. Its narrative styles reproduce aspects of that experience, including fragmentation of thoughts, a dissociative outlook, and decontextualized visualizations.

Cognitive psychology provides additional analytical tools with which to tease out subtle or hidden motives and emotional effects buried deep within a narrative. Cognitive frameworks are useful in the depiction of trauma in several ways. First, the narrator's limited or conflicted knowledge of the narrative situation creates internal contradictions or unwitting self-exposure signaling that the narrator is unreliable and perhaps unethical (Nunning 90, 100). Second, depicting social aspects of the mind helps identify a character's circumstances; these aspects are represented in characters' thought reports revealing their motives for action in relation to their surroundings (Palmer 76). Third, psychological constrictions can be read in the ways the narrator draws our attention, perhaps in directions we don't expect. For example, a narrow or obsessive focus calls attention to ways consciousness is predicated on emotions and memory is connected to the past. Scholars of narrative find that thought reports and focalization particularly induce readers to ascribe mental states to characters. Fourth, texts creating the illusion of details of lived experience, called qualia, give readers a sense of the "felt subjective properties of mental states" (D. Herman, "Nexus" 143). These analytical tools, drawn from a cognitive psychology context, help readers assess characters' ethical situations by providing, as the narrative scholar Alan Palmer notes, means for analyzing thought "in terms of motives and intentions, behavior and action" (66).

Cognitive-oriented narrative scholars believe interpreters can examine the problems of conflicted narrators by comparing their fictional perspectives with everyday conceptions of the human experience. Even in normative situations individuals do not understand much about their own mental states because of self-deception, misinterpretation, and inattention, according to John Searle (147–48). Social or other pressures can also distort self-examinations, causing individuals to invent mental states to explain their behavior in more socially acceptable ways. The cognitive scientist Antonio Damasio notes that our emotions are generally more observable to others than to ourselves (42). This is especially evident in traumatic contexts, where emotions are submerged and not accessible to the survivors who defend against them. Iris in *The Blind Assassin* can realize her behavior only belatedly, when she recalls how others—Laura and Alex—have seen her, and then she can break her trauma-induced haze and grasp her failure to recognize critical situations and to act. Remembering how her sister called her a "sleepwalker" and tried to persuade her not to marry a man who would control and exploit her, Iris is able to see that her sister recognized how she was distanced from her own feelings and the realities of her situation. Similarly, we must learn about Grace, Sutpen, and the women of *Paradise* from other characters' viewpoints or from indirect authorial narration, which provide additional insights, confirm behavior, and express judgment of the traumatized. These novels demonstrate the crucial effects the wounded have on observers and, through this focalization, on readers, whether they evoke sympathy, denial, or avoidance.

Cognitive scientists emphasize the role of the environment in cognition, finding that the mind is more "social, embodied, concrete, located, engaged and specific" than individual, rational, or abstract, as the classical view has it (Smith 769). Alan Palmer in *Fictional Minds* examines the narrative techniques writers use to show the connections of the "internal consciousnesses of characters to their external social and physical contexts" (49). He does not distinguish between thought and action because "the concept of an action necessarily contains within it mental phenomena such as intentions and reasons" (76). The narrative vehicle for expressing these connections is the "thought reports" of characters, which Palmer describes as having a "linking function, whereby the narrator, in presenting a character's consciousness, connects it to its surroundings. The use of this device emphasizes the nature of consciousness as mental action and thereby brings together consciousness and physical action. The mode of thought report is ideally suited to informative presentations of the purposive and directive nature of thought as well as its social nature" (76). Authors also provide reasons and motives for characters' actions by demonstrating their mental functioning and dispositions (81–84). Tracking these thoughts is useful to interpreting trauma, because though it is isolating, trauma makes us confront how the individual mind is situated in larger contexts because its causes and consequences are rooted in the social world. For example, in Atwood's *Alias Grace*, the protagonist-narrator's mentality has been afflicted by a gender- and class-driven world order. Her mind is social in its inhibitions and sense of duty, and operates within domestic spaces and other places of confinement (prison, an asylum) to which society has relegated her. By analyzing the social influences on this character's thinking, readers can link some of them to the causes of her traumas and her coping mechanisms. And yet the narrator-protagonist's social connections provide pathways to her dawning awareness of her wounds. In *Absalom, Absalom!*, readers must be able to see Sutpen's motivations for creating his landowner life within the contexts of Southern class, gender, and racial mores, and the male narrators' motives as connected to the wounds of the South's defeat in the Civil War.

The mechanisms of trauma, how it is caused and perpetuated, and the potential to heal wounds are all dependent on social interconnections, through witnessing or healing relationships. Unfortunately, social interests or opinions can retraumatize or cause rejection of the traumatized. *The Blind Assassin, Paradise,* and *Absalom, Absalom!* all feature adverse social environments in which trauma is denied and healing is thwarted. Denials, revulsion, and scapegoating characterize the responses of witnesses who are implicated in victims' suffering. Though such reactions are depicted as normative responses, the different authors also offer a critique of them by showing in detail the devastating isolation and abandonment others inflict on the wounded.

Gauging how a text creates a sense of direct experience of the life situation and mentality of a character is the most important goal of analysis in understanding how to interpret the situations of the traumatized. Reading narrative clues to thought and feeling provides a framework for this analysis. First-person narration provides the deepest sense of felt life in fiction and in life (Lodge 10). When immersed in the mind of a character, readers can become engaged in a version of what cognitive psychologists call "theory of mind," or the "processes by which humans attribute mental states, properties, and dispositions both to themselves and to their social cohorts" (D. Herman, "Cognition" 253) based on their actions. One technique used to achieve this is focalization, or "the method by which a narrator uses a character's consciousness as the perceptual viewpoint or angle from which the narration takes place" (Palmer 48) and other means by which the narrator guides readers' attention and focus to heighten our sense of knowing a character.

The extreme conditions of traumatic situations can reveal the intricate relationship between cognition and emotion, so readers must attend to how texts depict mental states, alive to signs of unresolved wounds and unrecognized affect and diminished cognitive and emotional functioning. Toni Morrison's portrait of Mavis in *Paradise* directs readers' attention to such an impaired thought process. When questioned after the event about why she left two of her children, infants, to suffocate in her car, Mavis does not react emotionally and can only report the specifics of what her husband, Frank, wanted her to get for dinner, underscoring his tyrannical hold over her life. As the narrative gradually homes in on her narrow, dissociated perspective, it plunges readers into the strange and terrifying world of a barely articulate woman and her responses to sexual and physical abuse by her husband and threats from her children. She does not feel she has control over her life, and her family's threats to avenge the babies' deaths shape her every thought and action. Readers must question how she has become the family scapegoat and why she is so passive, seemingly complicit, and paralyzed. Traumatic fears explain her incapacitated thinking, until Mavis comes alive to potential threats from her husband and children.

Realizing she may not survive, Mavis escapes and, once on the road, finds she is one of many abused women fleeing similar situations. Her behavior raises the difficult question of whether it was unethical or not for her to leave behind her children if she was so debilitated she could not carry out her motherly duties.

Another typical signal of traumatic experience is an uneasy relationship between past and present, signaled by the frequent invocation of defenses against potentially overwhelming emotions. This relationship has many manifestations: repression, splitting of the self between past and present, silence about the past (notable in Winterson's *Written*), feelings of alienation and not belonging (displayed by Iris in *The Blind Assassin*), and being haunted by the past (as in *Paradise*).

Other textual details may prompt readers to create in their minds a sense of a thinking being and their mental processes. These details, which resemble lived experience, are called qualia, a term coined by philosophers of mind and used by narrative theorists interested in the representation of consciousness.[1] Qualia may be defined as "the qualitative, experiential, or felt properties of mental states" that, according to David Herman, help readers envision a character's experience and, by extension, his or her consciousness (Levin 693; D. Herman, "Nexus" 140). Qualia usually include a sense of time, place, human qualities, and a "personalistic" view (140). Monica Fludernik notes that "the protagonist's emotional and physical reaction to [events as they impinge on her situations and activities]" is integral to creating this sense of a living mind: "since humans are conscious thinking beings, (narrative) experientiality always implies—and sometimes emphatically foregrounds—the protagonist's consciousness" (30). Faulkner imparts a vivid sense of the mental state of one of his narrator-protagonists, Rosa Coldfield, whose overdetermined emotions are encapsulated in imagery of birth, fecundity, and death that makes readers imagine her mentally reliving moments of a life once filled with potential and then disappointment when that potential is denied. These thoughts foreshorten her life, but also impute a haunting sense of hope.

Trauma writers can create a felt sense of life in their visceral portrayals of the intimate ways trauma is experienced in the body. Winterson's narrator-protagonist describes deteriorating body parts in *Written on the Body* as he or she—the gender is unclear—attempts to cope with the reality of the loved one's approaching death. The bodily experience and memory of trauma are also captured in Iris's visceral reactions as she relives rapes in her nightmares, and Mavis's fears in *Paradise* are characterized by a similar physicality.

Qualia and cognition can also be read in dream metaphors, which can be visual figurations of traumatic memory. Dream sequences provide writers like Atwood with a strategy for bringing readers into the fearful and conflicted emotions of the characters, emotions of which the characters themselves may not be aware. Dream sequences also afford authors an opportunity to use symbolic imagery reflecting the traumatic circumstances and give readers textual access to a character's innermost thoughts. Atwood uses dreams effectively in her novel *Cat's Eye*, but also in *The Blind Assassin*, where Iris, fearful, anxious, and unaware of what is happening to her psychologically, has perplexing dreams that reveal the fears she suppresses in waking life. With people long dead appearing in her dreams, figures both loved and hated, Iris's dreams represent what Robert J. Lifton calls the death imprint, or an "image feeling of threat to life" that trauma survivors experience (18). Such images reveal the victim's "vulnerability to death imagery—not only to direct life threat but also to separation, stasis and disintegration" (19).

Analyzing the creation of qualia, or the illusion of a felt sense of life that narrative gives readers, calls our attention to strategies authors use to involve readers in a kind of experience rather than to engage them in uncritical identification or condemnation. Depicting characters through the use of qualia is more illustrative of trauma than description because the trauma experience eludes straightforward accounts and is represented better in fragments, brief moments of action, or suggestions of emotions. This type of representation tries to capture the specific subjective qualities of human experience, the nature of our conscious and unconscious life. This approach to analyzing aspects of narrative and how and why they appear in trauma literature can elicit a more engaged reader response. Each trauma text provides a different challenge, and interpretation benefits from analysis that features the dynamic relations among authors, texts, narrators, and readers. Each text suggests the methods of interpretation (depending on narrative strategies and character depictions) needed to explore the complex interactions of the mind, body, and environment.

Narrative Theory and Ethics

Narrative theorists who examine how stories are told have come up with tools for describing how storytelling is designed to shape readers' responses and illuminate contexts of trauma. Cognitive psychological approaches have led narratologists such as David Herman to examine storytelling elements, contextual frames, and focalizations that draw readers' attention to what he describes as "attitudes of seeing, believing, speculating, etc." (*Story Logic* 325). Herman observes that the functions of narrative, such as who tells which part of the story and how, prompt readers to develop mental models that enable them to make inferences so they may be immersed in or relocated to the world of the text. Herman also sees texts as cognitive artifacts that are designed to mentally challenge us and tell us about our world ("Stories" 166–69). These theoretical tools help readers analyze narratives that are structured on symptoms of trauma. They help us see how such narratives stimulate readers' own perceptual and ethical frameworks by attempting to give readers access to experiences that are difficult to understand and sympathize with *because* they challenge normative Western conceptions of individual free will and trait-driven behavior. That is, traumatic experience challenges concepts of a consistent or reliable personality, focusing instead on the situational. This experience also raises the possibility that extreme circumstances undermine the capacity of the traumatized to behave ethically, for example being able to take responsibility for others and themselves, or to treat others fairly and compassionately (Root 247). Readers are a necessary part of the process of unraveling and evaluating characters' limits and their circumstances, and writers usually ease readers into traumatic material so they are not thrown into horrific situations without preparation or contexts.

These texts raise ethical questions about both the treatment of the traumatized and how they in turn treat others. Narrative theorists point to an ethical dynamic to the reading process as the viewpoints of the narrator, the implied author, and the reader interact, and as the reader considers whether a writer (or character) can successfully make his or her case. Ethical considerations surrounding the contexts of trauma provide a provocative framework for looking at the relation between text, author, and reader. The impact of ethical material in a text depends on how much readers can absorb and reformulate in their own minds. As James Phelan asserts, "Our emotions and desires about . . . fictional . . . characters are intimately tied to our judgments of them; and our ethical responses to narrative . . . are tied both to the ethical quality of characters' actions and to the interaction of our own ethical positions with the ethics of technique and the ethical positions of the implied author" (*Living to Tell* 160). The ethics of technique refers to how the narrative guides us, even stylistically or aesthetically, to consider ethical issues and behavior; the techniques themselves may include voice, dreams, symbols, or repetitions. The implied author is the conscience or consciousness underlying the overall message of a work; in a trauma narrative, this position can be inferred from how a text presents the causes and consequences of trauma. Are readers moved to accept the characters' wounds and their need for recognition, how they go about claiming it, and the costs of that claim? And what alternative, perhaps more ethical, behaviors does the writer or text suggest? The complexities of these characters often inspire conflicted feelings in readers and make ethical evaluation of them difficult; realistic depictions risk sacrificing readers' sympathy, despite their generally wanting to identify with a character and to be invested in a story. Characters can be compelling even when they are not likable.

Some considerations for looking at ethical dynamics in trauma texts are the following. Do authors' intended effects, such as creating awareness or empathy in readers, succeed? Are the limits of knowing and memory, common to trauma, acknowledged? And how do readers' understandings depend on contending with narrators' and characters' unreliable or unstable viewpoints? Unreliability, narrative theory explains, may manifest as failure to inform, but also, and more significantly, as a failure of judgment or ethics, which in the case of trauma narratives may be indicative of symptoms such as helplessness, faulty cognition or memory, shame, repression, or dissociation. How a reader may interpret ethical stances within a text is affected by how and where the narrator draws the reader's attention and by the relation between the worldviews of the text and the reader (Nunning 95). Additionally, one should consider whether the implied author offers an implicit value structure with which, or against which, a character or narrator's behavior is to be measured.

My approach assumes that reader engagement is unavoidable because readers are a part of the process of re-creating the text. If we look at the reading process as a transaction between reader and text, we can analyze how the text guides readers' responses to difficult material. This framework can provide interpretive direction to critical scholarship or pedagogical applications, which in turn can help readers better understand the critical nature of the issues, the behavior of the characters, and the intentions of the authors.

A reader's background and familiarity with a topic, and readers' sensitivity to others, all condition readers' reactions to texts. Research has shown that readers are transported by becoming engaged in or performing the work that narratives set out for them, in a variety of ways. (1) Readers apply their own experience and knowledge structures to interpret textual events, for they must either bridge or acknowledge gaps left by the text. (2) Readers develop schemas, attributing traits to characters more often than considering that their circumstances lead to behaviors. (3) Readers become engrossed in manipulations of causal structure (Gerrig 46). (4) Readers' investment in the consequences of a story or for a character is more likely if they are aroused by suspense, hopefulness, and the ability to use their real-world knowledge (Gerrig 8, 69, 17). Readers like to anticipate and make predictive inferences. These performative tasks, along with the dynamic relations between authors, texts, and readers, which are unique to each text, should disabuse anyone of easy conclusions about what readers might feel.

Louise Rosenblatt's work on transactional analysis of the reading process, which also addresses readers' cognitions and emotions, can also educate readers about their own responses and help them recognize the complex mix of fact and emotional life that is part of rendering traumatic situations. This approach helps readers appreciate how Faulkner and the other writers I consider complicate the notion of objectivity as narrator-characters are deeply embedded in their perceptions and defensive stances, all magnified by trauma. Rosenblatt's considerations of readers particularize elements of the reader's background that he or she brings to the process of reading and interpreting, including physical, personal, social, and cultural factors. Also, readers have cognitive, emotional, and associational matrixes and histories that texts tap into. Reading is a dynamic process: "Every reading act is an event, or a transaction involving a particular reader and a particular pattern of signs, a text, and occurring at a particular time in a particular context," Rosenblatt writes (7).

Rosenblatt breaks down reader-text interactions to the ways in which texts engage readers and move them into either efferent or aesthetic stances. The efferent position emphasizes "the cognitive, referential, factual, analytical, logical, and quantitative aspects of meaning" (12). Readers' cognitive engagement is important in assessing the situations of the characters. That is, readers must gauge textual information that may contradict or not be accounted for in the characters' perceptions. Readers have to note others characters' observations, or the author's or narrator's comments, that further clarify and contextualize those situations. Rosenblatt's aesthetic stance is concerned with the "sensuous, affective, emotive and the qualitative aspects of meaning"; the aesthetic is what is "lived through during the reading event" (11). Readers' sensations may be triggered by characters' sensations and help readers invest in characters' experiences. This book looks at how writers compose to engage readers on this level. Readers of trauma fiction often must find their bearings in multiple and conflicted accounts within a narrative and are left with effects that they must sort through and analyze, perhaps without a clear resolution.

Navigating the interweaving of the efferent and aesthetic stances has implications for how readers read trauma literature ethically as they weigh reliable facts against experiential effects. An example is how readers try to discern the causes of characters' actions and figure out what the characters feel, based on the characters' actions (thereby inferring emotion from facts), especially if feeling is deeply buried, repressed, or denied. Difficulties arise with unreliable narrators, who may present "facts" that are based in illusion, delusion, or misperceptions of a self-interested or defensive kind.

A fruitful communication between author and reader comes with shared "linguistic-experiential equipment," and with those "similarities, the reader is more likely to bring to the text the prior knowledge, acquaintance with linguistic and literary conventions, and assumptions of social situations required for understanding implications or allusions and noting nuances of tone and thought" (Rosenblatt 21). For example, texts communicate effectively if readers can connect literary allusions or imagery to trauma, or if their assumptions about social situations help them realize the brokenness of the characters' lives and relationships, or if the characters' painful sensations find some resonance in readers' own emotional lives.

Rosenblatt sets out some "tacit criteria" to facilitate readers' commiseration with authors "across social, cultural and historical differences between author and readers as well as among readers" (23). These basic criteria are (1) an awareness of the "context and purpose of reading," (2) the recognition that interpretation "should cover the full text," and (3) an acceptance that an interpretation should not propose claims that are unsubstantiated by the literary text (23–24). I would supplement these criteria with my own criteria for reading trauma texts, namely, recognition of the need to locate signs or symptoms of trauma and to consider the psychological and ethical implications that have been mentioned. A third criterion might be an awareness of how writers interest readers with words or phrasing or guide readers toward ethical considerations, what Phelan refers to as the ethics of technique. One point of reference here is the potential conflict in these trauma texts between what Rosenblatt refers to as the ubiquitous public and private elements of reading, even though the "criteria of validity of interpretation differ for readings at various points on the efferent-aesthetic continuum." Trauma texts may be best understood or served by the predominant aesthetic reading, whose criteria "call for attention to the referential, cognitive aspects but only as they are interwoven and colored by the private, affective, or experiential aspects generated by the author's patterns of signs" (24).

Readers can be made uncomfortable when confronted with the difficulties of considering relations between perpetrators and victims, who can be the same person (Iris, Sutpen). Though most texts give us sympathetic victims, they may still cause readers to inhabit an abuser's viewpoint, and readers may experience "empathic distress at feeling with a character whose actions are at odds with . . . [their own] moral code" (Keen 133–34). If readers want to understand the contexts of trauma, it would be valuable to see how someone becomes abusive, and even that a perpetrator might also be traumatized. We need to understand abusers' attitudes or experiences as well. Mental health professionals regularly comment on the dearth of services available to abusers. To deal with the subject fully and to have any hope of correcting it, accepting a simple paradigm of sympathy for the victim and wholesale rejection and condemnation of the abuser is insufficient. To be truthful, perhaps trauma texts might of necessity inflict pain or discomfort on readers.

Trauma writers are especially concerned with how narratives create empathy, or demonstrate the consequences if it is missing. Studies have found that novelists, and particularly women novelists, are more empathic than the average reader (Taylor, Hodges, and Kohanyi 376),[2] and that novelists clearly want to make readers care about certain individuals and issues. Jane Smiley fears empathy may disappear if people stop reading (Keen 124). Though not a focus of this study, Smiley's work reflects these concerns with empathy. She explores the consequences for the traumatized in her novel *A Thousand Acres* when those around the victims are unsympathetic or too uncomfortable to listen. As most of the characters in the story deny, reject, or are overwhelmed by the two protagonists' incest experience, the victims must try to heal themselves. Smiley counters these disconnections by directing readers to be invested in Ginny's and Rose's perspectives and by drawing the characters who reject them as less sympathetic by demonstrating how family members and the community willingly and generally accept women's illness and exploitation in exchange for prosperity (Vickroy, "Voices"). Smiley's work tries to produce in readers a locus of understanding of the sisters' anguish in the face of others' responses. Atwood's *The Blind Assassin* charts a similar course of broken relations between sisters because of an unsympathetic and repressive environment and a surviving sister who must discover her own path toward awareness and healing.

Trauma narratives complicate an already complex process of absorbing emotionally charged material. Narratives generally can make disturbing events palatable, even seemingly normal, by enabling readers to rethink framing categories of behavior (D. Herman, "Stories" 179–80). Narratives can offer context, a framework of cause and effect, and psychological insights that are not as readily available or as clear in real-life situations. Can these sorts of texts change us emotionally or cognitively? Can witnessing such events change readers' cognitive and emotional framework for considering trauma and identity? Empathy seems important to the reading process but may not have lasting effects after the actual reading is done (Keen 115; Comer Kidd and Costano 380). Discussion and analysis in the classroom or other forums could bring that reading experience out of the personal and into the social realm, where it could be reinforced to maintain empathy. Teaching can focus on processes rather than on horrific events themselves: we can focus on protagonists' ways of coping, and on finding parallels to our own defensive life responses. Reading about their situations can create sympathy for stigmatized groups and reduce the sense of social distance from them. A fictional text's recreation of ethical problems can alter readers' own ethical stances (Hakemulder 22, 53). A recent study published in *Science* in 2013 by David Comer Kidd and Emanuele Castano found that "after reading literary fiction, as opposed to popular fiction or serious nonfiction, people performed better on tests measuring empathy, social perception and emotional intelligence—skills that come in especially handy when you are trying to read someone's body language or gauge what they might be thinking. . . . Experts said the results implied that people could be primed for social skills like empathy, just as watching a clip from a sad movie can make one feel more emotional" (Belluck). If this is possible from just reading, then enhanced reading with guidance and discussion could reinforce the development of empathy. However, social influences on a person are more powerful influences than just reading (Keen 91). While reading may not make people act to aid others because of their empathic responses, or to treat others' suffering as prurience, a teacher or other guide could encourage or provide paths for responding to others more consciously. A theoretical approach that brings together trauma studies, narrative methods, and ethical considerations can create an engaged, critical discussion of these texts' complexities and can extend the private reading experience into the public realm in academic and social reading communities.[3]

ONE

Re-creating the Split Self in Margaret Atwood's *The Blind Assassin* and *Alias Grace*

Literary renditions of trauma offer important insights into human responses to stress. They allegorize and reconstitute such experience through the narrators' or protagonists' words and their motivations by way of defensive coping strategies. This literature substantiates that trauma is often evidence of forms of domination and misuses of human power, and underscores that people generally try to evade the psychological consequences of objectifying individuals. Through narrative juxtapositions, fiction can make compelling to readers the divisions within individuals (Emmott 170), showing how they exist inside and outside their traumas, wanting both to remember and to forget. Margaret Atwood engages readers in a critical reading process by immersing them in the flawed thinking and behavior of the traumatized and by illuminating the role of fear in motivating human behavior. Further, her protagonists engage in a critical rethinking of their situations that allows them and readers to challenge acts of power and complicity. Atwood's complex characterizations also demonstrate how identities can shift and flow according to circumstances. She and other trauma writers want to counteract the human impulse to blame victims and decontextualize victims' situations to protect themselves from feeling vulnerable (Root 232, 235). Activating large historical canvases, her novels *The Blind Assassin* and *Alias Grace* use the protagonists' haunting pasts to reflect on societal problems, justice, and ethics.

Atwood's works are particularly effective in exploring the effects of trauma on human personality, as observed in characters' split selves, dissociations, constricted emotions, distrust of others, and reduced capacity to love—all symptoms of trauma identified by clinicians such as Judith Herman and Ronnie Janoff-Bulman (*Trauma and Recovery* 42–47;

Shattered Assumptions 19–22). Atwood's depictions illustrate the personality changes consequent on trauma that Maria Root has described as the nonvoluntary survival response to perceived threat: "When the survival state is activated, the individual's perceptual, decisional, and relational processes are transformed; survival consumes and redirects all energy towards defensive strategies that may rapidly alternate" (247). In such a state, victims can no longer empathize with or identify with others. In their narrated accounts, Atwood's protagonists revisit and feel echoes of when they were more immersed in these mental frames of "depersonalization and disturbed identity formation" (J. Herman 125). As they begin working through their traumas, they must confront their fears, guilt, and feelings of shame and helplessness, and their resulting inability to connect effectively with others.

The Blind Assassin and *Alias Grace* exemplify literary texts' unique ability to re-create what Judith Herman calls the dialectical nature of this experience, caught between feeling and not feeling, remembering and forgetting, recognition and repetition (7–8). Atwood's novels demonstrate that intricate connections between power relations and personal trauma can be captured more compellingly by literary fiction. Though literary narrative can employ and depict the findings of psychological science, it also offers characterization and modes of storytelling that bring readers into "attitudes of seeing, believing, and speculating" (D. Herman, *Story Logic* 325). Such attitudes, when activated, enable readers to mentally and emotionally reconstruct the psychological and environmental complexities of, in this case, traumatic experience. Writers endeavor to change hearts and minds with their works by exposing readers to others' emotional states (Keen 5). They sometimes succeed, particularly if they address our most deeply held fears (Keen 71). The works I discuss in this book also engage readers' real-world knowledge of human psychology and trauma and their own psychological reactions to trauma (Gerrig 17, 20). However, trauma narratives, by emphasizing situational factors, can also run counter to readers' inclinations to attribute "causality to [human character] dispositions rather than situations," which Richard Gerrig calls the "fundamental attribution error" (54–55). This propensity for judging characters on the basis of free will might prevent reader identification or sympathy. However, if a literary narrative provides readers with causes for behavior and other means of engaging, it may win readers over to a more complex sympathy. To writers like Atwood, emotional investment on the part of readers is important.

Literary texts that deal with potentially upsetting and challenging material may not always overcome reader resistance. Because this literature raises the ethical issues of human agency, guilt, and responsibility, readers must measure their values and judgments against authors' and narrators' intentions and values. The outcome of reading always involves readers' perspectives and whether the text can effectively make readers believe its rhetorical or persuasive intentions (Phelan 18–19).

Reading texts through the lens of trauma theory helps identify for readers how a narrator is being presented to readers and how the narrator's characteristics are related to trauma; these theoretical tools include the illusion of quality of mind, and forms of perception guiding survivors. And here narratology proves helpful in identifying the literary techniques that ferry readers into characters' minds. For example, readers can locate evidence of traumatic aftereffects if they recognize ways that focalization, or the narrative's "perspectival filter," may restrict information (Jahn 94). Similarly effective interpretive tools are thought reports, which connect a character's consciousness to that individual's circumstances and actions (Palmer 76). Though multiple perspectives are offered in each novel discussed in this chapter, particularly in *Alias Grace,* Grace, and Iris of *The Blind Assassin,* are both the narrator-protagonists and the "central perceiving characters" (Jahn 95). Looking at themselves from within their own narratives, they offer the reader a chance to witness their situations through a particular lens that is not omniscient, is at times unreliable, and can only view events in a limited way. The characters' limitations offer something of this experience, but they also enjoin readers to process and perhaps fill in the gaps in the telling. Moreover, these two novels offer additional perspectives that reveal information not available to the protagonists and that, whether sympathetic or not, reveal "key issues and values within the culture" (Phelan 9) that can have devastating effects on the protagonists. These additional perspectives also provide social commentary or ethical insights that can be measured against the protagonists' perspectives. However, Atwood appears more interested in leading readers to explore her protagonists' thoughts and motives than in asking readers to decisively prove the protagonists' guilt or justify their actions. In fact, Atwood questions the processes by which such judgments could be made, and the underlying ethics of judging.

Grace and Iris are both reliable and unreliable narrators. Called on to reflect on their lives, they are able to report much in great detail, sometimes more than they can interpret. Both experience a confused sense of identity and a distance between their past and present selves as each confronts her own, possibly murderous, behavior. Bits of this haunting past and its consequences begin coming into consciousness as Grace and Iris come to terms with what they may or may not have done. At the same time, the picture of the past is often murky or repressed, or has undergone secondary elaboration in the manner of dreams. Despite some success resisting the suppression of their views, in the process of searching for clues and sifting through memory traces for fragments of evidence, neither Grace nor Iris succeeds perfectly in recovering the past. Nonetheless, their views are the most fully realized ones in the novels.

Atwood examines traumatic frameworks within two formative periods of Canadian history: the era of large-scale immigration and the 1837 rebellion in the nineteenth century in *Alias Grace*, and the effects of industrialization, the Great Depression, and World War II in the twentieth century in *The Blind Assassin*. She furnishes competing discourses, or points of view, for each period, and looks particularly at women situated in patriarchal and class-based contexts. While employing an array of detailed historical groundings for her readers, Atwood emphasizes the traumatic subjugation of women and the lower classes, providing them with the voices denied them in the past. As these novels particularly illustrate, punitive restrictions on women's bodies, choices, and sexuality can engender traumas of sexual violation and procreation that linger in personality and memory for decades and intergenerationally, beginning with the characters' mothers.

These two historical novels illustrate Hayden White's and Geoffrey Hartman's assertions of the historical and memorial value of literature in its broad capacities. These capacities include facility in presenting a range of historical cultural discourses and using specific kinds of stories or genres to translate discursive meaning (White 43) (e.g., events as tragic or psychologically complex). Also, literature is "more personal and focused than public memory," which can create cultural myths (Hartman, "Public Memory"). Literature can also open up interpretations or themes that other discourses may restrict. As White writes, "The narrative figures the body of events that serves as its primary referent and transforms these events into intimations of patterns of meaning that any literal representation of them as facts could never produce" (45). In other words, real events are imbued with meaning through the way "literature displays [them] to [a reader's] consciousness through its fashioning of patterns of 'imaginary' events" (45).

Alias Grace revisits the life of an actual historical figure, Grace Marks, who at best witnessed heinous murders of her employers and at worst participated in them. The historical and traumatic circumstances accumulate in novelistic ways that permit readers to see their impact on the characters emotionally, situationally, and relationally. Writers retranscribe a chronicle of facts into literary codes; they create allegorical narrative accounts of historical time periods. Atwood encodes history literarily in the epigraphs to her chapters, in which she juxtaposes discourses of the time, in Grace's view, and includes poetry as a legitimate, empathic voice therein. Using contemporary and historical knowledge of psychology, Atwood creates a psychological novel that deploys current theories of trauma in its descriptions of Grace. The passages unfolding Grace's split consciousness, evident in her visualizations of, but inability to normally remember, her traumatic, suppressed, but intrusive memories, allow readers some interpretive insight into Grace's responses to trauma. Such splitting is also evident in her capacity to dissociate in dangerous situations, for altered consciousness is a common symptom of the dissociative disorder suggested in Atwood's depiction of her (J. Herman 121). With the creation of the second protagonist, Dr. Simon Jordan, and other doctors in the novel, Atwood brings to the fore nineteenth-century views of mental illness and the representation of women through male authority figures, who can determine Grace's fate. She also intertextualizes and replicates some of the misogyny women patients suffered under psychoanalysis, as seen particularly in the case of Dora and Sigmund Freud (though this episode occurred later historically) (Darroch 109). Even the most humane of these views objectify Grace with what contemporary readers would recognize as outdated gender stereotyping.

Though Dr. Simon Jordan follows many of the progressive scientific views of the day (or perhaps of a later period, asserts Knelman 682), he is also hampered by his own emotional history with women and the gender norms of the time. These norms make him hold fast to his authority but undermine his ability to help Grace, though he loves her. Thus the novel demonstrates how emotional complexities embedded in culture complicate scientific, presumably objective, analysis. The Victorian moral and gender codes and the class system continually undermine all the characters and especially victimize the major female characters,

Grace, Mary, and Nancy. The novel demonstrates repeatedly how similar the stories of these three women are: servants vulnerable to their bosses, who want to seduce them, they are subjected to male violence and judged harshly for their real or imagined sexual transgressions, such as engaging in sex out of wedlock.

The Blind Assassin similarly presents historical events and discourses that shape the characters' emotional lives. The contexts here are different, however: turn-of-the-century industrialization, the violent suppression of labor unrest, and the trauma of two world wars. In keeping with Atwood's recognition that personal human relations absorb and mirror societal relations in contexts of power ("Notes" 7), the characters suffer many losses as the consequences of momentous economic and societal changes. Newspaper accounts codify the views of powerful interests, while Iris's memoir and Alex's fantasy stories of brutal regimes, the two principal narratives in the novel, unmask what the powerful try to hide. These alternative stories reflect the consequences of capitalist and political dominance over the lives of the characters and mirror Atwood's own fictional renderings of historical patterns. She also identifies patriarchal definitions of women that are internalized by Iris and complicate the sisters' lives as they become caught up in her husband Richard's grab for economic and political power.

Both novels illustrate new historical notions of historical complexity. Atwood makes use of the novel as a traditionally hybrid form to include multiple competing discourses by using actual historical documents and accounts, often recreating and critiquing media views (newspapers) of her subjects, in this way questioning whether objective representation is possible. The documents include Susanna Moodie's historical accounts of Grace (whom she actually observed), fictional letters that convey nineteenth-century medical views, and nineteenth-century poetry that matches thematically the characters' experiences in the novel. All demonstrate the various discourses (of media, law, religion, and science) prevalent during the nineteenth century. The news sources, whether actual ones in *Alias Grace* or fabricated in *The Blind Assassin*, exhibit a propensity for imaginative elaboration and emphasize appearances or sensational interpretations rather than facts or causational factors. The historical accounts appear more self-interested and uninformed than Grace's account, in which, emphasizing imaginative and subjective elements, Atwood compellingly recreates the circumstances of a servant's life and the emotional toll it exacts. The fabricated newspaper items in

The Blind Assassin acquaint readers with historical or public events occurring in the background of the characters' lives but distort or avoid important suppressed personal events that Iris covers in detail.

Further, these two novels enact a process of questioning how the past is remembered and who represents or writes it, through multiple contradictory perspectives from those times. For Atwood, "fiction is where individual memory and experience and collective memory and experience come together, in greater or less proportions" ("In Search of Alias Grace" 1504). Like other Canadian writers of the 1980s and 1990s, Atwood was interested in recovering repressed aspects of that nation's history. In those decades Canadian writers became more assertive about addressing their status as a former colony. They wanted to reexamine their own roots, even the ugly truths, of how Canadians arrived at their present condition, and the costs associated with the class structure, political struggles, and aspiring to wealth (1509).

Atwood recognizes the difficulty of recovering history because of faulty memory and the common propensity to repress painful or unpleasant knowledge. Repression can come from motivations as disparate as personal fear, ideology, or a desire to maintain the social order (Vickroy, *Trauma and Survival* 170). She has asked the ontological question, "How do we know we know what we think we know? . . . How do we know we are who we think we are . . . or thought we were . . . a hundred years ago?" ("In Search of Alias Grace" 1505). She recognizes there are some truths it is necessary to know, but that it can difficult if not impossible to arrive at them (1506). Atwood's background in Victorian studies and her familiarity with that era's preoccupation with memory, regret, and nostalgia for the past help to contextualize and complicate the nature of memory in *Alias Grace*. Further, Atwood took on an infamous true-life murder case complicated by a contradictory and incomplete historical record. Atwood notes in the novel's afterword that she made a point not to alter solid facts, that the major elements of the book had to be strongly suggested by the writings on Grace Marks from the time. However, the undocumented parts of the story Atwood felt free to invent (Atwood, "Afterword" 464–65). Many stories about Grace at the time had their own particular audiences with their own, usually moralistic, views of criminals and of women's nature and politics, which are arranged by Atwood in excerpted passages in book section epigraphs.

Believing "the past belongs to those who claim it, and are willing to explore it and to infuse it with meaning for those alive today" ("In Search of Alias Grace" 1516), Atwood asks us to reconsider Grace's situation in ways unimagined in her time. Embracing the complications, Atwood sets out to intrigue psychologically sophisticated contemporary readers by addressing the impact of trauma that challenges nineteenth-century religiously prescribed views of human nature as inborn and consistent. Knowledge of trauma also challenges assumptions of the law about personal responsibility and free will that contradict contemporary social science research on environmental effects and the behaviors people learn to adapt to adversity. She does this through revealing the social prejudices that guide most views of Grace, and by characterizing Grace's complex and painful relationship to memory and identity as she is subject to successive adverse, often traumatic situations in which she has few options and no power.

Though these two novels have common elements regarding the treatment of Canadian history, women's struggles, and narrative strategies, they deal with different time periods, traumatic experiences, and narrator motivations. Therefore, I will discuss them in separate sections. Each section analyzes the unique characteristics of each novel and the intricate renderings of historical trauma each provides readers.

Trauma and Narrative Motivation in Margaret Atwood's *The Blind Assassin*

Persistent themes of women in traumatic circumstances reoccur in Margaret Atwood's novels as she examines the effects of physical, sexual, and psychological violence on women situated in patriarchal and class-based contexts. Trauma victims, her female protagonists often begin in the throes of suffering and use psychological defenses—repression, emotional withdrawal, or rationalization—against punishing environments, and then go through the painful process of working through trauma (Vickroy, "Sexual Trauma" 254). The narrator and protagonist of *The Blind Assassin*, Iris Chase, writes a memoir that bears witness for the dead, and reconstructs a suppressed family history that includes her sister Laura's suicide and her own complicity in it. Iris's narrative is by turns revealing, poignant, self-incriminating, inconsistent, and self-serving. However, trauma can explain her thoughts, actions, and sense of identity and fuel the gaps, misapprehensions, and ethical failures evident in her self-portrait. Trauma's alteration of her memory and cognition is discovered in Iris's belated attempts to recall the emotional disconnection that had allowed her to survive at the cost of her closest relationships. *The Blind Assassin* exemplifies literary narrative's unique ability to recreate both what Judith Herman calls the "dialectical" nature of this experience, as the protagonist is caught between feeling and not feeling, remembering and forgetting, action and inaction, and the changes it wreaks on personality and perception (121–23).

It is important first to establish the traumatic contexts and the emotional patterns that arise from them. Atwood's characters regularly experience systematic coercion that, in the form of social demands to conform, demands silence, intimidates women, and protects perpetrators. Her protagonists also often experience emotional neglect early in life that makes them more vulnerable to subsequent traumas. Iris's experiences exemplify what Judith Herman describes as the humiliations associated with trauma that produce numerous symptoms and defenses that create a tainted and diminished sense of self, and that make victims protect themselves from shame, fear, and pain by repressing memory of experiences, avoiding recall, or dissociating (J. Herman 51–56). This shame and its attendant defenses come to define survivors' personalities, and their fear and distrust of others frequently jeopardize their relationships (42–47; Van der Kolk and McFarlane 15). Their repressed experience is not "remembered" in the normal sense but emerges intrusively; it is reexperienced rather than revisited (Laub and Auerhahn 288).

I am investigating the narrative strategies that lead readers through characters' mental frameworks. Knowing these strategies demonstrates how characters' mentalities illustrate Atwood's implicit contentions about the psychological effects of persistent coercion that destroy individual will and ethical judgment. An important strategy to examine is focalization, which refers to the ways readers' attention is drawn and readers are led to pick up on thoughts and feelings through the filter of a narrator's or character's perspective (Abbott 73–74). Iris's view is unusual in that she narrates as if she were both immersed in her own life story and outside it, with temporal shifts between past and present and emotional shifts, and a split narrative. Readers can better ascertain the narrator's claims, characteristics, and reliability through analyzing these storytelling elements, which highlight the traumatic fragmenting of the protagonist's memory, identity, and relational capacities.

To account for Iris's motives, readers must look for ways in which Atwood has Iris draw readers into her own and Laura's life history, and into understanding what made the sisters vulnerable to domination and subsequent traumas. Most of the early contexts of trauma are associated with the girls' parents. Their father, a prominent factory owner, was personally devastated by the deaths of his brothers in World War I. He is made to suppress his grief and rage by the girls' emotionally unavailable mother, who dies after a difficult miscarriage. Her daughters inherit her philosophy of self-sacrifice. Iris and Laura, only nine and six at the time, are urged to suppress anything painful or embarrassing (*Blind Assassin* 142). Iris became and remains especially vulnerable to culturally induced shame, to needing to save face because of her social position. During the Great Depression, the father's business falters, and he is forced to sell to an ambitious industrialist, Richard Griffen, who will break his promise to keep the factories going. The father persuades Iris to marry Griffen for her own and Laura's sake. Laura tries to persuade Iris not to marry him, but Iris succumbs to her father's needs, her own fears, and the powerful ideology of the time that women were in need of protection. However, giving in to such expectations reinforces past traumas and creates future ones, Atwood implies. Iris comes to realize Richard is a sadistic, controlling man who will ruin both her life and Laura's. He makes them his sexual prisoners. In fragmentary patches, Iris slowly reveals the sexual traumas she has sustained by alluding to her own bruises and recurring nightmares. Further, she eventually unveils the contents of Laura's posthumous notebooks, coded accounts of Richard's sexual coercion and his impregnation and incarceration of Laura, followed by a forced abortion. Another complication is the sisters' mutual affection for Alex, Iris's lover and a labor activist, whom they protect from authorities and whose death in World War II divides the sisters.

Iris has internalized her protected status as an upper-class woman who needs to be protected—so much so that she accepts the control of Griffen and his sister, Winifred (the primary enforcer), who forbid her access to money and her own mail. They assume this control to advance Griffen's career, and keep Iris in the dark to better manipulate her. J. Brooks Bouson has analyzed the many ways Iris buys into the culture's sexism and patriarchal diminishment of women, which limited women to social and reproductive roles. At Winifred's prodding, much of Iris's life is spent in the "women's culture" of high society, fashion, and charity work ("Commemoration" 262). Significantly, Laura rejects these trappings and immediately recognizes that for the Griffens, marriage is a business proposition (*Blind Assassin* 263).

As an elderly woman, Iris admits in her memoir the consequences of her life history, facing the fact that her younger self was crushed by many losses and denied an adult identity. If we interpret Iris's acquiescence to Griffen as symptomatic, we can see how Atwood leads us to infer that because Iris had so little say over her own life, she became emotionally numb, avoiding and denying feeling so as to tolerate a seemingly inescapable marriage and the Griffens' relentless control. She reports the feeling of losing herself: "I was sand, I was snow—written on, rewritten, smoothed over" (371). Moreover, she associates her marriage with intimations of her own death, an annihilation of self, which is typical of trauma survivors (Lifton 18). Iris learns to shield herself from Richard using the defenses of inattention and avoidance, but this stance detaches her from her emotional bond with loved ones, too.

The defenses Iris erects shape her personality in ways that elude her until she tries to reconstruct her past. Her narrow perspective then becomes evident when she must rediscover her situation through others' views of her and her losses. She recalls Laura and Alex as witnesses to her emotional withdrawal; Laura in particular described her as a "sleepwalker." Iris tends to minimize Laura's willingness to rebel, probably because Laura's strong refusals threaten the defenses Iris has built up to tolerate her situation. Discouraged by Iris's obliviousness, Laura stops confiding in her, resulting in their estrangement and Laura's gradual path to self-destruction. Iris exhibits similar avoidance with Alex, deciding too late that she would leave Richard for him.

Readers are absorbed into the dialectic of trauma as Iris alternates between present and past in her memoir, but she cannot fully integrate them. The disjunctions between her younger, emotionally defended self and inquiring older self are manifestations of her split existence and make her narrative task difficult as she tries to understand what happened and what motivated her. She belatedly recognizes painful details, or they intrude upon her. For example, at midpoint in the novel the older Iris stands near a bridge, indirectly (she does not mention Laura) recalling Laura's death (who had driven off a bridge): "I became conscious of my heart, and of dizziness. Also of breathlessness, as if I were in over my head. But over my head in what? Not water; something thicker. Time: old, cold time, old sorrow, settling down in layers like silt in a pond" (*Blind Assassin* 299). Triggers like the bridge or her writing force painful material to consciousness, hence her panicked and fearful response. In these confrontations with the past, Iris slowly begins to understand the powerful hold the past has on her and her lingering guilt over Laura's agonized life and suicide.

Similarly, Atwood has Iris confront repressed traumatic fears and draw in the reader by recounting character-defining dreams that reveal deeply buried emotions. Atwood's characters often report dreams but don't interpret them, so that readers may acquire knowledge about the characters that the characters themselves do not have. Nightmares about Richard wake Iris up regularly even decades after his death, and though she does not talk about them in detail, she acknowledges that past horrors relentlessly surface. "When you're young . . . you think you can get rid of things, and people too—leave them behind. You don't yet know about the habit they have, of coming back. . . . Time in dreams is frozen. You can never get away from where you've been" (396). Her dreams function like static traumatic memories, returning her to the fear and violence in her marriage that she fights to distance herself from when conscious. "I dreamt that Richard was back. I could hear him breathing in the bed beside me. . . . My heart was hammering painfully, as if I'd been running. It's true, what they used to say, I thought. A nightmare can kill you" (22). Atwood illustrates how vital to traumatic experience these sense memories are, remaining suspended in time and continuing to terrify because they're not subject to modification by subsequent experience or reevaluation, only reexperienced in repetitive, unconscious patterns (Van der Kolk and Van der Hart 441–42). Thus readers are brought into the fears that propelled Iris's past actions.

Readers must also reconstruct Iris's motives by comparing the two major narrative frameworks that constitute the novel, Iris's memoir and the novel Laura is purportedly writing, titled *The Blind Assassin*. Though for most of the novel we are not privy to the immediate connection between these alternating narratives, each nonetheless reflects on the other in a disguised fashion, and each tells crucial parts of the story, even if their relationship is not made explicit until the novel is almost complete. Readers need to note what Iris has not revealed and why, and the effects of Iris's emotional distance from Laura. Laura's novel describes an unidentified couple's affair, presumably Alex and Laura's. Alex is a union organizer apparently framed by Griffen for murder—which is explained in Iris's memoir. The man tells horrific science fiction stories with scenes recalling the violent oppression Griffen ruthlessly inflicted on Iris, Laura, and his workers. These stories demonstrate that Alex was more of a witness to Iris's life than she was, as he recognized the personal and larger socioeconomic frameworks controlling her and Laura's lives. They also suggest that one way of managing a traumatic past is through creation and witnessing. As Iris's first-person narrative progresses toward what caused Laura's death, readers are given the means to reconstruct how Iris was torn between the Griffens' demands and her secret affair with Alex. For it is Alex and Iris who are the couple in Laura's novel, which readers eventually learn was in fact written by Iris.

This embedded text also reveals Iris's great loathing of Richard and that her desire to rebel against him enhances the pleasure she experiences with Alex. Yet her fear of Richard transfers into a fear of being emotionally vulnerable with Alex. Consequently, she describes her desire for Alex in the embedded novel as a "humiliation. It's like being hauled along by a shameful rope, a leash around the neck. She resents it, her lack of freedom, and so she stretches out the time between, rationing him" (261). Sadly, the sexual traumas of her marriage structure and complicate her love for Alex, making it grasping, egocentric, and tragic because she is too emotionally stunted to reciprocate his love.

This double narrative is but one part of the split focalization in the novel that illustrates Iris's frame of mind. Her defenses lead Iris outside her own life story, and certainly outside Laura's. Her wedding photographs evoke little memory, and she regards the woman in the pictures, herself at age nineteen, as "her." "I say 'her,' because I don't recall having been present, not in any meaningful sense of the word. I and the girl in the picture have ceased to be the same person. I am her outcome, the result of the life she once lived headlong" (239). She realizes well into writing the memoir that her emotional splitting and fear distanced her from Laura's crises, especially Laura's trying to escape Richard's advances and being institutionalized so that Richard's baby could be aborted (which Iris doesn't know about until she reads Laura's posthumous journals). In her late admission of the extent of their rivalry over Alex, Iris further reveals why she's estranged from Laura. By allowing the Griffens to focus on Laura, Iris had protected her own secret: she was carrying Alex's baby.

Shame, though largely repressed through much of her story, surfaces early in the novel, long before her realization and recognition of her role in Laura's death. "Shame is the emotion related to having let oneself down [in traumatic situations]. . . . Victims may be unaware of its presence, and yet it comes to dominate their interactions with the environment. Denial of one's own feelings of shame, as well as those of other people, opens the door for further abuse" (Van der Kolk and

McFarlane 15). Readers are given examples of the way shame becomes a part of the tenor of her existence. Early in the novel, in the decades after the traumatic events, Iris expresses but does not seem fully aware of why she feels she's a "trespasser" in her own home snacking at night. "Standing there with the jar in one hand and my finger in my mouth, I had the feeling that someone was about to walk into the room—some other woman, the unseen, valid owner—and ask me what in hell I was doing in her kitchen. I've had it before, the sense that even in the course of my most legitimate and daily actions . . . I am trespassing" (56). Shame seems to be part of her consciousness, creating a sense of her own badness and illegitimacy, and her symptoms seem indicative of the guilt-producing actions she later admits.

Iris makes the ethical crux of the novel her failing Laura and having to face the shame of her failures as a sister, lover, and mother, which she avoids until the novel's final chapters. Iris remembers that Alex and Laura challenged her to leave Richard and change her life. She realizes her actions regarding them and her neglect and loss of her daughter to Winifred Griffen point to her moral deficiencies. She reports a long list of instances when she did not stand up to the Griffens' dismantling of her life and Laura's. Above all, she did not protect Laura, who Iris claimed was the pretext for her initial sacrifices, which she also admits resenting. Iris finally admits that in her last horrific conversation with Laura, Iris tried once again to wrest Alex from Laura. She destroys Laura's hope of reuniting with Alex, callously revealing he died during the war and that they were lovers, thus provoking Laura's suicide.

> My fingers itched with spite. I knew what had happened next. I'd pushed her off.
>
> Now I'm coming to the part that still haunts me. *Now* I should have bitten my tongue, *now* I should have kept my mouth shut. Out of love, I should have lied or said anything else: anything but the truth. (488)

At this point the victim has become the perpetrator; at the time of narrating she can feel shame about her past selfishness. Readers must assess whether there is sufficient evidence to make the case that trauma largely caused Iris's blindness and unreliability. Trauma can account for many of her failures to think clearly about Laura and Richard, and its attendant shame could account for the delay in speaking of her self-recriminations.

Shame was also highlighted in the past by her failures as a mother, which she cannot quite own and may make her speechless (or self-protective) when in her narrative she focuses more on her attempts to get Aimee back from Winifred. Self-recriminating, Iris recalls trying to approach Aimee as an adult; she describes Aimee's anguished drunken rants and her conviction that Laura was her real mother. Clearly, Aimee was deprived of love and stability, and readers might also implicate Iris in Aimee's death—Aimee self-medicates and kills herself in a drunken fall—though perhaps more so Winifred, who kept Aimee from Iris. Iris needs to make recompense and attempts this with her confessions and by revealing the truth about herself and Laura to her granddaughter, Aimee's daughter, through her writing.

When Iris is in survival mode, emotionally dissociated, she cannot account for her motivations. She begins to get in touch with her own shame through this writing. As the critics Van der Kolk and McFarlane have noted,

> The question of shame is critical to understanding the lack of self-regulation in trauma victims and the capacity of abused persons to become abusers. Trauma is usually accompanied by intense feelings of humiliation; to feel threatened, helpless, and out of control is a vital attack on the capacity to be able to count on oneself. Shame is the emotion related to having let oneself down. Being sensitive to the shame in others is an essential protection against abusing one's fellow human beings, and it requires being in touch with one's own sense of shame. Similarly, not being in touch with one's own shame leaves one vulnerable to further abuse from others. (15)

Readers can learn to recognize trauma symptoms in characters' self-defeating, defensive, and repetitive behaviors. These behaviors may elicit condemnation if readers do not understand that, though understandably self-protective, such behaviors also reinforce coercive circumstances and create mind-sets that can place victims beyond normal frameworks for considering ethical behavior. Traumatized characters may seem unreliable, but one can attribute this to their defenses against the fears that drive them. Unreliability, narrative theory explains, can involve failures to inform, but more significant are failures of judgment or ethics (Abbott 75–77), which, as I have mentioned, in the case of trauma narratives could be tied to symptoms. All are manifest with Iris: helplessness, faulty cognition or memory, shame, and repression, or dissociation. Atwood provides many examples of Iris's constricted emotional life, abuse, self-protective dissociation, and desperate grabs at moments of happiness. Readers may be more curious than sympathetic as to how Iris will admit her involvement in Laura's death. When she belatedly acknowledges the shame and sadness she feels about her actions, readers may admire her willingness to reach awareness ("I chose knowledge") and teach others. Atwood has provided more principled (or less traumatized) characters to indicate an implicit value structure Iris is unable to embrace. Laura and Alex are willing to sacrifice their lives for their beliefs, but Iris lacks both their integrity and any idea of a self that is capable of action until she learns why Laura died. Initially she blames Richard and avenges Laura's death by publishing *The Blind Assassin*, the embedded novel that exposes Richard's exploitation of Laura. His reputation ruined, he commits suicide, but Winifred retaliates and uses her influence and the legal system to take Aimee from Iris. Social and legal expectations about women's behavior are brought to bear in condemning Iris as she takes lovers for comfort after the deaths of Laura, Richard, and Alex. It takes longer, and the loss of her daughter, for Iris to recognize her role in both Aimee's and Laura's deaths.

Readers could test Iris's dilemma against their own concepts of meaningful sibling bonds. Iris could be given some consideration based on the technicality that Alex did not seriously consider Laura a potential lover, believing her too young and religious. However, if we take the whole story into account, Iris can be faulted particularly for failing to recognize Laura's feelings or to tell her about the affair until years later, when the shock of this, and Alex's death, leads to Laura's suicide.

If readers are led to see fictional characters' behaviors as the consequence of the emotional and cognitive limitations of adopting a survival mode, they can begin to consider to what degree trauma symptoms prevent individuals from bearing responsibility for themselves and others, the extent of misery they inflict on themselves, or whether they treat others fairly and compassionately. This demonstrates why terror and control are such effective methods of power.

Atwood's work features the unique properties of literary narrative that contribute to our knowledge of the intricate psychological ramifications of trauma, particularly as it is socially induced in contexts of domination and power. As Atwood has observed, "Power is our environment. . . . So many of the things we do in what we sadly think of as our personal lives are simply duplications of the external world of power games, power struggles" ("Notes" 7). Atwood often examines how her women characters are psychologically overwhelmed by personal relations that reinscribe dominance and submission in particularly gendered behavior codes. Some of the components of literary narrative, especially focalization and indirect characterization, such as by means of dream narratives, make available to readers how personality changes as a result of trauma. Often in Atwood's novels, recognizing the uses of power and its effects helps her female protagonists face their fears enough to break down defensive psychological patterns, to reconsider their lives, and to act in their own behalf. Iris breaks her patterns by writing and engaging in a growth process. And though her self-discovery is tragic because it comes too late for herself and Laura, she is at least no longer blindly destructive, as she warns future generations in addressing her memoir to her granddaughter.

Trauma and Patches of Memory in *Alias Grace*

The primary action of *Alias Grace* is the enactment of an early type of psychoanalysis (Knelman 684–85; Darroch 118) conducted by Dr. Simon Jordan with the convicted murderess, Grace Marks; the therapeutic context provides a framework for Grace to relate her traumatic history as a young immigrant woman. Simon is enjoined by sympathetic supporters to help Grace recover her memories so that she may be exonerated, or at least released from the prison where she has been incarcerated for ten years. Many facts of the case and trial were called into question, particularly her role in the murder of her employers, Thomas Kinnear and his partner, Nancy Montgomery. Grace has no clear memory of the murders. Her "accomplice," James McDermott, who had clearly instigated the crimes, was hanged right after the trial. Dr. Jordan is initially interested in the case in the hope that it will make him a great reputation as an alienist (an early type of psychotherapist). He eventually becomes personally invested in helping Grace; however, her reluctance and his own emotional baggage are substantial obstacles.

Grace relates to Dr. Jordan the many sources and contexts of trauma in her life: her family's poverty, her drunken father's physical and perhaps sexual abuse, and the difficulties faced by Irish immigrants to Canada. She is consistently affected by the insidious traumas often visited on those assigned low social status (Root 240) and associated with the desperate circumstances of the women who influence her life. First, she witnessed her mother's frequent births and her death on the family's sea voyage to Canada when Grace was twelve. Then she endured the suffering and death of her beloved friend Mary from an abortion after Mary was seduced by their boss's son. And last, she is further confronted with women's vulnerability to sexual and social class codes as personified in Nancy Montgomery, whose untenable position as both servant and then mistress of the house leads to her murder, along with the murder of Nancy's boss and lover, James Kinnear, by James McDermott and, allegedly, Grace herself. Whether Grace participated in the gruesome murders or was an innocent victim is the crux of others' judgments of Grace and the punishment she deserves. Only sixteen, she is treated leniently, sentenced to life in prison, while McDermott is hanged. Grace's memories of these terrifying events are repressed (Staels 431), gap-filled; her recall is dotted with only a few instances of scattered, visual traumatic memories. She cannot verify, even to herself, her own involvement.

A split consciousness is integral to Grace's characterization, denoting the lack of continuity in her sense of self, past and present, and consequently in the narrative structure. Grace is split between her youth and her older, world-weary self. Readers witness the split through her view as a narrator with deeper knowledge (Emmott 171) as she describes her younger, more naïve and frightened self. Many of the traumatic aspects of her past are unavailable to her because of time, repression, or dissociation. She cannot identify with her past actions that have so thoroughly determined her life, leading her from asylum to prison to becoming an object of pity. Like many trauma survivors, she must be of two minds about remembering and knowing repressed events. Though she feels thrilled to be talking about her life with Simon, she feels "torn open" (69) as painful details emerge. She desperately wants to be relieved from always living "inside" her traumatic story (298), yet she also fears exposure to terrifying memories, as well as the possibility of remaining incarcerated if she remembers she was in fact involved in the murders.

Though Grace's first-person narrative predominates, interspersed with her view is that of Simon Jordan, another central perceiving character presented through an indirect third-person narrative, which allows both his view and commentary on him to be expressed. He is sufficiently aware that Atwood can lay out through his perceptions and thoughts all the possible complex motivations Grace might have to evade him, and the uncertainties of her guilt or innocence that stymie his need for certainty. He sympathizes with Grace and wants to be helpful, but through him we see much of what Grace is up against with authority figures. A middle-class man largely protected from the harshness of a life like Grace's, he mainly views women condescendingly or as fantasy objects. Unexpectedly, he experiences a traumatic countertransference while delving into the horrors of her life story, which brings up his own hidden issues and seems to drive him to reenact some of the violence of her life. As one critic has noted, Simon's sexuality "erupts in brutality [with his landlady Rachel] and leads to his flight, [as he] . . . epitomizes a fear that the laws of class and social custom are easily transgressed" (Edwards 106). Though he is the most open and progressive male character, Grace's story brings out in him too many anxieties around sexuality and breaking with the social and moral order for him to be able to help her.

Many keys to Grace's character emerge through her immediate focus on the nature of her carceral life and as a servant in the governor's mansion, among people who want to free her. She adopts a dignified self-control because she realizes that to express emotion (she appears to have been psychotically enraged when in the asylum) or any resistance to authority brings punishment. She trains herself to suppress her views and feelings: "I've learnt how to keep my face still" (26). The context of her being Irish in an emotionally repressive British-dominant culture is significant; it does not encourage testimony or healing. This mask of calm is her only defense against the surveillance and control to which she is continually subjected. Through thought reports, the narrative technique whereby writers connect the "internal consciousnesses of characters to their external social and physical context" (Palmer 49), readers learn that Grace views the prison, domestic service, and even the bedroom as places that contain hidden traps, potential dangers, or punishment. She has to read or interpret what others want of her, usually obedience, placidity, and domesticity. Her skill at sewing is seen as a sign of emotional stability. These behaviors all exemplify gender norms of womanliness, far from her persona as the "murderess." And though she does not identify with this persona, it gives her a certain status and allows her human connections and insights into others' motives as they attempt to assist her.

Grace is bewildered by the many unflattering views of her expressed in the press and public, and with her steady and observant demeanor she does not seem capable of being the murderous temptress they describe. Carrying such labels makes her feel a critical loss of identity, and as she also realizes she must please sympathetic individuals such as Simon and the Reverend Verringer, she is left feeling "all the traces of me, soothed over and rubbed away as if they had never been" (342). Her thoughts underscore how she's had to bring her fears under control in order to fit in, and how trauma and lifelong punishment have driven her thoughts inward and changed her personality to one of passive resistance. Prison also teaches her a fatalistic awareness that women are punished regularly by institutions, society, and at home, even for not being able to prevent their victimization. Her fatalism extends to believing the souls of her mother and Mary remain captive and unable to find peace.

Readers learn of Grace's major traumatic symptoms not from Grace but from accounts by others who have witnessed uncharacteristic behaviors in her that point to an alternate personality. Grace, ironically, is dissociated from some of the most important events in her life. Atwood makes a strong case for Grace being severely traumatized and immerses readers in psychological details to emphasize this interpretation, starting with childhood abuse and subsequent worse traumas, which she depicts as causing Grace's dissociative disorder (Darroch 118). Atwood thus provides literary and historical grounds for the emergence of another personality. Many of the fictional characters, from the staff in the asylum and her employers to Nancy and McDermott and Susanna Moodie, report Grace's uncharacteristically inappropriate laughter or screaming or past aggressive sexual behavior. All these reports contradict Grace's self-characterized emotional and sexual caution (reinforced by Simon's observations). These accounts, and the emergence of Mary's personality within Grace after Mary's death, during the murders, and then when Grace is hypnotized late in the novel, represent the workings of dissociative identity disorder (formerly called multiple personality disorder), a rare and extreme manifestation of trauma, whose sufferers are known for "staggering dissociative capabilities" (J. Herman 124). As Hilde Staels has observed, dissociative identity disorder, labeled "double consciousness" in the nineteenth century, was often a diagnosis attached to hysterical women, and more recently has been recognized as an indication of childhood sexual abuse (Freyd 76, cited in Staels 437).[1] A person with dissociative identity disorder is typically split between a "primary passive identity and alternate identities with contrasting names and characteristics" (Favazza 247). Deborah Bray Haddock describes "alters" as "dissociated parts of the self that represent memories, emotions, and ways of relating. They are able to function independently from each other and are also referred to as 'parts' because they are parts of the individual's overall personality" (6). One alter may act out without the knowledge of the other: Grace appears to undergo what the psychoanalyst Judith Herman describes as a "passive influence experience of being controlled by another personality" (124).

As "Mary," Grace is able to act out the anger underlying such splits "that [typically] has had to be repressed over the years as a means of survival" (22). Grace looked up to Mary as a surrogate mother or sister; Mary had a strong personality and instilled in Grace a sense of class consciousness. Having identified with Mary, Grace reacts strongly to the injustices around sexuality and social class that Nancy and Kinnear embody. She may identify with McDermott's homicidal rage, but not consciously, she believes. Mary's traumas also become Grace's, as when Grace becomes hysterical at the sight of a surgeon with sharp instruments, associating him unconsciously with Mary's brutal abortion doctor. By indicating dissociative identity disorder as a diagnosis of Grace, Atwood offers a contemporary explanation for certain events, for the contradictory testimony about Grace's behavior, and suggests a pathway by which oppression and trauma can lead to psychopathology. A number of possible alterations of consciousness associated with this disorder can account for her amnesia, such as the reliving of experiences, depersonalization, and derealization (J. Herman 121).

Grace's sexuality provides further evidence of a traumatic split. Her reticence about sex can be easily associated with her mother's and Mary's experiences. Her prudish reactions to the crude accusations that she is a temptress and a murderess conform to the mores of the time, but they are also strikingly different from her alternate personality's behavior, which is sexually receptive, even aggressive, and in turn spurs male aggression, which puzzles her when she reverts to her primary mental state. For example, she infers from McDermott's comments that she eggs him on as Mary and then fights him off as herself. This is an example, too, of alters, the dissociated personalities, carrying out "highly contradictory patterns of relating" (J. Herman 125). Grace internally suppresses her desires for anything because Mary suffered for acting on her desires. Grace tells Simon about the dangers beds hold for women, connoting as they do sex, pregnancy, and death—something she has learned from her mother's and Mary's experiences.

Atwood creates dreams that are symbolically and metaphorically rich to suggest the associative functions of Grace's mind. Though Simon tries to unlock her past through her dreams, Grace guards them closely from him, but not from readers: "I need to keep something for myself" (101). Her dreams carry important unconscious material related to the murders, but it is disguised, imaginatively elaborated, not actual memories but seemingly her impressions of the horrific events—Nancy was killed with an axe blow and strangulation—something Grace does not remember witnessing. She has a recurring dream that she claims originally appeared just before the murders and in which she foresees Nancy's murder, but it's not a memory, and it is too incomplete and impressionistic to be conclusive evidence of her role in the murders.

Grace's memory gaps, dreams, and dreamlike visions engage readers in piecing together the fragments and uncertainties of traumatic memory. Natalie Cooke has pointed out that Atwood connects her narrators and readers with "fictive confessions" that "implicate the reader in the power politics under discussion" while appropriating to readers "the authority and the responsibility of a witness" (225). Grace's biggest memory lapses have to do with the details of the murders, particularly Nancy's. Her relationship to memory is complicated: she cannot recall some aspects of the murders but relives other parts visually in ways that indicate violence but neither confirm a narrative of events nor her role in them. She is also wisely hesitant to reveal some things she does know to protect herself from punitive authorities. Atwood creates richly symbolic imagery that evokes multiple associations with the murders in stark, visually intrusive reminders of Grace's traumatic experiences (Staels 437), which undergo a secondary elaboration in Grace's unconscious. She frequently "sees" red flowers, or red peonies, that she knows are not there. These images trigger a vision of Nancy, bloody, begging for mercy, with Grace's kerchief around her neck (*Alias Grace* 2). This image is a reconstruction, Grace claims, not a real memory, and is accompanied by her present wish, that she had helped Nancy. Readers could interpret this wish as a sign of guilt, or simply a wish to have been able to prevent events over which she had little control. Her visions are depicted as involuntary and repetitive, and remain isolated from normal, continuous memory, from which she remains dissociated. Grace indicates, "The soil for them is emptiness, it is empty space and silence" (297). She dreads the "shining red peonies, which appear particularly at night and are like satin. . . . I whisper Talk to me; because I would rather have talking than the slow gardening that takes place in silence, with the red satin petals dripping down the wall. I think I sleep" (297). Again, a split is evident: she wants to understand ("talk"), but sleep (or unconsciousness) indicates avoidance of the terror of the worst events. The primary association to this symbolic visualization is Nancy's peonies, red as they turned in the sunset the night before the murders. These could be examples of the alterations in consciousness associated with dissociative identity disorder. This type of dream could be a kind of derealization, an altered state of consciousness in which the reality of the world has been changed (J. Herman 121).

As the narrative juxtaposes Grace's thoughts, it creates a sense of lived experience as it immerses readers in Grace's confused, living memory experience of the night before the murders, where she cannot identify voices that go through her head. Here is the text as written, with my speculations in brackets about whose voices are rendered here, capturing the unreality of the situation, Grace's depersonalization, and her reliving of experiences (Mary's death):

> I'm in the back passage, feeling my way along the wall. I can scarcely see the wallpaper; it used to be green. Here are the stairs going up, here is the banister. The bedroom door is half open, and I can listen. Bare feet on the red-flower carpet. I know you're hiding from me, come out at once or I'll have to find you and catch you, and when I've got hold of you, then who knows what I will do. ["I" is Grace, then probably Kinnear to Nancy.]
>
> I'm keeping very still behind the door, I can hear my own heart. Oh no, oh no, oh no. [Grace]
>
> Here I come, I am coming now. You never obey me, you never do what I say, you dirty girl. Now you will have to be punished. [Kinnear teasingly to Nancy, but the overtones of the speech fit McDermott and Grace, too.]
>
> It is not my fault. What can I do now, where can I turn? [Grace, with echoes of Mary]
>
> You must unlock the door, you must open the window, you must let me in. [Mary, come to save Grace?]
>
> Oh look, oh look at all the spilt petals, what have you done? [Mary to Grace, Grace to herself?]
>
> I think I sleep.

Kinnear's teasing words to Nancy morph into the words Grace imagined Mary said after her death: "You must open the window, you must let me in. Oh look, oh look at all the spilt petals, what have you done?" (297). The petals again seem to refer to the blood of the murders, and to Nancy's peonies. The repeated "I think I sleep" renders an altered consciousness or dissociative state. As the murderous atmosphere is ramped up, along with her fear, Grace becomes more dissociated and depersonalized. She loses her identity in these dire situations of Mary and Nancy, as she envisions Mary with a red heart, triggered by Nancy's similar situation to Mary's—pregnant, helpless, and threatened—and signaling Grace's retraumatization and Mary's reemergence. Grace's closeness to Mary, the traumatic nature of her death for both of them, the terrors of the moment, and the historical background of communicating with the dead in Victorian times all make such hallucinations possible for a superstitious girl.

Atwood again creates qualia, the narrative illusion of lived experience, by immersing readers in Grace's thoughts. After the powerful red dreams she wakes in the prison in a liminal state among places of past and present. "I wake up at cock crow and I know where I am. I'm in the parlour. I'm in the scullery [Kinnear's]. I'm in the cellar [where Nancy is murdered]. I'm in my cell, under the coarse prison blanket" (*Alias Grace* 298). These simple statements convey the sense that past and present are not demarcated for trauma survivors. The past and its emergence control her: as she considers telling the murder story to Simon, she helplessly feels it "must go on with me, carrying me inside it . . . although I hurl myself against the walls of it and scream and cry, and beg to God himself to let me out" (298). She desperately wants to be "outside" the story as she tells it. And though telling may bring some relief, it does not bring enough memory for resolution. "When you are in the middle of a story it isn't a story at all, but only a confusion; a dark roaring, a blindness, a wreckage of shattered glass and splintered wood. . . . It's only afterwards that it becomes anything like a story at all. When you are telling it, to yourself or to someone else" (298). Though she realizes remembering could benefit her, and storytelling makes her feel better, and though she may be lying (Darroch 117), she does not try to concoct a story that proves her innocence, for Simon or the readers.

Grace repeats the phrase "I think I sleep" several times during her account of the murders as she loses the thread of memory, to indicate she has lost consciousness or gone into a fugue state, as she had at Mary's death. Readers could interpret this curious repetition as Grace trying to avoid looking guilty to Simon (Darroch 110). However, it could also be key evidence of a consciousness altered by trauma, provoking a state of dissociation and amnesia. When she repeats "I think I sleep," she appears to be trying to recall events around the murders, but privately, in her jail cell, not in front of Simon. This repression keeps her embedded in the past because she has difficulty assessing what she did. Grace is more open with readers than with Simon, and at no time does she admit to killing anyone. She could be guilty and could have repressed the fact of the deed, or she could be guilty and not saying so. Atwood depicts the many complications of Grace's situation and motives. Her limited memory and self-preservation techniques raise the question of her reliability, yet she is able to elaborate on her past and interpret her situation. She wants to please Simon and gain her freedom, yet fears the truth—and admits to this fear. Though readers are left with some doubts as to what actually happened (Atwood does not presume absolute knowledge), Atwood also provides enough evidence to sustain the trauma case and nothing to convincingly contradict this interpretation.

Though *Alias Grace* does not read like a Gothic novel, except perhaps in Grace's terrifying memories, Atwood interpolates aspects of the nineteenth-century Gothic genre, which typically created an atmosphere of fear and depicted helpless women who had nightmares about what could not be consciously expressed. The Gothic novel was a women's genre, used to talk about repressed experiences of trauma. Often it expressed women's fear of "being persecuted in domestic spaces . . . by men . . . women's fear of patriarchy and of where sexual desire for men may lead—to incarceration, abuse, loss of self and agency." Further, the Gothic novel served as a vehicle for female desire yet depicted it as a "symbolic threat to the protagonist" (Blackford 236). Much of this, along with the doubling of Grace/Mary, coincides with the nature of trauma, as when Grace is locked into a Gothic story as she recalls the murders. The Gothic is a genre that expresses well the terror and sense of mystery surrounding Grace's emotional experience, which cannot be conclusively explained, and thus the genre also supports a postmodern uncertain conclusion. Atwood, however, keeps these Gothic moments brief, focusing rather on Grace's more reflective voice, and through Simon and other characters she foregrounds the scientific and social views that contextualize Grace's traumas and engage readers more cognitively. Even if this approach does not bring certainty either, it elaborates causes and psychological complexities more satisfactorily than an explanation derived more largely from the Gothic genre.

After considerable reflection, Grace, interestingly, blames Mary's and Nancy's "weakness" for their deaths, and for leaving her with the fallout.

"It's the victims that cause all the trouble, if only they were less weak" (457). She cannot recognize the whole unjust economic, social, and moral apparatus that doomed these women. Atwood, however, thoroughly establishes the adversities in Grace's life such that contemporary readers readily recognize the tremendous restrictions on women in the past. Holly Blackford interprets Grace's anger at the two women and the quilt patches she uses to bring them all together as indicative of "women's anger at themselves and one another for perpetuating psychological imprisonment," a fetishizing of their objects (259). Grace feels abandoned by Mary and Nancy, two surrogate mother or sister figures, and admits as she imagines talking to Simon: "I had a rage in my heart for many years against Mary . . . and . . . Nancy . . . for letting themselves be done to death in the way that they did, and for leaving me behind with the full weight of it" (457). Grace concludes that these women borrowed trouble because they lived as individuals who did not play along with societal rules and thus made themselves vulnerable to the traumatizing punishments aimed at women's unauthorized sexual behavior. This interpretation on Grace's part allows her to sustain the illusion that they had some choice or control, and thus so does she. As Blackford notes, Grace can recognize only so much; she survives by not digging too deeply into her feelings: "With this quilt, Grace recognizes the other women as an intrinsic part of herself and her own ambitions. . . . This is an image of integration, but it is a dark one" [as the quilt contains pieces of garments associated with Mary's and Nancy's deaths] (Blackford 259).

It is also a containing image, like the cloth petals, a way Grace can live safely with the past while not denying its importance. The themes of the quilts correspond with those of the novel, raising questions of how to interpret the serpents on her quilt. Margaret Rogeron wonders whether they could be an admission of guilt, perhaps in the form of a memorial, or whether they might celebrate her crime (10, 21). No specific answers are forthcoming, but Grace indicates the necessary presence in her design of snakes, which connote evil but also knowledge in Grace's interpretation of Genesis: without evil, one cannot live or know life.

Atwood has created an associatively rich metaphor for attempting to live with trauma in a way that is manageable for the survivor. As Grace assesses her life toward the end of her prison sentence, she tries to construct memory through the pieces of fabric from the women she's known. Magali Cornier Michael interprets the patchwork as a template for multiple, conflicting and constructed stories that challenge linearity and objective accounts of history (436). Though they may be helpful reconstructions in a women's art form, Michael notes that they also highlight the limits to our ability to recover the past (437–38). Grace considers what scraps would be "truthful to my own life" (*Alias Grace* 382), thinking of a bloodstained petticoat (Mary's) and Grace's (once Mary's) Love-in-the-Mist designed kerchief, used to strangle Nancy. Quilting in *Alias Grace* also functions as an aesthetic and metaphorical marker of the search for identity and for a way to approach trauma, and as an analogy for imperfect memory. Quilting and sewing are daily domestic activities and points of pride for Grace. Quilting is Grace's way of understanding the world, and she likens it to reconstructing her version of the murders for Simon: "I could pick out this or that for him, some bits of whole cloth you might say . . . to supply a touch of color" (353). A quilt expresses the incomplete integration of Grace's thought-pieces.

Ethical Questions

Margaret Atwood makes the sociopolitical framework of trauma important in both novels as part of the characters' circumstances that will in turn affect readers' ethical evaluation of the characters' predicaments and treatment. Grace builds this framework indirectly, by referencing Mary's political awareness and class consciousness, McDermott's anger at his "betters," and the anxiety Nancy causes by living outside the social norms. In both novels, trauma is created in social and political contexts and is associated with power, class hierarchies, social mores, and gender codes. This raises the question, from which viewpoints are Grace's guilt and suffering being assessed? I believe Atwood makes the case for Grace by involving us in her story and setting out the adversities affecting her. By the end of the novel, it does not matter whether she committed the murders or not. She has been punished with thirty years' imprisonment and continues to be punished as her husband's prurience makes her revisit the story.

The novel raises the problems of victimization and personal agency and asks whether these can coexist in situations of powerlessness, of lack of choices under coercion, of the circumscription of women's lives and women's frequent subjection to violence or death. The way Grace is treated foregrounds the punitive rather than healing role of economic and political interests and the expediency of a legal system whose conceptions are inadequate to deal with the complexity of human psychology. The historical Grace was condemned by a large part of the public for being an "immoral" woman, someone of the underclass who "rebelled" against her betters by killing her employer—though, on the other hand, her status and age likely helped her escape execution.

The opinions expressed by the public about the actual trial and conviction reflected societal fears of the rage against class hierarchies manifested in James McDermott's actions, and many associated her case with the bloody rebellion of 1837, six years before the murders, which led a third of the population, especially the poorer and more radical groups, to leave Canada (Atwood, "In Search of Alias Grace" 173). As Atwood makes clear, the socially marginal status of teen servants like Mary and Grace made them vulnerable to rape and exploitation, and foreordained them to be potential victims of the insidious trauma experienced by the underclasses. Atwood underscores the public's tendency to blame trauma victims for the bad things they are associated with. Grace was viewed by the public as a temptress because she was good-looking, and seemed also to be viewed this way by medical professionals, as depicted in the figure of Dr. Bannerling in the novel. When the fictional Grace appears to have had a psychotic break as a result of having witnessed horrific events, she is still condemned by some professionals because of nineteenth-century views of human nature, which regarded inborn character, not circumstances, to be the cause of psychopathology.

Atwood also uses the social framework of *The Blind Assassin* to show readers how the abuse of power creates trauma. Wealthy social climbers, in the view promulgated in the novel, create traumas by dominating others' lives and forestall the healing process by intimidating and silencing their victims. Class interests control the economy, promote war, and are coupled with patriarchal control over women and their relations with each other (Bouson 253). In *The Blind Assassin*, Laura and Alex challenge these interests, as well as gender and class norms and hierarchies, by providing alternative paths that Iris might have taken. Alex organizes workers to strike and becomes a fugitive because Griffen wants to get rid of him; he fights against the fascists in the Spanish Civil War and World War II. Laura, well aware of the suffering around her during the Great Depression, works in soup kitchens. Sexually harassed by a childhood tutor, Laura is more aware than Iris of how people can abuse power. She is not invested, as Iris becomes, in maintaining their lifestyle at the cost of an unhappy marriage, and is willing to work. On the other hand, neither was she offered in marriage to save their father's business, as Iris was. Alex, Laura, and Reenie, the Chases' loyal servant who acts to save Laura from the asylum, all thwart Griffen but pay the price for it. After Laura's death, Iris finally brings him down with Laura's purported novel that starts an inquiry into the asylum that imprisoned Laura against her will on Griffen's orders. Iris's words damage the image of respectability Griffen needed for politics; however, she loses her daughter to Winifred, who vows vengeance and still has money and lawyers. Though Iris leads readers to feel satisfaction for her revenge and Richard's suicide, these do not bring her healing or the recognition of her own role in the destruction of Laura's and Aimee's lives. This becomes her ultimate insight as she writes her memoir. It could be argued that in trying to protect herself and survive, she became an accessory to their destruction, but sadly, her own wounds and appropriation by the Griffens prevented her from acting much on their behalf. The novel raises the ethical question of who is more to blame, the abusers or the people around them, who should know better but who deny or are afraid to acknowledge the harm abusers do. Does the public feel less threatened by agreeing with the reality abusers establish? Atwood implies that we must be aware of who wields power and how, and how much we are complicit in the operation of power relations. Iris may at times even have enjoyed the power she had when acting on behalf of the Griffens, the power of refusing responsibility for Laura or the world. Atwood clearly admires characters who resist and fight, and many of her novels feature female characters who help the protagonist become stronger and more aware (Vickroy, "Sexual Trauma" 254). Iris outlives all her good role models but, isolated, needs to remember her only close relationships, and still feels haunted by her past actions.

James Phelan speaks of the various levels of communication involved in the creation and interpretation of fictional narration as affording

> a layered ethical situation. Any character's action will typically have an ethical dimension, and any narrator's treatment of the events will inevitably convey certain attitudes toward the subject matter and the audience, attitudes that, among other things, indicate his or her sense of responsibility to and regard for the told and the audience. Similarly, the author's treatment of the narrator and of the authorial audience will indicate something of his or her ethical commitments toward the telling, the told, and the audience. Further, the audience's response to the narrative will indicate their commitments to and attitudes toward the author,

the narrator, the narrative situation, and to the values expressed in the narrative. (20–21)

By applying Phelan's construct of ethical layers to Atwood's texts, it is possible to see her narrators reporting much to gain readers' sympathies, but the works also complicate the idea of responsibility and question how much responsibility the protagonists can exercise in the novels' circumstances. The nature of guilt is undercut by uncertainty and by the protagonists' punishment for their deeds. However, Atwood avoids the notion of simple judgment. By focusing on the views of these narrators—not exclusively, but making readers live in their heads and see from their perspectives, so to speak—she wants readers to be affected by them. And in presenting so much detail and background, she seeks to make readers understand the protagonists' behavior as situational and not merely trait-driven. Readers' final judgments ultimately rely on their views of guilt and punishment, on how much they can be persuaded to view the protagonists' situations in a more nuanced, less judgmental light.

Phelan suggests our values are engaged as we read, and that literature is a "rich area for the exploration of ethical issues" because of its presentation of the "concrete particularities of human situations and their capacity to engage our emotions" (21). *Alias Grace* engages contemporary and progressive views of the treatment of women and the poor, raises doubts about legal justice for the poor, and views skeptically beliefs about human character that omit current knowledge of human psychology and the effects of the environment. These contemporary views make me consider why Grace wants to blame the other victims and is unable to question (even as readers must) her own deeply ingrained sense of what is possible for and expected of women like her. The sense of outrage the modern reader might feel about Mary's situation is undercut by the murders, and as such, we are meant to analyze how Mary's anger must be inflicted on a similarly powerless woman (Nancy). Mary could not even imagine acting against the man who seduced her because he was of the upper class and she was not, she was only a servant, but as a woman she was viewed as bearing the brunt of the responsibility for their sexual encounters. Atwood seems to be positing that we are socially and emotionally programmed to blame victims and protect ourselves from the crueler aspects of life. Grace exhibits a similar avoidance pattern: she can consider her connection to the important women in her life only from a safe distance, through her memorial quilt. Though such gender-role indoctrination and fear are more obvious in a nineteenth-century setting, they remain prevalent in the modern world.

The central ethical question in the novel concerns Grace's guilt, but the immediate follow-on questions are what she is guilty of, and who can assess that guilt. Atwood brings up mitigating factors: scant social justice for the poor, biased public opinion, gender attitudes, McDermott's guilt, moral views that victimize victims, and the limits of the law. *Alias Grace* raises the additional question of whether the precepts of human learning, trauma, and mental illness preclude or at least complicate rigid notions of moral responsibility—that is, to what degree is Grace responsible? If she cannot remember, and if she was young, ignorant, and terrified at the time of her arrest and her "confession" was a fabrication of probable events the lawyer insisted on for credibility in court (ironically, he believes she is guilty), what kind of justice is served? In his study of *Alias Grace*, Justin D. Edwards indicates that the law cannot accommodate a divided self and repressed memory because in its judgment, "the complexities of subjectivity are always vulnerable, fragile and subject to dissolution. This is because the body of the law . . . attempts to stabilize chaos by stabilizing identity. The legal process is thus a regulatory machine that imagines bodies in abstraction, permitting no differences between them and assigning fixed categories to identity" (107–8). Atwood realizes in novel form Edwards's point that "power operates on the subject [the individual] by way of asserting laws that result in a repression that carefully harbors a secret of the past" (108). She provides massive evidence of the behavior of individuals and institutions that reflects a private and public need to repress the chaos of violence and pain in order to maintain a social order that engenders much of this pain in the first place.

What is Atwood making readers confront with this approach? She takes on a similar task as Toni Morrison does in *Beloved*, of examining the life of a nineteenth-century murderess as a way to explore crucial historical legacies from an intimately human viewpoint. With limited historical information, Toni Morrison imaginatively reconstructs the inner life of Margaret Garner, a real slave mother who killed one of her children to prevent the child's enslavement and stood trial for murder. The case became a cause célèbre for abolitionists, who viewed the infanticide as proving the devastating effects of slavery, and this weight of public opinion won her clemency. However, Morrison imagines that Garner becomes a pariah among her own people, who are frightened by her actions. Morrison made some changes to the story to emphasize that a slave mother can love her children and still might kill one to free herself from the idea of being owned. Morrison understands the importance of Margaret Garner's story historically as emblematic of slaves' resistance to dehumanizing oppression. Rather than leading readers to facile judgment, Morrison endeavors to immerse us in the individual experience of terror, arbitrary rules, and the psychological or physical breakdown of victims so that readers might begin to appreciate such situations. The story is framed such that readers understand Sethe's (Garner's fictional name) love, suffering, and good intentions before revealing her deadly actions (Vickroy, *Trauma and Survival* 181).

Atwood follows Morrison's lead in presenting multiple perspectives on Grace's actions, and the effects of the sensationalized "murderess" label. Atwood's and Morrison's historical subjects both experienced the traumas of being low-status women in patriarchal and racially dominated cultures, objectified by class hierarchies. As such, they were powerless to control their own lives. Both made difficult choices, but from a human perspective, those choices were not really choices in that they involved avoiding a worse dehumanization: enslavement for Garner's children, death for Grace if she did not obey McDermott. Both novels deal with the question of building or maintaining an identity in impossible, trauma-inducing circumstances. Both characters in the novels psychologically avoid confronting their murderous actions and must talk around them because a narrative of what they have done is not cohesive or sufferable. Both protagonists want to tell, but ultimately cannot. As Morrison indicates on the final page of *Beloved*, remembering can be dangerous. Neither woman can resolve the question of her guilt. Sethe cannot forgive herself, and so must be confronted for her actions by her dead daughter. Grace, however, remains unaware, defended; she is haunted by events she is accused of but does not have access to a direct memory of the murders. They do not weigh on her as the lapses she remembers do: not using a good sheet for her mother's shroud, not staying awake with Mary when she was dying. It is others' projections of what they believe she has done that affect her. Atwood uses similar narrative techniques as Morrison to immerse readers in her characters' terror and psychic breakdown, as well as in the situations that brought them to that point. Atwood is fascinated by villainesses (see her lecture "Spotty Handed Villainesses") and plays with this idea with many of her characters. She is interested in creating portraits with the full complexity of what could underlie these women's motivations rather than making them merely likable or hateful, such that the simple condemnations visited on them seem crude.

Neither of Atwood's novels provides conclusive evidence of the protagonist's guilt or innocence. They present society's judgments (often inadequate and faulty) and characters' self-blame, but these narratives focus long on extenuating circumstances, on the why of things. The novels take advantage of the many benefits of literary fiction: its hybridity; the allowance of multiple perspectives, so that readers can weigh the relative worth of those perspectives; and the ability to take readers through a sense of experience (qualia) that is less concerned with providing answers than with raising questions about the role of trauma and fear in human history and with counteracting simplistic views of human behavior. They explore how characters live out their lives coping with trauma, elaborated in thick descriptions of living conditions and rituals that provide contexts for punishment or healing. They present social and historical phenomena that are replayed between the female protagonists and the other women with whom they are close: between Iris and Laura, between Grace and her mother, and among Mary, Grace, and Nancy. Most important, these novels chronicle understandable psychological responses to social and existential distress.

TWO

Fear and Commodification in the Shaping of America in Toni Morrison's *Paradise* and *A Mercy*

Toni Morrison's *Paradise* and *A Mercy* similarly reenact the traumatic American history of African Americans denied social status and self-respect in contexts of American capitalistic aspirations and white dominance. In *Paradise*, masculine success is predicated on a material and social success that protects men from "traumatic objectification" by the larger culture but keeps them bound and locked in the past (Read 529). In *A Mercy*, the combination of acquisition and religious rationalizations aids the proliferation of slavery and the homogenization of American culture. Morrison's characters exhibit the behavioral effects of insidious trauma visited on socially devalued people (Root 240). Morrison provides emotional contexts to historical knowledge for readers by embedding historical information into the consciousness and behavior of her characters, thereby plunging readers into the survival modes of thinking that compromise "the individual's perceptual, decisional, and relational processes" (247). In this way, Morrison establishes a framework that enables readers to cognitively and emotionally reconstruct the psychological and environmental complexities that create and perpetuate trauma.

Like Margaret Atwood, Morrison examines the exercise of power and notes the damage to personality that makes people replicate power relations in their personal lives. Both writers engage readers in a critical reading process by immersing them in, and providing a perspective on, the flawed thinking and behavior of the traumatized that develop from a psychology of fear driving individuals and society. Through this process, they want readers to understand individuals' roles in systems of power, how anyone can internalize systems' ideologies, and how awareness can increase perspective and reduce complicity.

Morrison is an exemplary producer of trauma narratives. Her works are significant examples of the numerous trauma texts published in the late twentieth century that recognized the catastrophic effects of wars, colonization, domestic abuse, racism, classism, and gender conflicts on the individual psyche while consciously incorporating traumatic symptoms and mechanisms into their content and formal strategies (Vickroy, *Trauma and Survival* x–xi). These texts introduce painful experiences that risk alienating readers while intending to enlighten them about the effects of oppression and power. They engage readers in uneasy relationships with characters who, while worthy of sympathy, also behave in destructive, complicit, or disturbingly irrational ways. And in this vein, Morrison works to illuminate the experience of African Americans in America.

Morrison exposes readers to the ethical dimensions of trauma and its representation in numerous ways in *Paradise* and *A Mercy*. First, she demonstrates that social and historical progress is obstructed when individuals are locked, cognitively and emotionally, into static defensive patterns. She also attempts to persuade readers that the by-products of trauma become versions of a perception of the best life, predicated on a binary of the chosen and the excluded. Finally, she shows how trauma becomes part of everyday life and normalized in particular social structures and practices intended to keep people silent and ineffectual.

Paradise and *A Mercy* cover a broad expanse of American history, from colonial times through the nineteenth century to the contemporary era, the 1970s. In both novels the characters are placed in historical contexts crucial to the situations and treatment of African Americans in America, from slavery to emancipation and the backlash against freed slaves in the antebellum South to World War II, the civil rights movement, and beyond. Morrison depicts this lived experience in gendered terms. For instance, in *Paradise* the patriarchs' murderous behavior is an attempt to reassert their control and sense of manhood in response to humiliations that reverberate back over a century to the "failure of Reconstruction" (Widdowson 321). As Andrew Read notes, "Morrison is severely critical of this method of enacting masculinity. It simply represses the traumatic consequences of racist oppression, rather than working through and overcoming them, ensuring that they will persist in some hidden but debilitating form within black psychology" (531). Besides wounded masculinity, Morrison focuses on women's multiple burdens arising out of being situated in patriarchal, racial, and class-based contexts. And, like Atwood, she foregrounds the traumatic subjugation of women and the lower classes, allowing them their once suppressed voices. These novels catalogue punitive restrictions on women's bodies, choices, and sexuality that engender traumas of sexual violation and mothering that linger in personality and memory intergenerationally.

Morrison's works exemplify the invaluable role of literature in presenting historical and cultural discourses, illustrating Hayden White's claim for the valuable historical role of literature in the ways it can display "real events to [the reader's] consciousness through its fashioning of patterns of "imaginary events" (45). Her socially marginal textual voices offer other types of historical consciousness that support her "social criticism" of American myths of expansionism and linear progress that require dominance of the "not quite human" other (Strehle 111). White also writes that "[literary] narrative figurates the body of events that serves as its primary referent and transforms these events into intimations of patterns of meaning that any literal representation of them as facts would never produce" (45). By juxtaposing perspectives and turning a spotlight on the destructive and constructive practices associated with different ideological stances, Morrison illustrates for readers "the limits of human vision, knowledge and judgment" and helps them "see the veils of history, ideology, subjectivity and divinity that shape one's vision" (Krumholz 31). Her characters challenge each other's views of race, social and economic position, gender, and religion. And sometimes their own stances are not absolute but conflicted and contradictory because of the damage and loss associated with these stances. Morrison's narratives are personalized allegories of historical situations, informed by current psychological and gender perspectives, that focus on the personal costs of those situations.

These costs are considerable. J. Brooks Bouson argues that "*Paradise* is a shame- and trauma-haunted work, dealing not only with the traumatic legacies of slavery and racial violence but also with the importance of shame and pride in the formation of racial and cultural identity" (*Quiet As It's Kept* 193). Morrison's recreation of the towns Haven and Ruby in *Paradise* refers directly to actual towns founded by African Americans a safe distance from white persecution; however, the inhabitants' social hierarchies and defensive behaviors created internal conflicts and exclusions "based on class, skin color and gender" (Crockett 49, 64). Morrison brings to life the complex matrix of town members and outsiders who engaged in these conflicts to show the psychology of racism, suggesting more broadly that the towns represent the larger failures of the United States to give African Americans "equal citizenship" (Widdowson 323). After Reconstruction, "blacks were once again" dispossessed and disenfranchised by Southern racists, Widdowson writes. Denied social value, "blacks concentrated on strengthening their community and surviving in the face of a patently unjust political and social order, rather than directly challenging the new status quo" (Foner 429). These retrenchments were necessary when black lives were at stake, but they were continued beyond their usefulness and hurt their people, Morrison reveals, because the people repeated the same ostracism they had endured. By depicting black patriarchs in *Paradise* as embracing European ideologies of manhood, including "autonomy, agency, and power, control over one's self, family and environment" (529), Andrew Read argues, Morrison shows that their idea of "masculinity . . . represses the traumatic consequences of racial oppression" (531).

Morrison and Atwood both recognize that human relations mirror social relations in contexts of power. Beginning with *The Bluest Eye* in 1970, Morrison's novels regularly show individuals internalizing the larger society's designations of them and suffering rejection and abandonment, socially and personally. Though both writers primarily focus on the mentalities and experiences of their characters, both also integrate historical situations through characters' thought reports, which position the characters in relation to their environments and their memories and private lives. The characters' experiences show the extent of injustice in the wounds and defensive repetitions they suffer. Like Atwood, Morrison is interested in recovering repressed or suppressed aspects of history that have been lost through either faulty memory, the marginalization of witnesses, or the human propensity to repress painful knowledge. Repression can arise from motivations as disparate as personal fear, shame, ideology, or a need to maintain the social order (Vickroy, *Trauma and Survival* 170).

Morrison sets *A Mercy* in 1690, a time of transition in America when powerful capitalistic and religious forces were establishing the ideologies of the culture for the next three hundred years. Morrison has said she depicted in *A Mercy* a "pre-racial" country, before race and racism "all got institutionalized" (qtd. in Cantiello 166). She shows readers that this process was already under way in the lives of the slaves whose story she tells. Her reference to Bacon's rebellion of 1676 (which took place fourteen years before the time of the novel) is important to Morrison because it marked a significant effort by nonwhite people to resist the hegemony of the English settler, even though the rebellion failed. Consequently, "the status of the European servile class was upgraded and a sense of racial superiority instilled" (Jordan and Walsh 212). But that superiority was not always a given. Settlers took over the land of native peoples whose populations had been decimated by European diseases (smallpox, influenza, measles) and whose homes and lands had been plundered (Stannard 68, 107). As Geneva Cobb Moore has written,

> Morrison's two striking descriptions of the colonies—peopled democratically by a diverse group of individuals and then divided violently and avariciously along the boundaries of an irreversible caste system—convey the idea of the gradual social manufacturing of race and class. . . . For natives and blacks had begun to be separated even from a formerly impoverished, downtrodden, backwater, throwaway group of European cultural upstarts. (7)

Morrison, like Atwood, analyzes the past through a new historical lens, revealing the complexity of life in 1690 through multiple voices and experiences of that time. The perspectives include English (Jacob, Rebekka, and the indentured servants Willard and Scully), African (Florens's mother), African American (Florens and the blacksmith—slave and nonslave), Native American (Lina), and mixed race (Sorrow). Each has a story about coming to America, or, in Lina's case, a story about the settlers' effects on those already here. Most embody in some way historical traumas from which they seek refuge, and each makes sense of the world in his or her own way, trying to take effective action in circumstances largely beyond any individual's control. None wants to be helpless, whether it's Florens's mother trying to save her daughter or Scully wanting to escape perpetual servitude. Morrison's indirect narrative and many of these voices construct an implicit critique of power: who has it, and how it is used. She locates the origin of people's need to exercise power in fear, and suggests it is instilled again when its use denies people the recognition and self-respect so essential to self-realization (Honneth, "Personal Identity" 43). This fear and the need to dominate are most apparent in the religious claims impelling the settlers' attempts to wipe out or force the assimilation of whoever is different from them. They are clearly gaining influence by the end of the novel.

Morrison's unique contribution to this literature is her ability to particularize historical trauma by infusing her narratives with multiple ethical dimensions. She does this by offering a range of dilemmas and responses to traumatic circumstances. Characters develop similar defensive behaviors, including fixed ideas and rigid personality traits, as part of the survival skills that are the residue of their psychic wounding. These defensive behaviors speak to the profound force of traumatic circumstances on the human psyche, affecting the powerful and the powerless as they try to survive and control their situations. Other characters act as counterbalance and represent ways of thinking beyond compunction, ownership, and the desperate need to control others. These countervailing views establish the ethical standards of the text, the conscience (or the consciousness) underlying Morrison's rhetorical gestures. And in trauma narratives, this position can be inferred in the textual presentation of the causes and consequences of trauma. What messages do readers get in transactions with these texts? Are they overwhelmed by Morrison's polemicism? Do they feel she gives a fair accounting of the trauma experience? Does she make the case that wounding explains extreme actions? The complexities of traumatized characters often inspire ambiguous feelings in readers and make ethical evaluation of the characters difficult. Judgment may depend on whether readers become invested in a character's struggles and on how much power that character has to inflict wounds on others, though of course even those who are damaged deserve some understanding (as in Morrison's unflinching portrayal of Cholly Breedlove in *The Bluest Eye*).

Morrison's characteristic shifts in her novels from one character's consciousness to another's, varying narrative perspectives, lead readers to absorb information from different viewpoints. These points of view are also filtered through a free indirect discourse style that places readers in the characters' minds while revealing the characters' flaws and contradictions through descriptions and juxtapositions. This technique enables readers to connect with the characters, but it also provides some distance from which to evaluate them. As readers are introduced sequentially to different perspectives, they are prompted to compare the different viewpoints that are presented. Morrison's aesthetic approach enhances the ethical implications of the texts, for the narrative simultaneously involves readers in the complexities of trauma symptoms and in competing views of traumatic circumstances, and enables readers to follow individuals as they lose or regain ethical grounding. Moreover, these narrative strategies mimic the alienation from self and others experienced by the traumatized by functioning simultaneously inside and outside the characters. Readers are also positioned inside and outside as they become engrossed in a story that moves beyond their own experience. As characters observe and ethically weigh each other's actions and motives, readers are enjoined to do so as well, but with more information than the characters have. Also incorporated in the narrative are survivors' typical struggles with knowing and not knowing the past. For example, what they have repressed may be revealed in repetitive and self-defeating actions and thoughts, in a resistance to memories, or in the recovery of partial awareness with memory fragments, if those fragments can be assimilated to other memories (Laub and Auerhahn 288). Morrison's characters are often caught between an unresolved, tainted past and wanting to endure into the future. Morrison equates their pasts with that of the American nation, provoking debate on American ideologies and treatment of nonwhites.

Paradise: Survival Mode and Insidious Trauma

The basic plot of *Paradise* involves the absolute, damaging control of an exclusively African American town called Ruby by a group of patriarchs from the town's founding families. The present time of the novel is the 1970s. The patriarchs see their position as irrefutable, arising from historical, familial, and even biblical precedents. The townspeople are products of a black diaspora from the post-Reconstruction backlash against African Americans in the late nineteenth century. Their grandfathers and fathers first built the town of Haven to ensure their safety and create their own community. Ruby was settled by the current generation of patriarchs as a new, post–World War II version of Haven. Because they have helped ensure the community's survival in the face of racist violence and rejection, the current leaders have appropriated the right to narrate the town's history, to take charge of the women and the young, to silence opposition, and ultimately to control even procreation as a way to protect their bloodlines. The names of the two most powerful men, Deacon and Steward Morgan, signal their direction of spiritual and material life.

As the novel commences, nine men, all town leaders, massacre a group of independent, runaway women living in a former convent outside the town, because the women's friendships with some of the women and youth of the town have encouraged them to resist the men. Most of the novel establishes the context for these killings; the final chapters present the aftermath. To many in the town, the convent becomes a magnetic place of refuge from the men's rules and gazes. Its unstructured inhabitants, women on the run from abuse and exploitation, seem to the men to threaten the town fathers' dwindling future bloodlines, though the real causes are too much inbreeding and their own tyranny. The myths the men have created about the fugitive women, that they have killed, performed abortions, corrupted the townspeople, and so forth, will be proven false through the townswomen's viewpoints. More important, the patriarchs' stances and actions throughout are a repetition of the persecution, intolerance, and victimization that have characterized the way whites have treated them.

Morrison's novels notably address the psychological effects of racism, and in *Paradise*, victims reinstitute trauma-inducing racial injustice in new forms. Readers, along with townswomen such as Pat and Lone, eventually discover that the patriarchs believe women's purity will bring them salvation, and come to understand that the men's conclusions are based in distortion, denial, and self-deception. The aftermath of the shootings shames some of the men, and one, Deacon, confesses his own role in events, noting further that the men's master narrative of the town's history leaves out shameful truths about its initial founders. Historical forces are forging a possible new future, however, in the persons of the activist Reverend Misner and his young followers. As the novel concludes, it's uncertain whether the town can change enough to survive or whether it will remain mired in the past.

As readers are gradually exposed to pieces of lives and history, the reconstructive nature of reading is highlighted in *Paradise*. As Bouson has written, "In weaving together the complex and interconnected stories of the people of Ruby, Morrison forces her readers to take on the role of historian and genealogist and to piece together the fragmented stories and conflicting versions of the past" (*Quiet As It's Kept* 195). Finding the story requires readers to engage in a challenging process of putting together disparate views and to draw connections between seemingly unrelated characters. Trauma, for example, links almost all of the characters, as does their persistent reconstructing of the past. Information is provided intermittently and in nonchronological order to keep readers in a constructive mode. Readers must commit to cognitive and emotional engagement as they process moments of extreme emotion, negligence, even violence, and then put together the pieces presented by the different voices in the text to figure out what brought about these moments. For events are presented without their accompanying causality: What brings the men to the point of shooting the runaway women? What circumstances lead a mother to fail to save her children from death, or another mother to violently attack her daughter?

Readers may feel frustrated by the obstacles placed in the path of a clear linear narrative, but it is the characters' thoughts and behaviors, and the temporal overlapping of past and present, that bring readers to the trauma experience. Similarly, the immersion of readers in fictional mind frames results in a kind of normalization of the characters' views within the bounds of the narrative. For example, readers enter into the contradictory minds of men skillfully narrating decades of historical injustice and heroic resistance while formulating grandiose atrocities. At other times the narrative follows the circuitous mental path of an emotionally numbed, abused mother. In this way, readers vicariously experience how defenses accompanying trauma distort characters' perspectives and trap them in the past or in insensibility. As Maria Root has observed, "Factors such as isolation, blame, loss of social status, and effect on ability to take care of one's self and/or family add to the trauma of the original event" (237). Characters who question the static groupthink of the town engage readers in analyzing the contexts and structures of trauma-related thinking that keep individuals mentally imprisoned and dysfunctional. In the following sections, I discuss in what ways representatives of three key groups in the novel—the patriarchs, the fugitive women of the convent, and the townspeople—each suggest a conflicted relation between trauma and ethical stances.

The Town Insiders

The narrative of *Paradise* reports information piecemeal, through competing viewpoints and claims on truth, in this way establishing a shifting rhetorical and ethical relation among author, characters, and readers. Readers must continually reprocess textual information to ascertain characters' positions and motives. In the opening section of *Paradise*, readers are located in the midst of an intensely brutal scene and in the thoughts of men shooting and stalking a group of unarmed women they believe must be eliminated. This episode is the pivotal incident that the rest of the novel attempts to explain and move on from. Though readers are ostensibly getting the men's side of the story, the narrative leads us to question their judgment, but to also assess their reasonable fears of the brutal world outside their town.

We eventually learn the men's actions are a misplaced response to the community's history of racial wounding, part of the survival modes that involve an obsession with race and birthrights that empower some but cost others dearly. The men's and their fathers' histories of racial oppression and humiliation, exhaustively detailed in the novel, are requisite to understanding the fear of being disenfranchised and unhomed by the larger society. These exiles are particularly wounded when denied shelter by lighter-skinned African Americans who internalize white racism and reject their own people. The original founders of Haven were on the run after a dramatic drop in their sociopolitical status and recognition. While they once participated in the running of states during Reconstruction, afterward they were banished from social and political participation in a society defined by whiteness and money. The list of historical trials survived by the townspeople is astonishing: the violent racial backlash after Reconstruction that deprived them of the vote, jobs, and social position they had previously won or been granted; migration to Oklahoma in the late nineteenth century; the Great Depression and World War II. Yet at the same time their fear that the convent women pose a comparable or even greater threat than all the above seems completely out of proportion.

Readers come to understand that the men's survival skills, learned in traumatic times, have led to materially successful lives and stability but have long outlived their usefulness. Trauma can be ascertained in the survival modes they adopt, especially in the rigid fixedness of their approach. Their view of others as either good or bad (according to whether those so evaluated threaten the men's defensive posture or not), a means of holding fast to their sense of psychic order and safety, exemplifies how "survival consumes and redirects all energy towards defensive strategies" (Root 247). As Bouson as noted, such strategies are the consequences of "the pain of intra-racial shaming, showing the intergenerational transmission of racial wounds and the damaging impact of the color-caste hierarchy on the collective black identity" (*Quiet As It's Kept* 193). In such a state the victim can no longer empathize with others, and the men exhibit this inability: "no taking the other person's perspective, no considerateness, no generosity, no forgiveness, no humor" (Root 247). As the men's own trauma-induced repetition of the abuse they have sustained, their emotional stasis, and their resistance to change are imposed on the town, Morrison implies that such defenses stand in the way of social and historical progress.

Readers' initial inclination to condemn the men's shooting of the women is likely to be tempered as additional historical and explanatory information comes out, in bits and pieces. The shootings lose some of their predatory quality as the logic of the trauma the world has created in the men's minds becomes available. We come to understand that fear of losing what they have drives them to violence. I do not think Morrison expects readers to identify with the men, but the text invites analysis of the necessities and costs of survival strategies and complicates settling into an easy or absolute judgment of these men.

The men's giddiness in hunting the women bears an emotional connection to the triumphs of their ancestors' survival, which obsess them more than the discriminations and dangers they themselves have had to face.

> The twins have powerful memories. . . . And they have never forgotten the message or specifics of any story, especially the controlling one told to them by their grandfather. . . . A story that explained why neither the founders of Haven nor their descendants would tolerate anybody but themselves. . . . . On the journey from Mississippi and . . . Louisiana . . . to Oklahoma, the one hundred and fifty-eight freedmen were unwelcome on each grain of soil from Yazoo to Fort Smith. . . . . What began as overheated determination became cold-blooded obsession. . . . . Becoming stiffer, prouder with each misfortune. (*Paradise* 13–14)

Stalking the women, the men feel "warm with the nocturnal odor of righteousness. The view is clear" (18). This is an essential mission for them, but because their mission is mass murder, it is chilling and ironic that their clarity leads them to such targets. Instead of taking revenge on the forces of white oppression, they focus on victims of gender and class oppression. The racial mix of the women does not fit with the men's pride in the town's blackness. Their scapegoating of the women "illustrates the causes and consequences of racial and social shaming: that is, the dismissive and inherently dangerous othering and demonizing of those people considered different" (Bouson, *Quiet As It's Kept* 194). The men are caught up in an ingrained pattern of inherited trauma. The defenses they inherited from their forebears and continued to develop were useful when they made their final move to Ruby after World War II. But more than twenty-five years later, this repeated form of threat resistance has become both fruitless and dangerous. The leaders' obsessive drive to preserve what they made turns the town into a timeless limbo. It is now 1976, and though the civil rights movement's struggles for social and legal equality have been ongoing for more than twenty years, they are just beginning to make a dent in Ruby, and are hotly resisted by the elders.

Ironically, the men's assertions of self and their masculinity, the denial of their weakness, so necessary for survival and self-esteem, cut them off from any sense of community and belonging that could also sustain them. Unmanned and dehumanized, they feel they have to re-assert themselves by activating nineteenth-century concepts of (white) manhood, by exerting "control over one's self, family and environment" (Read 529). If we conceive of the men as "cultural carriers" of trauma, this can help explain how a group's defensive responses to traumas might manifest in further persecutions. Cultural carriers are "collective agents of the trauma process"; that is, they construct the meaning of the past for their group by making use of historical situations and the symbolic resources at hand to project claims of group identity and interests to their audience (Alexander et al. 11). Morrison selects the communal oven as a symbol of contending group identities, the younger generation threatening the elders' hegemony. The oven, carried brick by brick from Haven, is supposed to represent town unity. However, it becomes a site of contention as young and old debate the wording and meaning of the motto written on it, questioning whether it says "Beware the furrow of his brow" or "Be the furrow of his brow." In other words, does one submit passively to God's will (the elders' view) or act as an instrument of that will (the younger generation's view)? The town leaders had once exerted a healing influence when they spoke eloquently of survival, but in the church debate over the oven's motto, it is clear that they no longer speak for their community, and try to strangle alternative views.

> Royal Beauchamp actually interrupted him, the Reverend! "What is talk if it's not 'back'? You all just don't want us to talk at all. Any talk is 'backtalk' if you don't agree with what's being said . . . Sir." Everybody was so stunned by the boy's brazenness, they hardly heard what he said. . . .
>
> Steward had the last word. "If you, or any one of you, ignore, change, take away, or add to the words of the mouth of that Oven, I will blow your head off just like you was a hood-eye snake."
> (85, 87)

They assert a moral framework of obedience to God, but they have lost their connection to their people in the name of defending them. The leaders' stubborn tyranny blocks any progress in the town on matters of race, gender, the power base, spiritual life, and even the town's future. They cannot see the young people's dissatisfaction with blind obedience or accept normal and inevitable change.

The Women Outliers

The men's voices dominate the town, but not the narrative. Most of the novel presents alternative views, largely women's, within and outside the town; these views shift and increase readers' points of focus. In the order of the narrative, after the patriarchs' opening sections comes the life and perspective of one of the convent women. Mavis's life stands as a compelling corrective to the men's simple formulas about female obedience. It also highlights in horrifying detail the traumas resulting from male cruelty toward women, the social sanctions underlying that cruelty, and the consequences for individual functioning and mothering capabilities. Her story is presented in the most depth of any of the runaway women's and is the most revealing of traumatic processes. Once again the narrative situates readers both inside and outside Mavis's mind, showing how others see her as well as her own thoughts; this dual perspective usefully suggests the difficulties of undergoing (the inside perspective) and understanding (the outside perspective) trauma.

Mavis's section begins with the neighbors' point of view: they are eager to condemn the family after Mavis's twin infants have suffocated in the family's car while in her care. "The neighbors seemed pleased when the babies smothered. Probably because the mint green Cadillac in which they died had annoyed them for some time. They did all the right things, of course: brought food, telephoned their sorrow, got up a collection; but the shine of excitement in their eyes was clear" (21). Mavis's losses and horrid life cannot be seen beyond the surface of her husband's ostentatious car in a poor neighborhood. The neighbors do not comprehend, or can deny, Mavis's particular circumstances because, like many abuse victims, she is isolated, frightened, and secretive. Readers, however, will be given access to her world, and will witness the painful course of her daily life.

Mavis is interviewed about the accident by a reporter, another oblivious witness. Meanwhile, readers follow Mavis's mental wanderings, from her noticing the crumbs on her sofa to trying not to react to her daughter painfully digging her nails into her. The two viewpoints, outside and uncomprehending, inside and experiential, are contrasted to great effect, as the reporter wants an explanation Mavis cannot possibly give: an easy summation, a cautionary message from Mavis to others so that "some good can come out of this awful tragedy" (22). Mavis's only available answer is to reproduce the urgency of getting what her husband Frank wanted her to get for dinner, how his wishes dictate her life. In this manner, readers are plunged into the strange and terrifying world of the benumbed and barely articulate Mavis and her memories of sexual and physical abuse at the hands of her husband and children. These weigh on her so much that she loses a sense of time, and may be dissociated when she leaves the children in the car for what she thinks is only a short time. Self-preservation in the form of vigilance, perseveration, or rumination is a common recourse by victims in these situations as well, a product of the survival mode they adopt (Root 248); in this case, however, self-preservation causes her not to live up to her motherly responsibilities, that is, to protect her children.

As the narrative follows the unfolding of Mavis's day, it records her utter lack of control over her life. She can only react to her situation, and, as with the Ruby men, vigilance about potential threats and fears shapes her every thought and action. Gradually Mavis reveals the cruelties hidden from the world that shape every moment of her dread existence. Readers are left to wonder how she has become the scapegoat of the entire family. Why is she so passive, complicit, and paralyzed? Clearly, she feels she has no power to behave ethically, no regard or standing in this family that deprives her of freedom and moral responsibility. She exemplifies how extreme fear incapacitates thinking, and that her cautious self-protection can be a "normal response to a horrible experience" (Root 237). That is, until Mavis comes alive to the hostile signs and threats from her husband and children, when they flash a razor at the dinner table after the babies' deaths and Frank says, "Maybe we can fix this, but I don't know. . . ." Realizing she may not survive, Mavis escapes. Again, readers are drawn into following each terrified moment of her flight, as she imagines Frank catching her, the car being traced, and so on.

The isolation of the trauma victim comes into sharp focus when Mavis has difficulty thinking of anyone who can help her. Her own mother helps little, does not fully believe her fears, and plots to return Mavis to her family. The mother reflects a normative thinking that cannot comprehend the notion of a woman running away from home. Such are the forces arrayed against Mavis, but her escape is hopeful. In contrast to the threats facing Mavis, the mother's view must seem out of touch, too simple for readers, because even if Mavis has nowhere to go, and little money, staying with her husband is clearly worse.

When Mavis hits the road, she finds she is one of many women escaping violence and entrapment, and she faces the fact that at age twenty-seven, her fears have made her unable to function as an adult. Is it unethical for her to leave her living children if she cannot fully act as a mother in this family? This decision haunts her, but she sees few choices. She returns several times over the years to check on the children but does not make contact. The children appear to have survived adequately without her.

In the safe space of the convent, Mavis thinks of her babies in memory fragments and fantasies, symptoms of connecting with memory and resisting an awareness of realities. And though she is stronger in the convent, Mavis still struggles between knowing and not knowing her traumas. Her emotional scars survive in self-punishing nightmares. She can also escape into pleasant dreams of reuniting with her dead infants, but these dreams end up costing her her life when they distract her from the men's inevitable attack. Hence, she is still not able to fully attend to the dangers facing her and preserve her life. The means to heal, and to become a whole person, are not available to her, Morrison suggests. Exhibiting telltale signs of traumatic rigidity, Mavis clearly resents and picks fights with Gigi, a young woman in the convent who asserts power through her body and her sexuality, whereas for Mavis these things became signs of her powerlessness. Once again, as with the men, the simple removal of immediate danger does not bring resolution or healing. The sole moment of exception to all this is an imagined scene of reunion between Mavis and her living daughter Sal, who seems to have survived well, near the end of the novel, after Mavis's presumed murder. The hope for reconciliation and renewal that binds the scene is mitigated for readers, though, because it lies outside the logic of the narrative.

When the convent women return from the dead to participate in similar healing scenarios near the novel's conclusion, what are readers to make of the way these possibilities are set apart from the rest of the novel in separately rendered, fictionalized or spiritualized spaces? Morrison's incorporation of religious elements in her works usually has essential connections to African American culture and history, associated with survival, hope, community, social action, and moral conscience. These references are usually tied to living situations and not moral absolutes.

Paradise, however, also shows that religion can become destructive and dysfunctional when it is used to rationalize patriarchy, murder, misogyny, and intolerance. So is it only divine or authorial intervention that can challenge the patriarchs' righteous punishment by saving the martyred women? The critic Linda Krumholz has argued that Morrison's purpose is to "teach readers to see beyond the visible, to see the veils of history, ideology, subjectivity and divinity that shape one's vision" (31). She thinks Morrison tries to offer as yet unavailable possibilities beyond repetition and stasis.

Is saving the women Morrison's wish fulfillment, a too easy solution, as some critics have charged? Women have not been part of the religious dialogue in the town and have not benefited from it, nor have they consented to the men's "spiritual" plans. Women's views of God in the novel are generally more personalized and therapeutic. After the mother superior's death, the convent women make up their own female-led rituals of survival that resemble mutual group therapy as much as religious practice. The convent-dweller Consolata tasks each woman to confront her own pain and fear. This practice could be seen as a kind of exorcism (Marouan 119) or as psychological flooding, depending on one's perspective. Consolata compels the women to lie in a circle on a cold stone floor, a kind of self-scourging, and confront their traumas. This gesture begins a process of working through traumas rather than perpetuating them as the men's faith seems to do. The women's "resurrections" at the end of the novel enable them to return to loved ones and either make amends or assert themselves in ways they could not when traumatized. Their rituals have prepared them to resume their commitments to others, have reinstated their capacities to act ethically. Their resurrections provoke some disappointment in critics and readers, however, because hope for change seems unreal, hypothetical, in the harsh context of the novel. Readers are allowed to imagine these "new visions [as well as] . . . the limits of human vision, knowledge, and judgment," as Krumholz maintains (31), but will readers buy this if healing remains unavailable without social supports?

Townswomen: Moving On?

Paradise underscores how trauma and defenses impede both thinking capacity and the development of fully realized emotions that would make ethical choices possible. Defensive spaces that protect survivors from reexperiencing trauma can also shut out new ideas and preclude communicating one's experiences to witnesses who could bring healing.

Immersion in self-protective behavior patterns can damage victims' relation to the present and the future because they avoid trying to think fully about, or emotionally working through, their traumas. Though driven by disparate causes and circumstances, the characters of *Paradise* function according to the same kinds of trauma mechanisms, including repetitions, irrational fears, and shutting down emotionally. These response patterns are made normative in the novel because they guide so many of the characters. All of them hope for a safe haven but live with a sense of being out of time, and a sense that the range of life is narrow. The exceptions to this general normalization of defense mechanisms appear in the women's lives in the convent (they know they are wounded, and attempt to heal by sharing their grief), and in the life of Pat Best, a schoolteacher, who actively thinks through the consequences of ingrained unreflective behavior.

Pat stakes out a place of greater knowledge and awareness than most of the women in the town, who often unwillingly go along with the men's moral agenda for them, frequently with traumatic consequences. For example, Sweetie is crazed from the burden of taking care of her inbred children (inbred because the town is so isolated). Arnette has to hide having a baby, and tries to kill it. Later, in denial, she tries to reclaim it from the convent women who had sought to help her. Pat's mother dies in childbirth because the men will not seek medical help for her. Finally, Dovey, Steward's wife, avoids him and fantasizes about a man who would love, listen to, and understand her because her husband is so preoccupied with his leadership mission.

Pat's narrative perspective seems similarly positioned to that of readers. An outsider, she is also embedded in Ruby's culture, with its secrets, exclusions, and conflicting views. And just as readers must deal with the intricacies of the narrative, Pat must sift through coded, incomplete, and unverifiable information to understand the town's belief structures. As the perspective shifts to Pat and her investigations, the town's deeply entrenched and hidden emotional history is revealed. One wonders, can it ever be sorted through? Like a new historicist, Pat illustrates that history amounts to varied experiences and competing views and cannot offer a singular truth about how to proceed. Her inquiring mind opposes the patriarchs' master narrative by looking to all kinds of viewpoints and information rather than imposing one version.

Her telling of the town's history focuses on the personal and psychological ramifications of the ways the town has survived its wounds.

Though she sometimes acts out as if traumatized, she also becomes aware of how learned defensive patterns guide her. By questioning them, she begins to outline ways to resist even if at times she participates in the town's hostile self-protectiveness. She has to continually reframe her own understanding of personal and town history. Her struggle mimics the contest between knowing and not knowing trauma.

Readers' attention is drawn to the contradictions within Pat as she grapples with them. Her attitude shifts from rigid control to a memory of her own spontaneous violence toward her daughter that terrifies her. She discovers that this act is connected to anxieties about maintaining a self-image that is really created by the town's male-dominated and self-righteous culture. Pat's reaction to her daughter's indifference to that image and her own obsession with the past also link Pat to the men's behavior patterns. However, *her* purpose in recalling the past is to *un*cover her family's story and to understand her own seemingly inexplicable behavior. Of the townswomen, she most attempts self-analysis and tries to think and work through her wounds, but is hampered by being forced to do it alone. Like many of the women in the book, she can resist patriarchal authority when she recognizes its influence in endangering her child's life. For instance, when her daughter's open questioning of the social order makes Pat anxious enough to attack Billie Delia with a steam iron, Pat starts to wonder what led to it, and why her family members have become scapegoats and shut out of the social hierarchy.

To find out, she tries to uncover other versions of the town's history, the hidden conflicts and motives, by sifting through the few clues provided in Bible records, her students' essays, and memories others sparingly share. "The town's official story, elaborated from pulpits, in Sunday school classes and ceremonial speeches, had a sturdy public life. Any footnotes, crevices or questions to be put took keen imagination and the persistence of a mind uncomfortable with oral histories. Pat had wanted proof in documents where possible to match the stories, and where proof was not available she interpreted—freely but, she thought, insightfully because she alone had the required emotional distance" (188). Her decoding of secrets and breaking of others' silences makes for exhilarating reading, especially as she discovers her own family's traumatic history. Her parents fell victim to the town's racial designations, which favored racial purity, or darkness over light skin, as a way of countering—but also, ironically, of repeating—the traumatic "disallowing" of their ancestors, that is, their earlier rejection by other African

Americans because of their dark skin. Pat tries to overcome her fellow citizens' obstacles to remembering: shame, repression, and avoidance of a painful past (as in her father's case). In doing so she is able to infer the reasons for the discrimination and the men's hidden goals.

The treatment of her family enables Pat to recognize and question the patriarchs' abuse of power. Her mother died in childbirth because the townsmen would not drive her to a white hospital because, Pat is convinced, she was light-skinned. Pat cannot get confirmation of their intraracial racism from her father, who seems to be in denial and unwilling to face the truth. She says to her dead mother, "We have quarreled about it and he doesn't agree with me that those 8-rock [very dark] men didn't want to go and bring a white into town; or else didn't want to drive out to a white's house begging for help; or else they just despised your pale skin so much they thought of reasons why they could not go" (198). She can well imagine her parents' suffering the personal anguish of the community's unwelcoming reception from the point when her mother joins it after the war (Pat's father met her elsewhere during World War II).

However, Pat also helps to perpetuate the town's cultural legacies of trauma. She is a Morrison character type that demonstrates how psychologically damaged people may turn on their own in response to oppressive forces, internalizing and practicing that oppression (see especially Geraldine in *The Bluest Eye* and Macon Dead in *Song of Solomon*). Absorbed into the traumatic history and defensive reactions of the town, like many, she's a hostage to dominant and narrow conceptions, in particular their view of her light-skinned daughter as "fast." She becomes aware of her own complicity and the deep conflicts she feels but cannot always access them cognitively until after she has acted them out. She knows the difference between the town's rigid morality and her daughter's nature and wonders whether she has not sacrificed her. "She, the gentlest of souls, missed killing her own daughter by inches. She who loved children and protected them not only from one another but from too stern parents lunged after her own daughter. . . . Have I missed something? Was there something else? But the question for her now in the silence of this here night was whether she had defended Billie Delia or sacrificed her. And was she sacrificing her still? The [iron] in her hand as she ran up the stairs was there to smash the young girl that lived in the minds of the 8-rocks, not the girl her daughter was" (203–4). This awareness shows her moving beyond traumatic repetitions and acting more ethically toward her daughter, ceasing their conflict even if Billie

Delia refuses to return to Ruby. Overall, their quarrel demonstrates the powerful allure of safety in defenses and habitual behaviors engendered in trying to survive traumas. Morrison here raises the question of whether awareness is sufficient to break long-held patterns.

Pat is a frustrating character for readers to evaluate because she is caught between stasis and change, and though her realizations could lead her and others forward, she seems unable to overcome resistance to change despite her considerable knowledge and her own family's victimization. Pat's view makes readers aware that the social support necessary to acknowledge trauma and healing is missing. Though she is engaged in the right struggle against lies and injustice, her acting alone is not sufficient to effect change. Pat comes to a powerful realization about the men's illusions of immortality (the town has not seen a death in decades) and women's necessary role in this. "It was clear as water. The generations had to be not only racially untampered with but free of adultery too. That was their holiness. . . . Unadulterated and unadulteried 8-rock blood held its magic as long as it resided in Ruby. That was their recipe. That was their deal. For Immortality. . . . In that case, she thought, everything that worries them must come from women. . . . Dear, Dear God. I burned the papers" (217). Just before this revelation she has burned her notes out of frustration with this lonely fight, so it is uncertain whether her knowledge can be shared with others. She is also defensive when a potential ally, Reverend Misner, asks her about the town's secrets and rigidity, and is surprised and disgusted with herself for discouraging him. Yet her self-consciousness, her students' openness about the past, the presence of potential allies, her devotion to children, and her own daughter's rebellion against male tyranny all are optimistic signs of the possibility of change, even if tension and resistance linger.

Readers might take the characterization of the Reverend Misner as Morrison's, or the implied author's, example of admirable behavior and a catalyst for change. He approaches the people and events of Ruby with sympathy despite their continued resistance to him, but he also points out to them their failures of action and vision. He provides a strong moral voice, not just because he is a man of the cloth but by his willingness to sacrifice and to work for racial justice and address the personal conflicts and wounds in Ruby. His stances and attempts at community and political action make him clearly a part of the civil rights movement, and he influences the town's youth in that direction, though to the patriarchs he is a threatening radical. Wondering why the community rejects social and political engagement, he recognizes that private and family wounds need to be revealed and discussed, and that the ultimate causes of these traumatic wounds, white oppression and internalized racism, must be resisted and defeated. Misner's attempts throughout the novel to provoke and question the community are really an engagement with the political and psychological aspects of trauma. He wants to be part of the town's "resurrection" (in a fashion other than what the patriarchs envision) and help the townspeople recognize the true origins of their wounds and fears. In the aftermath of the massacre he condemns the men's actions but understands the connection to racial wounding, and therefore renews his commitment to the town and its future, helping Deacon, the town steward, heal emotionally. Misner's view makes clear that a path toward the future is impossible if traumas are not healed collectively and if survival modes are perpetuated well beyond any direct connection to traumas.

Tensions still remain at the end of the narrative. Readers are offered both hope and discouragement that truth will emerge, a familiar dilemma for trauma survivors. Though some in the town try to cover up or justify the shootings, others express outrage, or penitence. Misner's young followers have replaced the oven's message of obedience with one of activism. The town's static patterns are loosening, and the town's isolation will inevitably come to an end with the expected opening of a gas station. Morrison's uncertain endings are a trademark. She provided some hope for the future in *Beloved* after the past nearly destroys Sethe. In *Paradise* the convent women have been killed, and it is difficult to redress that finality. However, their deaths do begin the return to Ruby of an acknowledgment of death (one of the sick, inbred children dies soon after), though the town's coming to grips with the women's deaths could also foreshadow the town's demise. The text places limits on possible healing and action in remaining true to traumatic experiences, which create fears and perceived threats that must be dealt with before the ethical treatment of others is possible. Conquering these fears is the necessary and most difficult work. The struggle against fear is enacted by the women who run away from abuse; it is similarly realized in the civil rights movement's resistance to violence and injustice, in Pat's analysis of the town's pathology, in the rebellion of Billie Delia, and more. As Krumholz writes, "At the end of the novel the people of Ruby must contend with mortality, knowledge of their own good and evil, and the uncertainty of truth exemplified by conflicting accounts of the events at the Convent" (31). The cumulative effect of these indicators of change, however, may not outweigh the destructive patterns lingering powerfully and emotionally in the text and in the world outside it. Morrison reminds us that climbing out from under that burden is an ongoing battle, even if signs of struggle and awareness offer some encouragement.

A Mercy: Orphans of History

As in her earlier novel *Jazz,* Toni Morrison continues the theme of orphanhood and exile in the face of social forces—in that case, captured in the story of African Americans' migration north in the early twentieth century to escape the violent racism of the South and the legacies of slavery. As Evelyn Jaffe Schreiber has noted, "While Morrison's earlier works investigate how the original core trauma of slavery persists in American culture, *A Mercy* reveals the seeds of slave trauma in the orphaned and disposed settlers" (164). In *A Mercy,* Morrison revisits America in 1690, in its birth stages, with migrations of people to the New World, among them the immigrant religious sects (Anabaptists, Baptists, Presbyterians, Quakers) claiming the land as their own; growing numbers of Africans brought in by the slave trade; and indentured servants of all colors. Women, people of color, and the lower classes are all owned to various degrees before, as Morrison points out, slavery developed an ideology of racialized insistence on difference ("Foreigner's Home"). As Morrison explains in that essay, she wanted to further explore "certain themes of cultural orphanage and shame that inform so much American literature. The promise and dread of displacement are major themes of early American literature. Along with the satisfactions of being reborn in a new country was the peril of somehow not belonging. The articulation of foreignness and dispossession, of utopianism and rootlessness, and claims of an infinite border, infinite frontier, become representations of the exiled's yearning, the isolate's despair."

In *A Mercy* the forces of religion and capitalism, which reach ascendency in the Reformation, sustain each other, and thus impose dominant views and structures on people's lives. European immigrants' confrontation with a seemingly endless wilderness, and with peoples of darker skin and different customs, fuels their fears and, Morrison implies, their need to control and dominate all they see. Lina, the Native American character, tells the story of an eagle observing the newcomers looking at the beautiful wilderness around them and declaring, "Mine. Mine. Mine." They then wound the eagle, sending it into a precipitous and endless fall. This story in a stroke characterizes for readers the acquisitive philosophy that will lead to the commodification and destruction of humans and nature that, Morrison suggests, become the basis for the founding of our country. Lina also articulates the Native Americans' view of the mental disposition and beliefs of white settlers who were outcast themselves: "like all orphans they were insatiable. It was their destiny to chew up the world" (54). These "orphans" in turn orphan others, creating a history of subjugation, dispossession, and recurring traumas.

The principle of ownership egregiously extends to human beings at this point in historical time and establishes the contexts of trauma that withhold human recognition and respect so necessary to human identity and agency (Honneth, "Recognition" 24). The slave trade is on the rise, indentured servitude encompassing generations is common, and fathers sell their daughters to husbands in marriage transactions in ways resembling the bondage and sexual exploitation endured by slave women. The voyage over, for most, involves bondage of one kind (or extreme) or another. Morrison's representative characters include slaves brought from Africa (Florens's and Sorrow's mothers), children born into slavery as a consequence (Florens) or born on a slave ship (Sorrow), men indentured for family debts (Willard and Scully), women sold in marriage (Rebekka), and women who were indentured because they were rejected by their families for "lewd" behavior or because they were prostitutes or thieves (Rebekka's shipmates). The commodification of the characters leads to wounds that must be survived, and that shape their personalities.

Morrison challenges the predominant expressions and institutions of faith of the time that were solely fear-based and oppressive to anyone not sharing those beliefs. She depicts this type of religious fanaticism as a defense against the harshness and newness of the New World and a contributor to the objectification of those considered "other." She gives us glimpses of the religious outcasts of Europe who dominated the American landscape, out of proportion to their numbers. In the novel, these characters hate the ostentatious Catholics who persecuted them in Europe. And they fear and despise those not like them, whom they seek to dominate with their austere Puritan views that reject the body, the emotions, and any kind of difference. Their rigid intensity comes from fear of God's punishment but flourishes and takes form in their traumatic encounter with the other. This is exemplified by the white

Baptist girl's terror at the sight of the black girl Florens, who seems (to the white girl) to be a walking manifestation of the devil's blackness; the white girl's involuntary reaction recalls the hysteria of the Salem witch trials. And the fixity of the religious outcasts manifests in strange behavior, as the group feels it is normal to examine Florens's nude body for signs of Satan.

Though these Protestant groups have a history of enslaving Native Americans and West Africans, it is the Catholic Senhor Ortega, from Portugal, who becomes the focus for most particularly embodying the rich and cruel colonialist slave master. He oversees shipments of slaves, who die horrendously of disease in the crowded boats or drown unnecessarily in shipwrecks as they are kept offshore until a full load of slaves comes from Africa. He and his wife also sexually abuse their women slaves. As Florens's slave mother says, "To be a female in this place is to be an open wound that cannot heal" (163). The Ortegas are particularly egregious in using religion to rationalize slavery and their ostentatious wealth, claiming that they do "God's work."

Morrison embeds history in her characters' thoughts and actions, making it briefly come to life in slaves' memories of the Middle Passage, in the immigrants' humiliating voyage to the New World, and in women's situations: even the free woman Rebekka's options were to be a "servant, prostitute or wife . . . the last one seemed safest" (78). Only in brief moments on the ship do women have moments of freedom: "Women of and for men, in those few moments they were neither" (85). Jacob describes America in 1690 as a conglomeration of "battles for God, king and land" (11) and describes it as in flux, an undetermined, often lawless place and rapidly changing, as town names shifted as often as ways of making money. Flux offers potential and some degree of freedom and mobility for those who are not of the underclasses (who must rely on the "mercy" of the better situated), but even for them that freedom is fragile, as we see when Jacob is taken by disease and Rebekka, alone, turns to the safer path of societal strictures.

Morrison's presentation of the effects of slavery and colonization highlights the ways in which trauma became part of the historical complexity of that time as the victims of those systems tried to survive within them. Readers are privy to the particular traumatic experiences that expose the characters' vulnerability, a result of their marginal status (as slaves, nonwhites, or underclass people), yet the trauma victims are able to analyze and critique their masters. Lina, the Native American servant bought by Jacob, articulates the situation of orphanhood that links all the characters. Lina's people, like many Native Americans, were wiped out by smallpox brought by the Europeans. She retains vivid memories of how they died and were eaten by animals, and of how the U.S. Army rescued survivors. "Terrified of being alone in the world without family Lina acknowledged her status as heathen and let herself be purified by these worthies" (47). She realizes she must placate the whites in order to survive, which entails allowing them to give her a new identity and going against her own customs by adapting to the Presbyterian view that the body is a vessel of sin, that emotions and idleness are sins. Lina's traumatic loss of her family is compounded by the white Christians, who deny her tribal identity and offer no social value or self-esteem except through their ways. They forbid other cultural or spiritual practices, cut her hair, and force her to adopt their language and customs. Lina represents the Native Americans' loss of land, culture, and identity, a loss that Morrison shows accompanies white settlement and establishes the parallel stories of the subjugation of Native Americans and African Americans so that whites can succeed in their claim of "mine." The settlers who take her in believe that the Indians died because they incurred God's wrath for their laziness, not from the diseases the Europeans brought. The Presbyterians sell her to Jacob as a servant, but once Lina realizes he is open and fair-minded, she is able to seek comfort in reclaiming her Native identity by readopting her own people's customs. She "found . . . a way to be in the world" (48). This exemplifies how in Morrison's works, "cultural and personal memory create the self, and the stability of one's personal memory and sense of self is a key factor in psychic survival" (Jaffe Schreiber 161). Lina maintains a cautious approach to memory, wanting and not wanting to remember: "She sorted and stored what she dared to recall and eliminated the rest, an activity which shaped her inside and out" (50). "Memories of her village peopled by the dead turned slowly to ash and in their place a single image arose. Fire" (49). Her trauma is distilled into the image of fire, the reminder of when her people's bodies, halfeaten by animals, were set ablaze—an image that is partly cleansing, yet haunts her every day when she lights a cooking fire. Her one relationship with a man is so brutalizing she does not want to repeat it, but she acquires a measure of healing, and fulfills a need to love, through nurturing Florens, a black slave girl Jacob reluctantly agrees to accept as a debt payment from Ortega. Lina also protects herself from Sorrow, who "dragged misery like a tail" (55), and thinks Sorrow's misery a curse that causes the death of Rebekka's children. In this instance Lina shows her own wounds in not helping a fellow sufferer, one who perhaps threatens Lina's well-cultivated self-control.

With her Native American way of thinking, less focused on the individual than on the collective, Lina judges the Vaarks' life as a "selfish privacy" and believes that by their refusing their clans, pride leads to their downfall, with no heirs. These views could reflect a Native American inclination of mind, but one that perhaps has absorbed some of the settlers' ideas of sin and punishment. Ironically, Lina condemns the Vaarks' independence as "like Adam and Eve" (58), despite having the most freedom with them. She turns to her oppressors' beliefs because once Jacob dies, "they were orphans, each and all" (59). She again feels separate, abandoned, as the Vaark household falls apart and Rebekka cannot hold it together, turning instead to her neighbors for approval.

Sorrow, another servant on the farm, is an orphan rescued by Jacob. She is a mixed-race child raised on a slave ship, the progeny of perhaps the captain and a slave, and she is groomed to be a sail mender. Readers can cobble together from her patchy, repressed memories that she was apparently abandoned during what seemed to be a slave revolt and responded to the bloodshed and her sudden isolation by dissociating. When she recovers self-awareness, her personality has been split into two parts, her "Sorrow" self and an identical other named "Twin," whose friendship makes it possible for her to function, even in a delusional state. When she first appears on the farm, aged only eleven and a charity case accepted by Jacob for goods, she has no memory of her past life "except being dragged ashore by whales" (51). Sorrow, the most outwardly traumatized of the group, in her inwardness and dissociated state puts others at a distance. Others (especially the women) tend to be frightened of her lack of control and blame her for her heedless, dissociated state. Men take advantage of her distanced affect, turning her into a sexual victim, and her inwardness (she talks mostly to Twin, because others ignore her) isolates her further from the other women on the Vaarks' farm. This suggests that the damaged may want to avoid even one another if they trigger each other's traumas, and also that they fear otherness. Her looks, resulting from miscegenation (kinky red hair, gray eyes), and her black teeth (from surviving on the ship's molasses) mark her as strange and other even to Lina and Rebekka, who isolate her. She is haunted by the death of her premature baby, which Lina has sent floating down the river. Sorrow imagines the child to be breathing water, and feels more alone without it. The novel suggests the actions of memory shaping her mentality: "Miles of hemlock towered like black ship masts"—these images transport her back to her life on the ship. She can only tell the horror story of the ship's slaves at a safer distance, through Twin. As she recovers from a vaccine the blacksmith gives her for smallpox, in a still semiconscious state she involuntarily remembers the screams of people on the slave ship, the frantic whinnying of horses let loose, the dull sluice of molasses pouring out of the barrels. Her preoccupation with images of white clouds is an example of her defensive ability to disguise—or cover up, as clouds cover—these traumatic events. She then remembers being able to search the ship and leave it because Twin is with her. She begins a healing process when she awakens to the passive impersonality of her own sexual encounters while witnessing the mutual pleasure of Florens's and the smith's encounters. She recovers a coherent sense of self only when her third baby survives and Twin disappears, a sign that her defensive splitting is not useful for caring for her baby. In Sorrow and Lina, Morrison raises the possibility of healing through caring for others and bearing responsibility for them—the only ways available for such women to transform their lives, and to create purpose for themselves. The women most feel this need to nurture, but Jacob and even the blacksmith feel it too.

Florens and, later, her mother are the only first-person character narrators and the most important focus for establishing the broken relations caused by slavery and the resulting mind wounding in Florens. She is haunted by what she perceives as her mother's abandonment of her and becomes "fixed" in this scene of rejection (Wyatt 134). As is typical of a traumatized child, she internalizes others' rejection of her as her own fault. Scully describes Florens as a "combination of defenselessness, eagerness to please and, most of all, a willingness to blame herself for the meanness of others"; she could easily be victimized, he thinks (*A Mercy* 152). She carries a sense of being tainted, referring to the "darkness" within her that she thinks may have caused her mother's actions: her "inside dark is small, feathered and toothy. Is that what my mother knows? Why she chooses me to live without?" (115). Her mother begged Jacob to take Florens as a child because, we learn later, she feared Florens would be sexually abused; the plot turn encapsulates the difficult choices of slave mothers that Morrison similarly depicted in *Beloved*. Florens, however, does not understand her mother's motives; she believes her mother chose her brother over her and feels perpetually unwanted at the slightest reminder: "Mothers nursing greedy babies scare me. I know how their eyes go when they choose. How they raise them to look at me hard, saying something I cannot hear. Saying something important to me, but holding the little boy's hand" (8). This implies her mother tried to explain what she did but Florens was too hurt to hear it. Throughout her sections of the novel she is visited by "a *minha mae,*" which is Portuguese for either "my mother" or a voodoo spirit, an image of her mother as she was with Florens's brother. This coded form, and the nonspecific article "a," highlight the term's double meaning, indicating the vision partakes of both the mother's spirit and an illusion in Florens's mind. She confirms her mother's death early in the novel. These visitations from a spirit terrify her because she cannot hear the message it is trying to communicate—her mother's important message that Florens was not rejected (which is explained by Jacob and later her mother at the novel's conclusion). Once again, Morrison employs supernaturalism, another reality, to express the possibility of resolution and healing. This possibility also arises as Florens lies unconscious, haunted by her mother, wanting and not wanting to know what motivated her to give her up.

This early separation makes Florens so desperate and greedy for love that she alienates the man she wants. This is the tenor of the narrow and fixed quality of her mind as she addresses her story to the blacksmith she loves obsessively, an emotional substitute for her mother ("You are my protection. Only You" [69]). The smith is a free black man who uses her for sex but then rejects her for having a slave mentality and for physically harming a young boy, Mailik, whom he's raising. The boy's fear of her becomes associated with Florens's own "traumatic separation scene" with her mother, and she "conflates [Mailik's fear] . . . with her own hiding behind her mother just before being sent away" (Jaffe Schreiber 167), the painful emotional exile she cannot seem to escape. Reverting to survival mode, she focuses on herself and not on whether she might frighten or mistreat the child. She recognizes the similarity of the situation: "full of danger and I am expel" (136). When the smith protects the boy from her, her mother's choice seems reenacted: "As if he is your future. Not me" (136). This situation triggers her woundedness, and in these moments she has a weak sense of self: in a dream she looks into a lake but cannot see the reflection of her face; then a friend who helped her escape the Baptists consoles her: "You will find it" (138). This dream could be interpreted as revealing an unconscious conflict between losing one's identity to trauma and wanting to recover it. The *minha mae*, or spirit of her mother, appears to Florens just before she hurts Mailik; the *minha mae* is holding his hand, perhaps trying to clarify that the situation with Mailik is different, and that Mailik is not Florens's brother. If it is the mother's viewpoint that is represented, Florens is too afraid to hear the message ("I hide my head in [the] . . . blanket" 138), but she interprets the appearance of her mother as further proof of the similarity between her brother and Mailik, which makes her crueler toward him.

When the smith sees the wounded child it becomes obvious, even to the distracted Florens, that the man cares much more for the boy than for her. He tells her that she has made herself into a slave: "Your head is empty and your body is wild. . . . Own yourself, woman. . . . You could have killed this child" (141). Susan Strehle argues that the smith lives like a white man and condemns Florens "in terms that differentiate her from the elect but also from himself . . . [according to] the logic of an exceptionalist culture" that privileges mind over love and desire (119). Living as a free man, a valued laborer, like a white man, he cannot imagine or sympathize with the effects of being raised in slavery. He shocks Florens into confronting his rejection, and she responds by fighting him, attacking him with a hammer, not accepting his cruel (if true) accusations. Even after these events she still loves him and wants to explain her nature, to be understood in the context of her life. Her telling her story to him is a significant part of the book, now the way she survives. However, she repeats her mother's fruitless attempts to tell her side because she knows the smith cannot read. She writes it on the walls of Vaark's now empty house. Jean Wyatt makes the argument that Florens remains a needy child emotionally, unable to surmise that her mother may have had different motives for letting her go, which supports the idea that Florens is a case of "arrested development" (138). Insofar as she repeats her mother's impotent explaining, there is some justification for this view. However, on her journey to the smith, she exhibits a quick mind and an ability to survive.

Florens makes some progress toward becoming aware that something is controlling her, repeating the "claws of the feathered thing" (160) metaphor for her violent desperation, her inner traumas, which she knows she must fight off. Because it's something she feels inside herself, she is also still internalizing her rejection, wanting to know what happened and yet still defending herself from it. At the end of her story, in some measure more aware of the complexities of her life, she describes herself in more assertive and complicated terms: "Unforgiven. Unforgiving. Slave. Free" (161).

Florens and her mother personify the broken relations that are the legacy of the abandonment and rupture caused by slavery. Strehle observes that "the novel's perspective and structure effectively isolate each witness, emphasize their absence of understanding, and replicate at the formal level the failure of connection and communication at the thematic level" (120). Their failures to communicate show us the isolation of trauma; Florens cannot discover her mother's motives because she is emotionally locked into that moment, a survivor who cannot get outside it enough to reevaluate her mother.

Florens's mother tells her story last, and expresses Morrison's views on power and domination in the final lines of the novel. She too wants to be understood, and to explain why she asked Jacob to take Florens: knowing that her son would not be abused as Florens might be, she tries to prevent her daughter from experiencing the humiliations she has. She judged Jacob a better kind of man who would not exploit Florens. She also remembers the horrors of the Middle Passage, a misery so great that the slaves wanted the sharks in the water to devour them. While with Ortega, she realizes the full extent of her commodification and objectification as a slave, sexually abused by the Ortegas and forced to breed with other slaves. She puts her faith in Jacob and regards his taking Florens as "a mercy. Offered by a human," since godly mercy is in short supply. She takes the action available to her, saving her daughter for a while, although as the novel ends, Rebekka plans to sell Florens, so she may, ironically, end up in exactly the position from which her mother tried to save her.

Reading according to the complex interactions of the efferent/aesthetic modes helps explain some of the difficult dynamics of traumatic situations. For example, the rational basis for the mother's actions is outweighed by the emotional baggage and loss they produce in Florens. Morrison puts this mother in the ethical dilemma of having to abandon her child to save her. Can a child ever understand this decision? Florens and her mother repeat a seemingly endless loop of self-recrimination, as does Sethe in *Beloved*, who almost dies from her guilty conscience. Readers might consider from Florens's viewpoint whether the separation of mother and daughter to avoid abuse is preferable to a life with abuse but remaining together. If the mother is the spirit, she worries that her daughter will be traumatically stuck and give herself over to abuse. The spirit could also be a metaphor for Florens's mental repetition of the mother's attempt to speak that she could not hear. Florens's deafness has a parallel in Denver's hysterical deafness in *Beloved;* her resistance to hearing a schoolmate connects her mother to her sister's death.

In the final lines of the novel, Florens's mother's message about the complexities of domination is designed to help Florens understand trauma-inducing circumstances, and that one responds ethically as best one can under impossible circumstances: "I stayed on my knees. In the dust where my heart will remain each night and every day until you understand what I know and long to tell you: to be given dominion over another is a hard thing [like Jacob]; to wrest dominion over another is a wrong thing [like Ortega]; to give dominion of yourself to another is a wicked thing [like Florens]. Oh Florens. My love. Hear a tua mae [Hear your mother]" (167). The mother wants to free Florens from her sense of rejection and emotional exile. Her repetitions indicate a traumatic separation for the mother as well, in a continual struggle to justify her actions to Florens. This is Morrison's message to readers as well. Both she and Atwood understand that trauma traps individuals in circumstances that foster helplessness and internalized oppression, and look for possible routes out of this stasis. One route is not to embrace your own oppression, which is very difficult, given the realities of how trauma works on personality. However, when there are opportunities for resistance or greater knowledge, they should be pursued. Fear must be overcome, pain refused when possible, as when Florens attacks her abusive lover.

In *A Mercy*'s historical time, only whites with money, most often men, could give legitimacy to nonwhites and the underclasses or break the cycle of trauma for those who would become victims or property without their sponsorship. Jacob's compassion and fair-mindedness, which Rebekka shares, sets a tone of freedom, both religious and cultural, on their farm. The Vaarks have allowed their subordinates to have their own identities before they are appropriated by capitalism and religion, respectively, as they succumb to their losses. Readers are meant to initially identify with Jacob, who expresses contemporary progressive views against slavery and religious excesses. Unfortunately, holding these views does not deter him from participating in slavery. He seeks a place in the scheme of things that will not compromise him. Nevertheless, when he unwillingly accepts a slave (he chooses Florens when her mother begs him to) as payment for a loan, he begins a descent into further involvement. He accepts indirect participation in the slave trade when it serves his own interests, making money in the rum trade, which requires slaves to raise sugar cane. Jacob's family's failure to nurture him deprives him of self-worth, and he wants to assert himself as a man and to leave something behind. Readers can see him as deprived of his moral sensibility, and his situation raises the ethical issue of whether anyone can stand against prevailing economic, social, and cultural systems.

Though Jacob and his family try to be self-sufficient, they cannot avoid connection to others and social pressures. Despite his contempt for Ortega, and the knowledge that he is a more substantive man, Jacob, like Faulkner's Thomas Sutpen, feels a keen sense of class inferiority as he leaves Ortega's mansion, convinced he will not feel equal unless he has something similar. "Jacob felt the shame of his weakened position like a soiling of the blood" (23) as Ortega taints him with a slave as a debt payment. Jacob's embrace of the European ideology of manhood to enhance his life and the need for recognition (represented, as in *Absalom, Absalom!*, as a huge house he builds on money earned from slavery) allows him to deny and distance himself from collusion with slavery. He wants to save the enslaved (Florens, Lina, Sorrow), yet he is still their owner, if benevolent. Like many of the other characters, Jacob is an orphan, and his compassion for orphans leads him to take in Florens and Sorrow. His uncertain status and the deaths of all his and Rebekka's children produce in him an obsession with acquiring things and lead to building the house that seems to be compensation for his lost children: "What a man leaves behind is what a man is," he tells his wife (89). The house is incomplete when he dies of smallpox, and Rebekka will refuse to live in it. Jacob's aspirations cost him his values and his moral perspective (fairness toward others, owning people); the house he builds represents sacrifice (of trees, of others' freedom), a legacy his own wife rejects.

After the death of Jacob and her children, Rebekka is devastated. These traumatic losses change her worldview and the way she treats the other women, not allowing them the freedoms they had before. Once she had the confidence and skepticism to assess the religious fanaticism and rigidity the Baptist women around her as "convinced they were innocent . . . [but they were] children without the curiosity of a child" (92). People so locked into their fears, this description implies, cannot be open to anything different. They must also absorb everyone and everything that surrounds them into their own worldview. Fueled by fear of everything around them, and careful not to indulge in pleasures, they are nonetheless confident that God has already chosen them. Unfortunately, Rebekka absorbs this fear and reverts back to her parents' bitter religious fervor, as now the death of her family seems like a punishment when she sees the religiously observant children alive and well. She adopts the personality traits associated with trauma: rigidity, fear-based motives, and splitting others' behavior into good and bad, rejecting the "savagery" of Lina bathing in a lake, and hitting the pregnant Sorrow for urinating in town. Rebekka plans to sell Florens, who once again becomes a commodity. Lina thinks that without Jacob and with Rebekka ill, they are now "wild game for anyone. . . . Female and illegal, they would be interlopers, squatters, if they stayed on after Mistress died, subject to purchase, hire assault, abduction, exile. . . . They were orphans, each and all" (58–59). Rebekka's reversion allows the prevailing culture to draw apart misfits who were once a comfort to one another. As she did with the convent in *Paradise,* Morrison created a haven for damaged women still vulnerable to outside invasion. Here too she creates possibilities for healing that are not yet part of the social realities.

Morrison's characters' responses to extreme situations highlight their emotional and psychological similarities: they are all either orphaned or abandoned in various ways, which creates in them all a crisis of identity, a need to search for something to replace that emptiness and to feel safe in the world. With that early denial of recognition, all struggle to create a consistent and strong sense of self within their limited environment. Jacob, childless, looks to money and status. Rebekka once turned to Jacob, then to her children, and then to religion to make sense of her life. Lina and Sorrow each find solace in nurturing a child. Before Jacob's death, the farm sustains a collective support system. Rebekka and Lina become close; Lina nurtures Florens; and though they have an arranged marriage, Jacob and Rebekka are well-suited and happy. Jacob is the linchpin, however. When he goes, Rebekka cannot sustain the group: no children means no future.

Morrison's message is clearly articulated through Florens's mother's statement regarding dominion. Also, she suggests the importance of nurturing children and the importance of taking back one's life in order to heal from trauma and oppression. While males, the social structure, and whiteness are forms of protection, these things also define others and create trauma. *Paradise* and *A Mercy* share a number of themes: dispossession of particular groups; the goal of creating a perfect world where fear and trauma are cause and effect in the process of exclusion; the absorption of white, largely Puritan values; and the passing along of destructive behavioral patterns with the anxiety that children will bear their parents' burdens and perpetuate them. These subjects should raise the issue of how we as readers might conceive of a good world. If we see the novels as an analysis of the process of exclusion and its consequences, do they convince us that we must shift to paradigms that help heal from a traumatic past? What might these new paradigms be? Rejecting exclusionism seems necessary, as it's tied to binary thinking that defines by opposition and makes value judgments on that basis (Strehle 109). Morrison's work demonstrates the key role of trauma in perpetuating oppressive systems, explaining why people need to create "others" that are not as worthy. A psychological fear response to perceived threat is part of the human makeup. Moral accountability toward others does not flourish in environments of fear and commodification, which remain insidious frameworks for our thinking and our treatment of others.

THREE

Obsessions and Possessions in William Faulkner's *Absalom, Absalom!*

Like the other writers in this study, William Faulkner employed trauma narratives to help readers recognize extreme human responses to situations of crisis, in this case the scars of Southern slave culture. Faulkner examines the traumas of objectification and commodification of individuals in capitalist and class systems that are themselves elaborate defenses against recognition of their effects. The costs of this version of the American Dream are dehumanizations lived out in legacies of pain, lost connection, and regression (Porter 154). "In *Absalom, Absalom!* Faulkner imagines how the initial insult of reducing human beings to instruments of labor and commodities of exchange dooms a society to concussions of brutality, domination, and revenge" (Mathews 174). His narrative strategies pull readers into the persistent repetitions and stasis he witnesses in Southern thought and behavior before, during, and after the Civil War. *Absalom* unveils the traumatic origins of the elaborate illusions of Southern manhood, and of protagonist Thomas Sutpen's "design," or dream for success, as a form of avoidance and denial. The novel immerses readers in the fears and obsessions that powerfully motivate human beliefs and actions. It calls our attention to silences around the effects of slavery and miscegenation that are elaborately unacknowledged, forbidden, and camouflaged to avoid facing the tragic consequences of rigidly drawn color lines.

Faulkner's depictions of defensively rigid personalities reflect the perverse traumatic logic that shapes their willingness to jettison human feeling to maintain concepts of race and gender that necessitate breaks between deeply connected individuals. Rigid designations of race and gender manifest and perpetuate trauma because they become the basis for destructive conceptions of truth and identity. Faulkner's characters insist that white men's regular abuse of these designations be kept secret, lest the myriad contradictions of miscegenation and the black "stain" on families, as the racial categories and ideologies of the time would have it, be revealed. This secrecy masks how white patriarchs betray blacks and women by disavowing their black family members and denying women their futures. The men are protecting themselves from their own trauma, that is, the disconnection between the realities of Southern heritage and the ideals of the American Dream (Woodward 21). The men refuse to recognize blacks and women and deny them self-respect and rights in this social context, illustrating Axel Honneth's points that these rejections create traumatic consequences ("Personal Identity" 133).

Reading Faulkner's characters as traumatized has several advantages. It helps readers recognize the impact of severe stress, and it establishes both men's and women's traumas and suggests men and women suffer comparably (as Sutpen and Rosa do) even if their gender roles lead them to different symptom manifestations. Further, analyzing the causes and workings of trauma allows readers to see fully how the social environment affects human psychology and shapes responses to stressors. These responses include how individuals defend themselves from feeling, or act out rather than remember; how emotions or memory can emerge involuntarily; the forms of cognition that develop; and what happens when individuals do not find a supportive environment. Rosa and Sutpen repeat, repress, and dissociate from their own and others' suffering. Both construct identities around the pillars of pride and single-mindedness. Many factors may contribute to a trauma survivor's view: one's emotional state, social thinking, circumstances, relations to others, and social and cultural contexts and values. Recognizing that Sutpen's society values and devalues people according to class, race, and gender, for example, is key to understanding the nature of his traumas.

Faulkner's narrators relay remembrances of Southern history through the characters' recurring behaviors and what those behaviors come to mean within the structure of individual consciousnesses. Many critical studies of this novel explore the significance of racial trauma, but I also want to look at how Faulkner presents gendered and class trauma, and how the construct of Southern masculinity required the commodification of both blacks and women. The primary focus of this chapter is on analyzing Sutpen and the impacts of his traumas, his sister-in-law Rosa's scathing critiques of him, and Rosa's appropriation of his values, as well as the similarly defensive emotional frameworks of all the narrators.

Faulkner's Narrative Strategies

Faulkner immerses readers in the traumatic consequences of Southern life on personalities and relationships. He achieves this immersion through the use of narrative devices that approximate trauma-inflected cognition, such as characters' limited or conflicted knowledge and perspectives and their emotional constrictions. The first-person narration helps convey mental states and creates the illusion of quality of mind and experience. For Faulkner and other modernists who address "cultural trauma and personal bereavement," observes Suzette Henke in *Post-Traumatic Fiction*,

> early twentieth-century narratives were imbued with pervasive symptoms of post-traumatic stress: dissociative thinking, hypersensitivity, obsessive repetition and flashbacks, compulsive fear of intersubjective relations, and a "disintegrated" sense of self reflected in linguistic fragmentation. For the modernist author wrestling with irreconcilable issues of loss and cultural mourning, trauma overloads the psyche to such an extent that intrapsychic conflict evinces a dissociated stream of consciousness that rescripts the narrative bricolage of a tessellated interior landscape and revises our understanding of artistic production as a formally experimental, therapeutic response to shattered subjectivity.

Faulkner's narrative framework reproduces the levels, vagaries, and gaps in consciousness that cause the ethical failures perpetuating traumatic wounding, and captures for readers some of the cognitive distortions of a traumatized mind.

As a modernist, Faulkner compounds the contradictions and crises of the mind as he re-creates them, but his approach also embraces the uncertainties of knowledge and perspective seen in Morrison's and Atwood's more contemporary narrative and epistemological approaches. All three writers depict characters who may observe their own behavior but do not have the means to feel or interpret the depth of the traumatic effects on themselves and others, instead acting out the damage by repeating their wounds and obsessions. The views of other characters and certain narrative or linguistic devices also help readers infer what the protagonists do not know.

The seeming inexorability of the characters' actions, though articulated by Faulkner as resonant of biblical and Greek tragedy, can as well be seen in all its complexity through the lens of trauma. One could argue that this story is not a typical tragedy in that the focus is not exclusively on the tragic hero but on how others make meaning of Sutpen's actions: of how he has made them his victims, and of the social and economic intricacies that fuel the traumatic stress that shapes his fatally flawed conception of a successful legacy. He does not exhibit much awareness of his failings, either. The Southern defeat that threatens men's historical position as patriarchs is devastating, and the men in Faulkner's novel try to defend their positions through "collective fictions [that] affirm the legitimacy of a system that affords . . . advantage, while justifying the disadvantages borne by everybody else" (Mathews 182). The encounter with the other becomes traumatic because the other's presence and suffering would, if the men acknowledged it, remind them of their own lost status and reveal the human, emotional toll of their designs. My interpretation attempts to account for the male characters' fears and the nature of their repression of feared truths as trauma-driven behavior.

The narrative structure slowly reveals trauma: first in the characters' symptoms, then gradually by revealing some of its causes. Also indicative of trauma are time shifts, conflating past and present; a narrowed perspective; duration, or length of narrative focus; and the frequency with which such elements as repetition occur, suggesting obsession. All these elements in aggregate make the connections with trauma part of the storytelling.

A preeminent sign of a traumatized state of mind is the existence of an inextinguishable link between past and present, and particularly a past so fully present that it drives current action. Faulkner has summed up his view of memory and the past dominating the Southern mentality: "The past isn't dead; it isn't even past." He attempts to re-create the confusion resulting from conflation of past and present that characterizes the mental experience of trauma by using a dense narrative style that reflects the uncertain, repetitive, and conflicted contours of that experience. Often, he conflates times within a single rumination. For example, Rosa imagines a simultaneous curse on her family and on the South carried forward by Sutpen's first discovery of Ellen in a church; Rosa traces the curse back to the actions of an ancestor, who "had elected to establish his descent in a land primed for fatality and already cursed with it" (*Absalom* 14). The past becomes present in the ways that memory takes on corporeal form: a man's voice haunts Rosa's voice (4), and memory is felt in Quentin's body when in 1909 he "breathed the same air as in 1833" (23). Further, Rosa describes traumatic memory as intimately felt in the body and repeated as if hard-wired: "That is the substance of remembering—sense, sight, smell, the muscles with which we see and hear and feel—not mind, not thought: there is no such thing as memory: the brain recalls just what the muscles grope for: no more, no less: and its resultant sum is usually incorrect and false and worthy only of the name of dream" (115). Moreover, Rosa's incantation of her sister Ellen's past directive to her, "Protect Judith at least" (10), provides the impetus for her going to Sutpen's mansion. Duty to family and the desire to protect her niece embolden Rosa to enter the "ogre's" lair. She must continually remind herself of this when she takes herself to task for becoming involved with Sutpen. She is not referring to normal memory, which can be considered from a distance and acted on, but traumatic memory, a blind, automatic response to a past that is buried in the unconscious and irrevocably shapes the present. The past can never become a memory if one cannot get over it.

Other uses of narrative elements also demonstrate a sense of time and action driven by past traumas. Focalization, or the use of a perceiving, directing consciousness to focus the reader's attention, is complicated by Faulkner's narrative because there are multiple "central perceiving characters" or narrators with different perspectives and different access to information. Consequently, readers must analyze them in relation to each other, which makes their testimonies less certain as readers are brought into the narrators' self-serving stances in attempting to make sense of Sutpen's life.

Another narrative feature, the order of the storytelling, as opposed to the chronology of the events related in the story, is not chronological because time past repeatedly overwhelms time present. There is no linear progression but rather a sense that the past catches up to and destroys the present and future (as we see in the deaths of Sutpen's children and grandchildren and in the destruction of Sutpen's estate). Narrative duration, or the length of time a text devotes to particular events, alters clock time as past events are extensively replayed in the character's minds and reflected on in minute, repeated detail. Also, frequency (how many times an event or thought is narrated) is used to produce the effects of obsessive and repetitive replaying of particularly harrowing moments and feelings that become part of the characters' personalities. Examples are Rosa's repeated "I offer no brief for myself and ask no pity," saving

Judith, and Sutpen's repeated warning to Henry about Bon and Judith: "He cannot marry her, Henry" (133, 283).

These narrative techniques carry readers deep into the consciousness of the narrators and into their self-imprisoning thoughts. Readers experience difficulty gaining perspective on traumatic events as they are immersed in fragmentation, in characters and scenes revisited from different viewpoints, with the liminality of past, present, and future a cognitive given for the characters.

These storytelling methods help us understand Faulkner's larger points about the complexities of the human experience of history and the question of whether any kind of coherent understanding of the past, especially a traumatic one, is possible. Peter Brooks's analysis underscores these points, starting with the missing plot: Faulkner's narrative has no linear progression, no climax, and important information is made either inaccessible or anticlimactic. Brooks discusses the irony of Sutpen as the "master plotter" of his life, attributing to Sutpen an "abstract, formalist sense of what the future shape of his life must be. Yet his repeated attempts to found a lineage do not work, no doubt because one cannot postulate the authority and outcome of a lineage from its origin. The authority of genealogy is known only in its outcome" (Brooks 301). The resulting genealogy is disastrously broken because Sutpen objectifies those close to him by treating them as mere functionaries in his plan, denying them both recognition and the achievement of their own desires.

Narrators

The narrative focuses on how each narrator's version of the story transpires in his or her thoughts rather than as a chronological sequence of events. Minrose Gwin characterizes Faulkner's plural narrative structure as a hysterical text in "its mysterious and ceaseless disruptions of meaning, its stubborn resistance to analysis. . . . [We] experience the back-and-forthness, the tautness of this discursive space in which female and male voices do battle" ("Silencing" 166). She describes the novel as enacting "an intense struggle for narrative authority. On the one hand, Rosa's woman's voice, like the voice of the hysteric, resists and refracts the cultural text of patriarchy. On the other, the male voices continually struggle to distance and disavow women's bodies and stories" (168). Mr. Compson calls Southern women "ghosts" (*Absalom* 12). Writes Gwin, "Mr. Compson constructs women who are absent to their own historical voices. For the most part, they are seen, gazed upon, but like Cassandra, avoided when they have something to say" (171). These are largely silent women (Judith, Ellen, Clytie), except Rosa.

In trauma contexts, silence can be forced, but it can also be a self-protective device. It may signal "defeat, it serves [victims] both as a sanctuary and as a place of bondage" (Felman and Laub 58). Silence can represent a traumatic gap, connected to repression, isolation, loss, and hidden knowledge. Words may be withheld out of terror, guilt, or coercion. Traumatic memory is characterized as wordless, visual, and reenactive rather than cognitive and verbal when facing the unspeakable. For a writer like Toni Morrison, silence is insidious and harmful, indicative of impotence and isolation (Vickroy, *Trauma and Survival* 187). It can serve a similar purpose for Faulkner's women and for Sutpen, who is silent about his shame and others' suffering. In much of Faulkner's work, women and slaves are silent because they are unrepresented by his male narrators, and this befits their exclusion from the symbolic order. Even with few words, however, they can leave a powerful impression, like Caddy or Dilsey in *The Sound and the Fury* or Judith in *Absalom*, whose silences prove men's deafness to those they have neglected. They need to remain emotionally distant from the suffering they cause.

Readers infer from the characters' own words but are also guided by narrators' limited access and unreliability. Mr. Compson and his son Quentin draw readers to their viewpoints as they re-create Sutpen's and Rosa's complex lives according to their own understanding and motives, which are hampered by second- or third-hand knowledge of events and their own prejudicial assumptions. For example, the Rosa narrated from men's perspectives lacks the self-conscious suffering of her own first-person account. Quentin is also an emotionally charged narrator, self-invested in the past and its effects. Though too young to be directly involved with much of the central story, he becomes absorbed into the past and the thoughts of the other characters he talks about: he "absorbed it already without the medium of speech somehow having been born and living beside it, with it, as children do" (*Absalom* 172). Further, his low affect, his "curiously dead voice, the downcast face," indicate that for him there is a traumatic inevitability to retelling these stories (208). And in the telling, some of these voices echo each other, as Quentin and his college roommate Shreve "become compounded with Henry and Bon [Sutpen's sons]. . . . Who is speaking here? the text replies, Everyone and no one" (Brooks 303). Quentin says, "maybe we are both father" (*Absalom* 210), whereby he and Shreve repeat, multiply, and recreate the past, with little choice. "I shall never have to listen to anything else but this again forever so apparently not only a man never outlives his father but not even his friends and acquaintances do," says the resigned Quentin (222). The ways in which the narrators fictionalize the past are intimately associated with their emotions about their own circumstances in the Southern context, where everyone is denied their desired place in it.

Some of Faulkner's multiple narrators exist within the central story of the alliance of the Coldfields and Sutpens (Rosa), or have some indirect acquaintance with the protagonist. Sutpen's story is principally told indirectly, by all the other narrators (Rosa and the three generations of Compson men). The exception to this is a few pages in chapter 7, where Sutpen's own words to General Compson are reported by his son, Mr. Compson, through *his* son, Quentin.

Sutpen's struggle and the effects of his actions on the storytellers receive the greatest share of attention in the book. Rosa, the second protagonist and a major narrator, tells her own story with Sutpen in chapter 5, but she is also described by Mr. Compson and Quentin in chapters 1, 3, and 7. Quentin Compson is the principal narrative filter of the novel, but he has direct connection to the story only through Rosa and a brief meeting with Sutpen's son Henry. Quentin assimilates details of Sutpen's story from his own father, Mr. Compson, who has gleaned them from *his* father, General Compson, who actually knew and talked to Sutpen.

The last narrator, Shreve, Quentin's college roommate, has the least direct connection to the participants, with a third-hand interpretation culled from Quentin's storytelling. He is the Canadian "Yankee" outsider, marveling in the early twentieth century at the tragic and harrowing stories of the South since before the war.

Rosa and Quentin in particular remain haunted by Sutpen's life. These narrators have their own traumas, related to or triggered by Sutpen's struggles, which raises the question of whether Sutpen's life is the emblematic, defining narrative of the South. Does his story explain Southerners' complicity in their own defeat, as Rosa would suggest? Or is he a heroic figure (according to Mr. Compson), or a fated (tragic) one (as Quentin may see him) who, in trying to change his fate, only brings himself and his family repeated loss and devastation?

Sutpen's Story

The contexts of trauma in the novel are multiply framed in Sutpen's rise and fall. The Southern social structure before the Civil War was one of rigid class privilege and enforcement of white male power over women and black slaves. Faulkner explores how the norms of this society were overwhelmingly at odds with the nature of social identities and human feeling in their strictures. Rigidly enforced class divides and status based on material consumption, and particularly the commodification of black slaves and marriageable women, become the contexts of Thomas Sutpen's traumatic devaluation as a lower-class white and his repeated attempts to overcome it. He "seeks revenge on the artificial standards that make one man inferior to another, not by trying to do away with those standards, but rather by founding a dynasty, by establishing that same artificial standard of superiority for his family and bequeathing it to his son[s]" (Irwin 55). The frequency of racial mixing, despite the taboos against it, bring inner conflict and trauma to mixed-race Sutpen family members and confer legacies of emotional, moral, and cognitive decline on the family.

Sutpen is the patriarch around whom all the other characters' and narrators' lives revolve. His traumas shape or capture the other characters' imaginations. Both victim and perpetrator, he is compelled to distinguish himself in a social system that devalues him, and *Absalom* is a catalogue of his abuse of others in his quest. He is presented through narrators who try to fathom this seemingly possessed man as he attempts to create and re-create the ideal material life that will give him self-worth. He is described as having demonic energy and determination, in a fever of activity when readers first see him and before they learn why he is trying to establish a second home and family. Faulkner foregrounds Sutpen's actions over his inner life, and narrators and readers must speculate as to the motivations for his behavior and read for signs or symptoms. First, readers learn of his actions through others' horrified and astounded observations. Rosa's is our first view of him. She refers to his swagger, his being "stronger in fear" (10) and capable of hunting down his slaves, and then notes that her family is cursed with him and help him conceal himself behind a cloak of respectability. Quentin, through his father, describes Sutpen as someone forged like clay by a "furnace experience" (24–25): "his flesh had the appearance of pottery, of having been colored by that oven's fever either of soul or environment, deeper than sun alone beneath a dead impervious surface as of glazed clay" (24). This image connotes his emotional and mental hardness, his trauma-induced rigidity, something that cannot bend away from its purpose ("forged"). Compson reports townspeople observing him erecting his house, rebuilding his fortune, with a "grim and unflagging fury" (31).

Eventually, in chapter 7, Faulkner presents Sutpen's own revelation of the origins of his hardness. His primary trauma, being told by a black servant to go to the back door of a plantation owner's house before he can deliver a message, teaches him as a boy that he is not deemed worthy because of his social class ("He never gave me a chance to say it" [191], he repeats incredulously). He begins to hatch his plan as he processes the signs of affluence—clothes, house, slaves, and so forth—that he needs to attain landowner status. This original trauma scene sparks his relentless pursuit of an identity of social legitimacy through money, land, and power that necessitates the ownership of slaves and the white purity of his bloodlines. He develops a sense of shame about his status that is confirmed by his drunken feckless father and his sister, working like a "beast." He becomes cognizant of a perpetual social devaluation, a typical cause of insidious trauma, whereby individuals are automatically rejected from being part of a group (Root 240). Closing off those emotional avenues, he becomes determined to create a better legacy of prosperity and respectability. As he suffers these realizations, readers see Sutpen internalize these social designations, which take over his identity. Thus, "Sutpen determines his fate—to repeat periodically that traumatic affront but in a different role. Henceforth, he will no longer receive the affront, he will deliver it" (Irwin 50).

Sutpen must leave his family to pursue his fortune in Haiti. This abandonment of his imperfect family members may indicate another trauma, as he repeats similar abandonments several times in the novel. He faces many obstacles and lacks the education, social graces, and sensibility that would make him part of the class he desperately wants to join. But by the force of his will and obsessive efforts, he lures and ensnares other characters, particularly the Coldfields, into his projects. His associates often end up damaged and tainted in their dealings with him. Propelled by a mission to fight time and mortality, he experiences numerous setbacks in working toward his goals. The first is what he views as the necessary abandonment of his first wife and son, whose mixed race precludes attainment of white Southern respectability. While establishing his second household, at age twenty-five, he is described as "at this time completely the slave of his secret and furious impatience, his conviction gained from whatever that recent experience had been—that fever mental or physical—of a need for haste, of time fleeing beneath him, which was to drive him for the next five years," until he completes his house and marries Ellen Coldfield (*Absalom* 25).

Though driven by the past, Sutpen appears to block any memory that might make him feel or distract him from his plan. The narrators' descriptions and Sutpen's actions indicate a personality distorted by the trauma of his discovery, which comes on him like an "explosion," that the way to fight the upper class is to have what they have. His trauma-based mind-set, described by Compson as his "innocence," becomes his primary motivation. This "innocence" is the simple formulation of his design to achieve greatness and in turn becomes his excuse for every cruel or immoral act he will commit. His rationalization is part of an array of defenses that fend off trauma and come to constitute his personality: a dissociated splitting of self from emotions and self from others, evident in his cold determination to jettison people who no longer serve his purposes, leaving others stunned and in his power; a fear of intimacy that keeps him focused on his singular goal; and his obsessive cognitive frameworks, which lead to repetition and rigidity.

Though a powerfully compelling figure, Sutpen is largely silent, acting, and acting out, more than he speaks. Silence may be a trauma symptom, indicating shock or avoidance, and in Sutpen's case perhaps reflects a need not to reveal shameful information that would ruin his reputation and his design. Faulkner emphasizes Sutpen's silence and lack of self-reflection, his avoiding acknowledgment of the consequences of his "design" on others, which indicates the repressed or suppressed nature of his consciousness. Sutpen is seldom depicted communicating with others, implying his disconnection from them; he is even laconic with Judith and Clytie on returning home from the war: "Well daughter . . . Henry's not [here]" (128). Further, his silence seems necessary to avoid what the narrators reveal of his need to conceal shameful secrets, such as the existence of his first wife and child. His most powerful silence is directed toward his three children, Bon (the first, mixed-race son), Henry (the second, white son), and Judith (his white daughter). He first suspects and then confirms Bon is his son, but keeps the secret so long that Henry and Judith expect Bon to marry Judith. Sutpen must tell Henry but cannot until it's too late (wanting perhaps to hide the truth about Bon's race). The Civil War intervenes, and only at the end of the war does he finally break the silence to tell Henry repeatedly "he cannot marry her" (283), in this way letting Henry resolve the situation (which he does by killing Bon). Sutpen's own shame and trauma prevent him from accepting responsibility for the situation his children are in and brings about their rebellion and the family's destruction in the process.[1]

A mark of Sutpen's trauma is his reenacting his own early rejection with his children (Irwin 50). What Sutpen cannot say or acknowledge because of his shame destroys any relationship he might have had with Bon, and destroys Henry's life as well. Mr. Compson and Quentin surmise the effect of Sutpen's silence on Bon and of his failure to recognize his first son, a failure that probably destroys Bon's sense of himself as a man and makes him hinge all his hopes on this recognition, which would enable him to do the right thing—not pursue Judith. Instead, out of revenge for Sutpen's failure to acknowledge him, Compson and Quentin believe, Bon deliberately puts himself at the mercy of Henry, hoping first that Henry will kill him in the war, and then finally provoking him by not giving up on Judith: "I'm the nigger that's going to sleep with your sister. Unless you stop me, Henry" (286).

Sutpen illustrates the distortion of an individual's perceptual, decisional, and relational processes that allow him to avoid the long-developing dilemma of Bon and Judith's possible marriage and accounts for his failure to prevent Henry from murdering Bon. Sutpen's implacable design, his way of coping with or fighting his designation as inferior, compromises his moral and ethical judgment. Compson indicates as much: "The ingredients of morality [to Sutpen] were like ingredients of pie or cake" (211)—that is, already measured, and meant to produce only the predicted result. His ethical judgment is thrown off by his design, which reduces his capacity for feeling and caring for others. Sutpen represents, in broader scope, the South's rigid adherence to social designations of class, gender, and race, which deprives individuals of rights and explains the devastating betrayals within families and society of people who are deeply connected to one another (Sundquist 125–28; Gwin, "Silencing" 157).

Faulkner's portrayal of Sutpen's ways of coping with his traumas illustrates through character and psyche how, as Eric Sundquist notes, slaveholding Southerners continued to defend and feign innocence of a violent and oppressive way of life that continually brought shame on them (108–9). Racial divisions enable the "psychological division" required of people engaged in sexual and violent behavior as slave owners (127). Miscegenation during slavery resulted in the exploitation of black women and affronts to white women, and enhanced racial and gender divisions. The tragic and traumatic ironies of Sutpen's situation multiply as his obsessive and ill-adapted plans repeatedly fail, and in the process others become merely functional for him, mere instruments of his "design" to achieve respectability, not family members with whom he can make the deep human connections that would give him the solace most people require. The dishonorable and shady means by which he desperately creates (steals) a new fortune ironically deprive him of the ethical structures required to be a gentleman and, more important, to appreciate connections to his own family members. Further, by adhering to rigid class and racial proprieties, he repeatedly reenacts his own rejection as a boy with his own son Bon and his girl child by Milly at the end of the novel, ultimately destroying his family.

The traumatic consequences of Sutpen's obsessions for his family are Faulkner's focus. Many Faulkner scholars have noted that the repetitive behavior and fixed ideas of his characters tend to be inherited and reproduced down through the generations.[2] I would posit that Sutpen's traumas are revisited on the children, who bear their consequences and whose circumstances compel them to repeat them. Henry is likened to the biblical Absalom, a son who must uphold honor in the family because of his father's betrayals and the father's abandonment of his other son, Bon. Henry and Bon become embroiled in Sutpen's design against their will and despite Henry's far stronger feelings for Bon, for whom he repudiates his father. Henry is also willing to let Bon marry Judith despite the incest. Their passions work against the father's plans for a while, but as the triangle is played out—Bon is killed by Henry, Judith is abandoned—Henry recognizes how they have fallen into the father's disastrous design. Henry thinks the three of them "are just illusions that he [Sutpen] begot and your illusions are a part of you like your bones and flesh and memory" (277). Some critics explain Henry's reasons for killing Bon as a denial of his own homosexual desires for Bon (Roberts 35), which seems to be substantiated textually when Judith is described as a proxy for Henry with Bon. The men's bond could also signal a recognition of familial connection, of their hidden origins.

Bon becomes subject to the trauma of unbelonging once he knows of his father's existence, and particularly after he realizes his father will not acknowledge him. This is how Compson imagines him. Bon's comfortable identity in New Orleans, a place of moral and racial flexibility where he can take a mixed-race partner, is crushed under the rigidity of nineteenth-century Mississippi racial views and Sutpen's manic quest. The Bon-Judith union continues to represent for Faulkner the "racial and sexual anxiety" of Mississippi even as he is writing the novel (Roberts 36). In 1930 the state passed a law against racial mixing. Bon carries the racial stain that creates the distance between Sutpen's hopes and the reality of the losses he perpetuates. The ways his children are sacrificed to social pathologies, to individual injuries and shaming in relation to social mores (felt by Sutpen and passed on to Bon), seem to mock Southern codes of decency and honor.

Sutpen's rejection of his children and the traumatic legacies of the racial stain are further reenacted in his family after his death in the destroyed lives of Bon's son and grandson. Charles Etienne Bon, part black, like his father, was raised in New Orleans to be white. Like Bon, he cannot flourish in the harsh racial environment of Mississippi, despite Judith's and Clytie's efforts. To avoid the racial stigma attached to his father, Judith and Clytie, Sutpen's white and black daughters, try to raise Charles Etienne as white as well, but they cannot break the influence of the racial divide inherited through Sutpen's and Southern society's consciousness. This inherited sense of division confuses and splits Charles Etienne's identity to the point that he must insist on his own blackness despite his white appearance. The trauma of a lost identity results in a double consciousness that cannot be reconciled. He acts out his inner conflicts with compulsive and self-destructive fights with African American men, both asserting and denying this identity. He also marries a dark and crude black woman, thereby demonstrating his revulsion with his black self, leading to a short, unhappy life of twenty-five years. Like his father, he is unhomed; he no longer feels acceptance anywhere. The racial divide of Mississippi is internalized, and Charles Etienne grows up acting out the unresolvable conflict of a mixed-race identity. His son, Jim Bond, the last surviving Sutpen, is depicted as feeble-minded and an object of white anxiety as Shreve jokingly dismisses him as the inevitable future consequence of miscegenation.

The father's sins are visited on the daughters as well. Judith remains haunted by the loss of Bon and her brother. She is described as hopeless, like a marionette, and yet has incredible, suffering endurance as she gives Bon's letter to General Compson's wife and tells her to read it or not, as she sees fit:

> Because you make so little impression, you see. You get born and you try this and you don't know why only you keep on trying and you are born at the same time with a lot of other people, all mixed up with them, like trying to, having to, move your arms and legs with strings only the same strings are hitched to all the other arms and legs and the others all trying and they don't know why either except that the strings are all in one another's way like five or six people all trying to make a rug on the same loom only each one wants to weave his own pattern in to the rug, and it can't matter, you know that, or the Ones that set up the loom would have arranged things a little better, and yet it must matter because you keep on trying or having to keep on trying and then all of a sudden it's all over and all you have left is a block of stone with scratches on it provided there was someone to remember to have the marble scratched and set up or had time to, and it rains on it and the sun shines on it and after a while they don't even remember the name and what the scratches were trying to tell, and it doesn't matter. (100–101)

This is Judith's longest speech in *Absalom*. As we will see with Rosa, there are two portraits of Judith. In this passage she expresses a life spent in fruitless effort and controlled by others' wishes, fighting against oblivion but with the knowledge that all traces of existence may fade. She is typically depicted by the male narrators as a figure of ghostly silent stoicism: a paragon of the purity and the passivity of women. Though she has endured traumas, her silences may as likely be imposed by the male narrators of her life (Roberts 39). At key moments of supposed trauma, such as Bon's death, she demonstrates great calm and control (as Rosa tells it), and she performs occasional acts of disobedience, strength, and will. Faulkner allows her one emotional outburst, when she tells her father Henry killed Bon. Despite the depiction of her life as a "truly scary drama of self-denial" (Mathews 181), she also struggles for a place and name. She runs Sutpen's Hundred and raises Bon's son with Clytie until he and Judith both die of yellow fever. In her attempts to commune with the past and to raise the son she never had with Bon, she reaches for a family legacy counter to her father's racial fears.

Diane Roberts discusses this double portrait of Judith. As the male narrators tell her story, writes Roberts, "she is a dutiful daughter, faithful sister, forgiving lover, surrogate mother, and nurse, living and dying on the father's land: a tribute to the plantation patriarchy" (25). However, the ideal image of the chaste and silent woman gives way to Faulkner's evidence of Judith's spirit, the way she flouts feminine conventions, leading us to the idea that the Southern lady is a construct, says Roberts, that camouflages men's fears about a white woman who wants to sleep with a black man (Roberts 37).

When Judith sells her store, her source of income, to buy family tombstones, she appears to be equating family with death. One could read this act as her succumbing to trauma, symbolically choosing death over life, whereby honoring the dead and considering legacies are more important than her present life, as they are to her father: his sole obsession is that his name endures. However, Judith notes in the above lengthy quotation that it doesn't matter if in the future one cannot read the names on the stones. She has made her family connections in life, accepting and bonding with the children in her family whom Sutpen rejected or didn't acknowledge. Her legacy seems to be passing on Bon's letter in which his voice is vividly heard, and she leaves it up to others to read and remember.

While they may not endorse Sutpen's actions, General Compson and Mr. Compson refer to the "innocence" that causes his misadventures, the adherence to his doctrine of success. They do not analyze the trauma and destructiveness but rather see his actions as tragically flawed. Mr. Compson is deeply affected by Sutpen's life and portrays him as some sort of glorified figure, bigger than the defeat by the Yankees. Compson marvels at the "fine proud image of the man on the fine proud images of the stallion. . . . The apotheosis lonely, explicable, beyond all human fouling," and he remembers Wash, the man perhaps most like Sutpen in the novel, saying:

> He is bigger than all them Yankees that killed us and ourn, that killed his wife and widowed his daughter and druv his son from home, that stole his niggers and ruined his land . . . bigger than the scorn and denial which hit helt to his lips like the bitter cup in the Book. And how could I have lived nigh to him for twenty years without being touched and changed by him? Maybe I am not as big as he is and maybe I did not do any of the galloping. But at least I was drug along where he went. And me and him can still do hit and will ever so, if be he will show me what he aims for me to do. (230–31)

However, Sutpen's stunning rejection of Wash's granddaughter, Milly, comparing her to a mare, because she has not given him the son he expected, creates a traumatic break in Wash's illusion, and he must, ironically, kill Sutpen, who has defined Wash's own sense of honor, to defend his and Milly's honor. Some critics interpret Sutpen's actions here as suicidal (Strobel 168), bringing on his own death in the face of his mortality without a son. One could also attribute his actions to a heedless narcissistic fixation on his goals that is generally consistent with how he is portrayed throughout the novel. This example of his disloyalty and his body comically falling out of his coffin are two of the numerous ways in which Faulkner undermines the ironically tragic and heroic Sutpen constructed by the male narrators.

Sutpen similarly tears up the Coldfield family: while needing their respectability, his ambitions compromise and destroy them. He taints the respectable Mr. Coldfield's life, perhaps through blackmail or by involving him in illegal activity. Sutpen's relationship to Ellen is not elaborated on, but the town's rejection of Sutpen by refusing to attend their wedding and throwing objects at them as they emerge from the church could well have been for Ellen a traumatic "public humiliation" leading to her withdrawal into an imaginary world (Urgo and Polk 26). She copes with Sutpen's indifference and—to her—bestial behavior by living in a fantasy world of frivolous activity, denying his disconnection from her and their children, Judith and Henry. His most potent effect, however, is on her sister, Rosa, who survives them all.

Rosa's Story

Unlike their admiration of Sutpen, Compson, and to an extent Quentin, who sees much through his father's eyes, the male narrators view Rosa and other women through a differently biased lens, often blind to women's circumstances and feelings. Through their voices Faulkner demonstrates how a patriarchal perspective can prevail and reproduce itself over generations and defend itself against recognition of the effects of male dominance. Like Morrison's patriarchs, Compson and Quentin need to remain unaware of or insensitive to the pain they inflict. Covering a fear of helplessness and repressing "their own loss of control, their de-centered subjectivity, their castration" (Gwin, *The Feminine and Faulkner* 67) in a defeated masculine culture, they embrace the comfort of subordinating women and African Americans. Faulkner's depictions expose the male narrators' own illusions and lack of compassion. Their mentalities reveal, Gwin argues, "how they join together in a symbolic order which configures woman as Other; how the exclusion of the feminine [and blackness] actually becomes the necessary element for the masculine to order itself and its interactions" ("Silencing" 176). Particularly revealing are Mr. Compson's views: he can see symptoms and patterns in women's behavior, but he does not know how to interpret them. Compson claims women live in illusions: "In very breathing they draw meat and drink from some beautiful attenuation of unreality in which the shades and shapes of facts—of birth and bereavement, of suffering and bewilderment and despair—move with the substanceless decorum of lawn party charades, perfect in gesture and without significance or any ability to hurt" (*Absalom* 171). He does not recognize their inner lives or these forms as a kind of emotional self-defense against their narrow range of options, economic, social, and sexual, particularly in their role of chaste ladies perpetuating white bloodlines. For instance, the ridicule and shame Ellen endures at her wedding would be expected to have a traumatic effect insofar as this ritual and celebration, which confer a sense of identity and station for a woman of her time, are disgraced. Additionally, as dependents, women are ensnared in men's traumas as men's fortunes shape women's lives. Compson would rather see women as constitutionally irrational than face that their behavior is situationally linked to male control. Faulkner's men generally fail the women, even as protective patriarchs: they fail to take care of them (Coldfield and Sutpen), or else destroy their hopes, as Henry does to Judith by murdering Bon, or else, like Sutpen, regard women as merely breeders of their children (Rosa, Milly). Though women are essential to male status, perpetuating the male bloodline and giving men the cover of moral respectability, it is in these men's own psychological self-interest to establish systems of gender and racial inequality and ignore the consequences.

Faulkner's silencing of women and African Americans in much of his work demonstrates their voicelessness in this male-dominated culture, offering only rare opportunities for them to question or resist. "Much of the narrative's force, in fact, derives from Compson's, Shreve's, and even Quentin's efforts to master Rosa's text by distancing and diminishing her as a subject" (Gwin, *The Feminine and Faulkner* 68). In *Absalom*, though, Faulkner also allows women—Rosa, her aunt, Sutpen's first wife—to express their passionate need for revenge for Sutpen's failure to maintain duty and honor toward women as established in the Southern codes he seeks to follow. The women's anger, expressed and lived particularly in Rosa's voice and fruitless life, endlessly regenerates in the face of lost promises and lost existence, of which there remains only the sense of a tainted life and a longing for some sort of vindication.

Rosa is presented as a living wound, the product of elders' embedding her in the past such that her memories are not really reflections on that past but traumatic, recurring fixed ideas about Sutpen's perpetual wounding of her family. Compson and Quentin describe Rosa's life from childhood as a living death. Her mind is filled with the family's bad feelings toward Sutpen for using them to gain respectability and shaming them with criminal financial transactions. Rosa suffers particularly gendered traumas in relation to her family and Sutpen's thwarted goals. Her vindictive aunt directs Rosa's attention to her sister Ellen's suffering in her marriage to the "ogre" Sutpen. Rosa's father continually reminds her that her mother died giving birth to her, and he essentially abandons Rosa, letting her feed him and take care of the family business as he locks himself in the attic, where he dies, to avoid the Civil War, and absolve himself of responsibility toward his family (Wagner-Martin 237). Compson insists she hated her father, yet she dutifully kept him alive.

Compson and Quentin characterize Rosa as a "crucified child," "embattled in virginity and in a 43 year old insult" (9), and Cassandra-like: knowledgeable, but without power. Rosa grows up disappointed in men, who seem to withhold from her the normal woman's life, as defined then. Deprived of a mother, Rosa is referred to as a "living reproach" to her father for making his fragile wife pregnant, as she may unconsciously find him responsible for her mother's death in childbirth (perhaps why she seems to act out, according to Compson). She is deprived of her childhood in that she is made to participate in and absorb the world through the sense of being wronged that her aunt instills in her in relation to Sutpen; and according to Compson, she lives in a "grim mausoleum air of puritan righteousness and outraged female vindictiveness" (47). "Each adult left the child Rosa not only alone but without emotional or financial resources. And so Rosa became both the agent for [the family's] vengeance and its victim" (Wagner-Martin 237). She is depicted as repeatedly invoking Sutpen's injury of her, endlessly re-creating a loop of this "long dead object of her impotent yet indomitable frustration" (*Absalom* 3). To Quentin she represents the past ("the deep South dead since 1865" [4]). In her company in the present, 1909, he feels he is made "to listen, to one of the ghosts that had refused to lie still even longer than most had, telling him about old ghost times" (4). He hears the "ghost in her voice" (6). The male narrators focus on her pathological reactions, not on the keenly felt sense of loss articulated that is in her own narrative.

For Rosa, her family's and Sutpen's family's traumas mostly revolve around Sutpen:

> I saw Judith's marriage forbidden without rhyme or reason or shadow of excuse; I saw Ellen die with only me, a child, to turn to and ask to protect her remaining child; I saw Henry repudiate his home and birthright and then return and practically fling the bloody corpse of his sister's sweetheart at the hem of her wedding gown; I saw that man return—the evil's source and head which had outlasted all its victims—who had created two children not only to destroy one another and his own line, but my line as well, yet I agreed to marry him. (12)

Rosa enters "Bluebeard's" house after her father's death out of material necessity, wanting also to "save" Judith as her sister has asked, and as an "instrument of retribution" (48). However, his proposition (that she give him a son before he will marry her), which deeply insults and infuriates her, seems the principal cause of her anger and emotional investment in hating him, according to the male narrators. Her own words focus more on lost opportunity.

Like the other narrators', Rosa's perceptions of events conform to her own ideas and needs. Initially she enters Sutpen's house after Bon's murder, terrified, coming "not by mortal mule but by some chimera-foal of nightmare's very self" (113). She is soon disabused of the idea she will save Judith, who seems calm rather than grieving. She feels she traveled "twelve miles and nineteen years to save what did not need the saving and lost instead [herself]" (113). If her life at home was a living death, she describes an alternative identity in chapter 5 as her desires are awakened in her stay in Sutpen's house, with Judith and Bon modeling some idea of love, and later, with the possibility of becoming Sutpen's wife. Even after her hopes are destroyed, she finds a purpose in continuing to revisit thoughts of him, if only to revile him and replay her lost opportunity. She obsessively repeats these moments of crisis during which her life could have gone one way or another.

Though Compson portrays her as the embodiment of outrage and vindictiveness in chapter 1, her own words and final actions in chapter 5 mitigate this and present different manifestations of trauma as she holds herself responsible for the past, repeating, "I hold no brief, I ask no pity" (133). Imagining she might have had a choice is a classic defense against feeling helpless, and though she is also left with questions around her own actions, she reaches some insight into Sutpen's shattered and disconnected life:

> Because he was not articulated in this world. He was a walking shadow. He was the light-blinded bat-like image of his own torment cast by the fierce demoniac lantern up from beneath the earth's crust and hence in retrograde, reverse; from abysmal and chaotic dark to eternal and abysmal dark completing his descending (do you mark the gradation?) ellipsis, clinging, trying to cling with vain unsubstantial hands to what he hoped would hold him, save him, arrest him. (139)

An ellipsis is a perfect metaphor for his traumatized disconnection, silently representing the missing elements of his life and referencing his lack of grounding as a man in eternal movement. Rosa also recognizes that Sutpen had "sacrificed pity and gentleness and love and all the soft virtues for [Sutpen's Hundred]" (124). The blind animal imagery and flailing in darkness link his and her trauma symptoms and function as another metaphor for unawareness: instinctual, or in this case automatic, behavior. More important, Rosa implies that his death instigated her central trauma: a childless future.

Rosa's consciousness is enlarged within the new environment of Sutpen's house. The terrors bequeathed in her family give way to new ones, but she also discovers possibilities. She recalls hoping to see the family intact when she arrives, but with Bon dead and Henry gone, she must rouse herself: "Wake up Rosa. . . . Wake Rosa—not to what should, what might have been, but to what cannot, what must not be; wake, Rosa, from the hoping" (113). Upon her arrival, still embedded in long-taught fears, she must confront the only family she has left. "I found only that dream-state in which you run without moving from a terror in which you cannot believe, toward a safety in which you have no faith, held so not by the shifting and foundationless quicksand of nightmare but by a face which was its soul's own inquisitor, a hand which was the agent of its own crucifixion, until the voice parted us, broke the spell" (113–14). This is Judith's voice—calm, capable Judith. The dream state and quicksand metaphors recall Sutpen dwelling in his design, caught in a kind of dream or illusion, while Rosa wants to avoid drowning in that state of mind. Rosa feels she glided toward her hopes, but she also knows in retrospect that she moves inevitably toward unfulfilled potential—her trauma—and punishes herself for hoping. Her thoughts alternate between believing there was no choice and hoping that there was, even if the "choice" was to refuse him.

Rosa's monologue is filled with images of her potential, of fecundity, of her being overdue, particularly during the wistaria summer, when she was fourteen. The idea of herself opens out, like an image of blooming flowers. Even when this sense of self seems lost, she holds on to hope in comparing herself to a "warped chrysalis": "But root and urge I do insist and claim, for had I not heired too from all the unsistered Eves since the Snake? Yes, urge I do: warped chrysalis of what blind perfect seed: for who shall say what gnarled forgotten root might not bloom yet with some globed concentrate" (115–16). The image of the warped chrysalis suggests the body's memory for reproduction. Despite being damaged, Rosa still retains potential, which might be awakened with the right stimulus. This image hovers between life and barrenness (death), not conceding to the living death to which men have relegated Rosa.

Rosa's notions of memory do not have the reflective quality of normal memory but instead are inculcated in the deepest sense, as traumatic memories and history arise through the body and the senses. She accepts what cannot be "remembered" in the conventional way; such memories cannot be accessed consciously and therefore cannot be escaped or let go. Her youthful desires continue to reemerge in old age; she associates them with flowers:

> Once there was—Do you mark how the wistaria, sun-impacted on this wall here, distills and penetrates this room as though (light-unimpeded) by secret and attritive progress from mote to mote of obscurity's myriad components? That is the substance of remembering—sense, sight smell: the muscles with which we see and hear and feel—not mind, not thought: there is no such thing as memory: the brain recalls just what the muscles grope for: no more, no less: and its resultant sum is usually incorrect and false and worthy only of the name of dream. . . . Ay, grief goes, fades; we know that—but ask the tear ducts if they have forgotten how to weep. (115)

She recognizes the limitations of this type of memory, caught in time and lacking perspective (the false dream) but she also must recognize the powerful emotional impact that surfaces through the body and keeps her desires alive.

Sutpen's seed and his existence become part of Rosa's meditations on love, and what that could mean. She needs to construct a view of Judith and Bon to help her see herself, her own desires, to help her conceive of the love that had been denied her: "I who had learned nothing of love, not even parents' love" (117). When Judith calmly oversees Bon's burial, Rosa's dream of love seems to die. For Rosa, it is the trauma of a loss she can only imagine, the hope of a complete sense of being and connection, figured in the idea of Bon's corpse (the viewing of which is denied her by Judith, though neither does Rosa try to see him). "That was all. Or rather, not all, since there is no all, no finish; it's not the blow we suffer from but the tedious repercussive anti-climax of it, the rubbishy aftermath to clear away from off the very threshold of despair. You see, I never saw him. I never even saw him [Bon] dead. I heard an echo, but not the shot; I saw a closed door but did not enter it" (121). This is a huge loss, but there is an unreality to it. She recognizes at a certain point where she was fixed in life. In the midst of Wash's comical making of Bon's coffin she realizes, "There are some things which happen to us which the intelligence and the senses refuse just as the stomach sometimes refuses . . . occurrences which stop us dead as though by some impalpable intervention, like a sheet of glass through which we watch all subsequent events transpire as though in a soundless vacuum, and fade, vanish; are gone, leaving us immobile, impotent, helpless; fixed, until we can die" (122). No resolution is possible for her because she has not seen it, so she is able to psychically deny its finality to keep that hope for life, her life, alive: "I became all polymath love's androgynous advocate" (117). Did she want not to see Bon's corpse?

The male narrators dismiss Rosa as neurotically hysterical, but Minrose Gwin's reassessment of the concept of hysteria suggests that Rosa's narrative, through its emotional intensity and recognition of the madness around her, acts to subvert the male narrators' master narrative ("Silencing" 168). It has also been noted that Rosa's narrative shows readers the damages inflicted by a patriarchal perspective. For Gwin, Rosa "erases the boundaries between the conscious and the unconscious and so shows the father to himself in disconcerting ways" (177). It also helps locate Faulkner's views of psychology at the time, which were influenced by Freudian theory.

At this point I'd like to turn to trauma theory to further elaborate on how Rosa is presented psychologically. Though hysteria and trauma share symptoms such as dissociation and emotionally overdetermined reactions, interpreting Rosa as traumatized has several benefits.[3] It helps explain the impact of severe stress, and by avoiding the solely female association with hysteria it establishes that both men and women experience trauma, and suffer comparably. Trauma allows us to see a full process of the social environment's effects on human psychology: the nature of the stressors, the ways individuals defend themselves from feeling or act out rather than remember, how emotions or memory emerge involuntarily, the forms of cognition that develop, and whether suffering individuals find a supportive environment. Rosa and Sutpen repeat, repress, and dissociate from their own and others' suffering. Both construct identities on the edifice of pride and single-mindedness. There are moments when Rosa seems to be working through her emotions, though she still seems enraged at the end of the novel (again, from a male perspective), believing she is trying to save Henry—but Clytie may also have saved Henry by burning down the house with them both in it. Are both Rosa and Sutpen doomed to no resolutions? Or should we see Rosa as forcing the fire and bringing down Sutpen's house and family line, as Wagner-Martin (231) suggests? Should we think that he has broken the spell of his design, and in defeat does he deliberately (or unconsciously) provoke Wash to kill him when he rejects Milly (Strobel 168)? These are brief, anticlimactic moments in the novel, however.

The greater focus in the novel is on Rosa's traumas, and her willingness to address them in her narrative presents a challenge to male definitions and authority in recognizing the suffering they all experience but that the men deny. The male narrators want to devalue her experience and diminish her by referring to her as a "ghost, a vampire, a girl with dangling legs, which never grew" (Gwin, "Silencing" 173). However, through Rosa's voice, Faulkner "lets a whole sisterhood of abused plantation women—wives, fiancées, daughters, sisters, aunts—denounce the mad misogyny of masters who commandeered women's physical labor, administrative and financial skills, personal fortunes, and sexual lives so as to create domains they ruled, then venerated female chastity to safeguard the patrilineal descent of property and wealth" (Mathews 179). She is also a catalyst of the story, leading Quentin to an encounter with Henry (which she seems to avoid), during which he learns the important fact of Bon being part black.

Rosa attempts to understand her appropriation by Sutpen, who represents the white patriarchal culture that she condemns. Rosa's question of "Why, Why, Why?" (*did* she give in to Sutpen?) suggests a traumatic loss of self. She discovers her own desires were awakened and caught up in his desire, his design: "Forty-three years later she still struggles with the question underlying her own madness, her own un-interpretable willingness to negate her own identity and become 'whatever it was he [Sutpen] wanted of me—not my being, my presence: just my existence, what it was the Rosa Coldfield or any young female no blood kin to him represented in whatever it was he wanted'" (Gwin, "Silencing" 159). A disconnected sense of self and origins is apparent in the ways she describes herself: as a blind subterreanean fish, existing on the edge of knowledge, not allowed to be a child or a woman:

> instead of accomplishing the processional and measured milestones of the normal childhood's time I lurked, unapprehended as though, shod with the very damp and velvet silence of the womb, I displaced no air, gave off no betraying sound, from one closed forbidden door to the next and so acquired all I knew of that light and space in which people moved and breathed and I (that same child) might have gained conception of the sun from seeing it through a piece of smoky glass. (116)

It's as if she is unborn, looking at the living, not yet among them. Not a living death (a vampire) but existing outside a life she might enter, a nonexistence with potential. Quentin echoes her existence; he has not really lived either, and relives what's not even his own past.

Rosa's disappointing encounter with Sutpen, the realities of his forceful nature and the sexual life he might offer amid the desolation of war, and the hope he gives her for a meaningful life, produce a traumatic split in her twice. She is divided between her upbringing, which proclaims him a monster, and her experience of him as someone who might fulfill her desires even at the price of her being lost in his design. Her sense of self has been defined in opposition to him, and yet she is a tool for her family: both they and Sutpen objectify her for their own purposes. The second split comes as her hope is crushed with his humiliating demand that she produce a son before marriage. This is delayed information, told by another narrator instead of her, so the narrative focus is more on her outrage and his madness (as she perceives it). What is the nature of her trauma? Is it her sense of disappointment? That she was willing to lose herself with him? That she was helpless, having given him the power to make her hope, only to humiliate her? This splitting of her identity under the powerful agenda of white patriarchy is also evident in the way she absorbs and comes to identify with the white man's fear and unethical devaluation of blackness in how she denies Clytie's humanity and thereby "enacts her own loss of humanity and power" (Gwin, "Silencing" 157). His effects on her, and the stain of race, dominate her thoughts in ways that overshadow her own experience with an unrelenting and unresolved past that haunts and compels her forty-three years later to find out if it's Henry hiding in Sutpen's home. The thoughts and imagery used to create Rosa testify to the effects of a brutal man's world on her, which she construes as savage and black, referring to Sutpen's "black, naked and outrageous words." With this racial imagery we see her, like the men, create a sustaining illusion, linking herself to the myths the men use to perpetuate their power. This happens despite her own experience, for she at one time bonded with Clytie in surviving the war together with Judith, and she knew Clytie recognized her as a subject, unlike the men in her life. Though she comes to realize that men have denied women their desires, she is not similarly able to see the same disservice to black people. In this frame of mind, Rosa rejects Clytie forty-three years later, as Clytie tries to defend Henry from what she believes is Rosa's desire to expose him.

Clytie is also tragically caught up in Sutpen's world years after his death. Clytie, compared in the novel both to Clytemnestra and Cassandra, figures of knowledge, revenge, and impotence, also linking her to Rosa, is freed as a slave but remains tied to Judith, helping her raise Bon's son and grandson. Judith and Clytie cannot overcome Southern society's outrage at racial mixing, which permeates the children's upbringing and destroys them. Clytie dies doing Sutpen's will, burning herself with the house and a dying Henry, forty-three years after he has murdered Bon, the last family secret. Symbolically, as women and blacks, they are caught up, as Sutpen was, in self-annihilating class, gender and racial structures of the old South.

Ensnared in class hierarchies, Rosa denies herself connection by refusing (like Sutpen) to ask others for the help that would be freely given while she resists increasingly fluid class boundaries after the war. She resents that Milly, the subordinate Wash's daughter, becomes an acceptable mate for Sutpen (if Milly can produce a son). So destitute that she picks vegetables from neighbors' yards, Rosa will not acknowledge the shame that she is bereft of others' caring, her pride or class status forbidding she express this. Her feelings can only publically emerge in rage, but her inward thoughts reveal her vulnerability in a stream of undefended emotion and need.

In conveying Rosa's anger at the unspeakable insult that has undone her life, "Faulkner begins the effort to relate how a certain kind of abusive mentality was responsible for the South's mis-conceiving, perpetuated itself through rippling acts of brutalization, and so thoroughly infected its victims that they ended up replicating its horrors even as they sought to redress them" (Mathews 178). Rosa lives one of the profound paradoxes of trauma: that one can end up absorbed by perpetrators, or perpetrating systems. Quentin similarly can only echo voices of the past, feeling his impotence as a man, and, like Rosa, will die childless (but thus perhaps breaking a destructive cycle).

Lurking death, their inevitable mortality, the loss of self, and their failure to fulfill their obsession with producing offspring bring Rosa's and Sutpen's traumas together. On a subterranean level they do not give up the struggle, the imperative to reproduce. Both have a profound sense of their limited time. Sutpen continually races against time. Rosa's memories and impressions of Sutpen's house after Henry shoots Bon are described with a plethora of death imagery: "desolation more profound than ruin, holocaust" (109). Her views of love, which become real for her with the possible bond of Judith and Bon, and some hope with Sutpen, are shattered. Rosa's reference to Moloch, the god who sacrifices children, fits with the aforementioned ironic sacrifice of Sutpen's own offspring (109). Moloch becomes a metaphor for Sutpen's self-annihilating obsessions.

Thomas Sutpen and Rosa Coldfield embody the effects of trauma on personality, particularly the constriction of emotions and distrust. They illustrate the dialectical nature of trauma: feeling and not feeling, remembering and forgetting, recognition and repetition. Finally, they manifest the rigid and absolutist thinking that perpetuates trauma and links them with the patriarchs in *Paradise*.

Ethics and the Reader

What ethical issues does Faulkner's novel make us confront as he explores these characters' traumas? Readers can analyze these issues with the help of narrative theorist James Phelan's conceptions of a reader's ethical position being created in a dynamic interaction within four ethical situations. These are (1) how characters "behave and judge others," (2) the reliability of narrators, and how narrators focus readers' attention, (3) how implied authors' "narrative strateg[ies] . . . affect the audience's ethical response to the characters," and (4) readers' reactions to the "values, beliefs, and locations operating in situations 1–3" (*Living* 23).

The first ethical considerations are the significance of characters and their behavior. In *Absalom*, readers have to look at the narrating characters' shock or pity regarding Sutpen, or their judgment of Rosa. Readers have to decide how to feel about Sutpen and Rosa both in those characters' own words and through the other narrators, and as such will have to measure their feelings about trauma survivors and victimizers against these characters, and their views of women and African Americans. The nineteenth-century values readers absorb in these narrators' mind-sets must seem relatively intolerant and simplistic from a twenty-first-century perspective, as in Atwood. And yet readers witness how those values take a deadly toll. *Absalom* details the exacting standards of behavior, of Byzantine elaborateness, that Southern men demand of women and people of color (exemplified in Compson's description of New Orleans' mixed-race concubines). These standards create proscriptions around human connection, feeling, and compassion that seem to destroy everyone in Sutpen's orbit. Because we are immersed in these narrators' thoughts as they try to decipher the possessed actions of Sutpen, and because they contradict or undermine one another in their judgments of Sutpen, the stain of Sutpen's individual guilt broadens to a sense of a society (and generations) collectively trapped in fixed ideas. As readers, we can be swept up in the experiences of characters that try to avoid such deep conflicts even as they reveal them.

Phelan's second category involves narrators and their relation to telling. In *Absalom*, narrators are rendered as self-interested, lacking knowledge or understanding of other characters. Much as they try to piece together the story from multiple sources, it's still not complete. They seem capable of making sense of Sutpen and Rosa only on their own terms. The relations of the narrators to the stories they tell are often tenuous, and the reader must not accept them at face value. Some narrators (Compson) are unreliable because they wish to cover up the failures of a patriarchal and racialist Southern society. Other narrators, like Rosa and Sutpen, do not lack observational acumen but are in thrall to their own passions and have a certain blindness to their situations, so that they draw readers' attention to the wrongs done to them. To consider an ethical accounting of the past, the novel puts readers in the position of having to recognize the uncertainties of reconstructing traumatic history. The lack of plot and linear narrative, the urgency of narration, and the echoing voices in *Absalom* all call into question the possibility of a coherent understanding (Brooks 308–12). What glimpses of the past are available despite the uncertainties? To what extent is the narrators' witnessing accurate or ethical? The narrators offer scenes, slices of dialogue or action from which readers must infer, weigh contradictory information, try to fill in gaps, or assess the influence of the narrators' states of mind and self-interest. Most often female and black voices (rarely heard) reveal the origins of the problems, and critiques of the status quo (Gwin, "Silencing" 152).

As readers become aware of the unreliability of these narrators, they must consider some of the narrators' failures of judgment or ethics as collateral to trauma-related faulty cognition, shame, repression, or dissociation. Men like Compson and Quentin preserve patriarchy, their status, and manhood in the face of defeat in war, a lost way of life, and the distressed women, who reveal the costs of the men's drives and obsessions. Do these symptoms prevent the men and Rosa from bearing responsibility for themselves or others? Do they guide them to inflict misery on themselves and others? Sutpen narrates his drive toward self-worth as necessary, not acknowledging that it occurs at the expense of others: he rejects the women who do not provide the legitimate white sons he needs. Seeing him as traumatized reveals to us the process of his self-deception and avoidance, which Faulkner suggests motivate societal norms to avoid acknowledging human costs. No one narrates the emotional toll on Sutpen as he loses his wives and children. Are readers to infer from his silence the extent of his denial and repression? Do we consider ways he cloaks his own suffering?

The third element of Phelan's schema is the implied author and his or her relation to telling, in this case Faulkner's narrative strategies and how they lead readers to an ethical evaluation of his characters' situations. Faulkner's narrative highlights the psychological dysfunctions of the South, the scars of the Southern defeat, men's and women's traumas, the lingering traumas of the denial of black family members, and the decline of social values that his characters play out and only occasionally recognize. What are readers' reactions to how Faulkner has immersed us in these characters' minds? He encourages us to resist their racial views, but we might also recognize the difficulty of whites' encounters with others, with difference. *Absalom* unveils how the South "is full of unrecognized cast off sons and daughters who jeopardize the integrity of blood and family" (Mathews 186–87). In depicting who speaks and who does not, Faulkner's strategies demonstrate who has power to control a master narrative, but in the margins, in the fissures, readers can see alternative versions. For instance, writing about the women in the novel (Judith, Clytie, Ellen, Rosa), Susan V. Donaldson observes,

> These are characters who seem to live in the breaks and empty spaces of the narrative, who threaten to disrupt and even destroy the continuities of history woven by the narrators. As such they form their own narrative of sorts, a muted story underlying Sutpen's dominant history (to borrow Elaine Showalter's terms), a muted story, moreover, of gaps, disruptions, discontinuities and even precipitous endings. If the story told by the four main narrators, then, suggests the making of history, this muted story hints at its unmaking (21).

Women, she continues, do not fit well into the narrative sequence that the men are trying to recreate out of bits of Sutpen's story. The women are subordinated to this masculine story (23), but Faulkner lets them emerge out of fissures, things we see briefly that are mostly hidden, suppressed, repressed, because he is telling us the men do not want to hear from them.

Mathews analyzes the ideologies of abuse that he sees at work in *Absalom*, linking them philosophically to a long history of European rationalism:

> Faulkner ties the abusive treatment of individuals to an epistemology, the very way we process reality and arrive at conceptions. For him, as for many other moderns, the project of European colonialism, the surge of capitalism, the spread of slavery and racism, the rise of violent nationalisms, the eventual birth of modern fascistic states, all stemmed from an excessive devotion to abstract reason. Whatever the progressive legacy of the Enlightenment . . . slavish obedience to abstraction also desensitizes people to the claims of particular experience, logical contradiction, categorical mixture, the uniqueness of living bodies. Faulkner makes Sutpen an example of this mentality as he links him to a cold, unfeeling "logic and morality" as he tries to find the flaw in his design . . . It's the madness of reason that sustains the unnatural fantasy of property, whether of land or other humans. (193)

Adding to Mathews's analysis, I would like to consider another dimension of Sutpen's programmatic thinking suggested by Faulkner: that this rationalism is part of the capacity to deny or rationalize the consequences of misuses of power, and to create an idea of the self in a seemingly necessary narcissistic self-assertion in the face of wounds, fear, and annihilation (Vickroy, *Trauma and Survival* 125). Sutpen's identity is a provisional self, created out of the ruins of a destroyed identity. I focus on the psychology and traumas of the characters because of the narrative strategies Faulkner employs to immerse readers in the mind-sets of his narrating characters. These mind-sets are constructed on and act out emotional overdeterminism, defensive reactions, and the fragmented storytelling whereby readers and narrators struggle through conscious and unconscious thoughts, and in which the point of view is far more important than notions of historical accuracy. These elements are most visible and acknowledged in Rosa's narrative, whereas the male narrators present the mythmaking façade that camouflages traumas consequent on systems of greed and power ingrained in this Southern version of the American Dream. To maintain this ideology, the pain inflicted on others by commodifying them must be repressed; otherwise lost human connections (among families, between black and white) would be felt. The trauma of the Civil War was reenacted through one hundred years of racism. Whiteness is an abstract and irrational idea that once seemed so right, but it was so powerful because it was a defense reenacted to cover the wounds of defeat.

How can readers detect Faulkner's stance on ways of valuing male and female in his representations? Faulkner shows his men compensating for the Southern man's loss of authority and sense of manhood in their need to diminish and belittle women and African Americans. The men's disrespect of these others becomes a defense against their own traumas. Faulkner mainly silences or demonstrates how men silence his women characters in his works broadly. His women also chafe under male constrictions (Caddy in *The Sound and the Fury*), or challenge men's rigid race definitions that destroy their personal relationships. However, as Gwin notes, Rosa's women's text "overflows" into the men's; the men seek to contain it but cannot. Rosa unmasks what is hidden and feared, much like Roth's mixed-race lover in the "Delta Autumn" story in *Go Down, Moses*, who simply confronts and uncloaks the white men's repressed connections to blackness and the terror that these will undermine their status.

Like the patriarchs in Toni Morrison's *Paradise*, Faulkner's men are obsessed with ideas of salvation that come out of their own fear of losing power and identity as male leaders and of losing the ability to define others in ways comfortable for them. Faulkner's men's views of the women are called into question as they define women according to their own fears or suppress women's distress, which reveals the men's own failures to keep a community connected and to allow any input from others, be it women or young people. For Faulkner, the elder generation eats its young, and in *Paradise* women are killed or driven away: as if modern views have to find a new space in which to grow (significantly, Morrison's character the feminist girl Billie Delia, who represents progress, can no longer live in the community). Women are given more of a voice in *Paradise*, and some are on the way to healing, though some also lose their lives to men's violence. Faulkner and Morrison make women's voices and wounds available to readers but not to their male narrators. Men's voices are more overtly discredited in Morrison's novel, but a gender-sensitive interpretation of *Absalom* must recognize how Faulkner depicts Compson's perspectives of women as simplistic, unsympathetic, and prurient, suggesting that women are not worth the care that men were expected to give them. Again, we see the pervasiveness of splitting, men alienated from themselves, their own ideals, and others who bear witness to their wounds and failures.

Each of these first three ethical dimensions stimulates readers' responses to how trauma is portrayed and contextualized. Readers also bring their own values to these complex narratives. They must first be willing to understand traumatic depictions, to be open to exploring psychological complexity and questionable ethical responses of the characters. Along with the text, their views of human character and subjectivity will influence their judgments of these characters and their situations. Further, they will also bring their views of the contextual elements of trauma situations. In this case, twenty-first-century views of race, gender, and class, which stand in marked contrast to the nineteenth-century views presented in Faulkner's text, perhaps make it easier to recognize historical injustices leading to trauma.

FOUR

The Traumas of Love and Death in Jeanette Winterson's *Written on the Body*

As Atwood focuses on how characters reveal societal problems and become victims of them, Jeanette Winterson explores the emotional lives of adults who were neglected and abandoned as children in her novel *Written on the Body*. The narrative underscores the role of neglect in prompting survivors' traumas, which are acted out in seeking and destroying different kinds of love; as a consequence, survivors are left without love or the recognition necessary to feel alive and needed. The pursuit of love and the failure of love leave the narrator-protagonist empty, in a kind of emotional death. Winterson's novel takes on nothing less than the traumas of love and death. Love, its pursuit and loss, is traumatic, particularly as Winterson associates love with illness and death; but through the power of art and narrative, the lover's imagination transforms and staves off death within the story world she or he creates. For the protagonist and the author, *imagining* becomes first a coping mechanism and then a way of holding back death and recovering the beloved.

The narrator-protagonist is not identified by name or gender in this fictional work; for ease of exposition, I use "she/he" and "N" to refer to this character in the following discussion. The anonymity of the narrator and the nonspecific conflation of gender underscore, I believe, Winterson's attempt to make this novel's meditations on love and death inclusive.

Winterson's story line consists of the narrator's retrospective reflections as the character tries to understand "where I went wrong" (17) in a history of aborted relationships, particularly the one she/he most regrets, with a woman named Louise. "Why is the measure of love loss?" are the first words of the novel and suggest that the prerequisite for understanding failure is to sufficiently understand and care for a beloved. The narrator's central purpose is to convey regret and apologize to Louise, and simultaneously to try to reframe and redefine tired ideas of love and explore why love should be pursued honorably. She/he further explores how love can be expressed in an honest and beautiful language, and not in self-deceiving platitudes. N attempts to grow out of emotional adolescence by analyzing past mistakes and by absorbing Louise's honesty and suffering, with the emotional support of a friend, Gail. The plot consists of the narrator recounting several former relationships, an ongoing devotion to Louise despite their separation, and why she/he felt it necessary to leave Louise as the latter develops cancer, with an uncertain conclusion in the novel about the couple's reunion.

The narrator's voice dominates the storytelling, addressing Louise at times, but often readers too, in the course of philosophizing about the nature and expression of love. N's viewpoint is only occasionally supplemented by other characters' words, introduced at crucial moments to offer other perspectives that put into question the protagonist's motives. The narrative directs readers into the narrator's internal thoughts, which exhibit mistaken beliefs and frequent failures to appreciate or understand others' feelings. N's unreliability lies in failures of judgment and ethics, which in this traumatic context manifest in feelings of helplessness, faulty cognition, avoidance, repression, and dissociation. These deficiencies of judgment help develop the narrator's consciousness and become key to understanding the effects of trauma on his or her state of mind. However, this narrator-protagonist is motivated by the need to reassess past behavior and learn how to love another. By considering how much the narrator is willing or able to talk about past and present feelings or to represent others, readers can discern stages in the teller's emotional quest. Very focused on immediate experience, the narrator offers little explanation of past influences, suggesting repression or avoidant omissions; readers are engaged to imagine the emotionally deprived origins of this character through his or her current relational mistakes.

Winterson's identification as a postmodern writer is evident in her use of fragmentation, mixed genres, and techniques of metafiction. She often alternates between semireal confessionalism, on the one hand, and fantasy and fiction on the other, as in her earlier work, *Oranges Are Not the Only Fruit*. As in Atwood's and Palahniuk's novels, Winterson's employment of postmodern self-consciousness and fictionalizing helps her represent trauma through her narrator's avoidant storytelling. In

Atwood's *The Blind Assassin*, metafictional elements amplify textual themes and provide a space where the narrator can cloak herself before she is ready to reveal the extent of her wounds and her complicity. Winterson's protagonist similarly deflects wounding with defensive and self-protective multigenre comedic versions of failed love. Eventually the narrator will address these failed relations in textual and linguistic questions.

Winterson's narrator-protagonist, like the author, has the inclinations of a writer, questioning the ways language conveys meaning and decomposing clichés to create new concepts of love and ways of expressing it. Through her protagonist, Winterson offers traces of the potentialities of love and life in the face of the lover's impending death, as a warning against the living death of social prescriptions, by presenting a revised engagement with life that shatters categories and runs on creative imagination and intense connection.

Winterson's work also exhibits a postmodern sense of identity that is contingent on circumstances, multiple, and established self-consciously in language and stories as well as through realistic life circumstances. Winterson's sense of fractional identity as conveyed in the work is also shaped by traumatic contexts. Her novels, even the quasi-autobiographical *Oranges*, use metafictional and intertextual techniques to reconfigure identity outside the oppressive social and linguistic structures within which her characters live. Both postmodernism and trauma narratives share a view of the self as fragmented and lacking continuity. Postmodernists tend to reject stable definitions of self as limiting, fictional constructions. However, traumatic breakdowns of identity produce in survivors destructive or avoidant personality traits and cognition, and often induce in survivors the need to impose on themselves constricting structures that bring temporary relief but limit their ability to live, connect, and feel fully. For childhood abuse victims, "Fragmentation in consciousness prevents the ordinary integration of knowledge, memory, emotional states, and bodily experience" (J. Herman 107).

The traumatized create a provisional identity to adapt themselves to adversity (Lifton 30; Vickroy 125; Langer 121–61). In *Written*, the protagonist adopts narcissistic roles, like that of Lothario and the absent lover, that help him or her avoid painful emotions. These roles are depicted comically, at an emotional distance. These defenses are connected to an ungrounded, underrecognized identity that is driven by a seemingly unfillable emptiness—an emptiness that is to be feared and avoided. Winterson's and Palahniuk's protagonists are alienated from social norms and from the landscape of people or institutions that use individuals. They rarely refer to their early emotional lives, and they depict unsettling, ungrounded lives that leave them wanting true connections.

Reading through the interpretive lens of traumatic wounding helps bring to light the missing evidence a reader would expect to find provided by a narrator attentive to concerns of inner life and views of intimacy but who nevertheless denies readers typical markers of identity, such as gender and family history. Winterson has her own philosophical reasons for omitting this material: so that it doesn't limit the scope of her inquiries about love.[1] And while I do not want to make the simple equivalence of the narrator with the author, the author's own childhood struggles in a neglectful and abusive family, which she has fictionalized (in *Oranges*) and documented in nonfiction (in *Why Be Happy When You Can Be Normal?*), suggest a level of insight into and preoccupation with how neglected children struggle to achieve intimacy with others in adult life. Unsustainable love is a frequent theme in her novels (*Oranges, The Passion, Sexing the Cherry*).

Readers must locate identity and trauma from symptoms and behavior in *Written on the Body* because Winterson does not provide much other evidence; there is a deliberate vagueness about gender identity and virtually no record or recognition of early nurturance in the novel. The symptoms of trauma include a splitting of the self, into the part that abandons Louise and the part that loves her, as well as a split between the lover devastated at the married lover's callousness and the braggart who "cracks" marriages. Other symptoms of trauma include constricted emotion, distrust, and a reduced capacity to love as the narrator-protagonist embraces a survival mode, after Root's formulations of trauma and personality. The narrator's state of mind exemplifies the dialectical nature of the experience of being caught between feeling and not feeling, remembering and forgetting, action and inaction, and alterations in personality and perception (J. Herman 121–23).

While burning love letters from a failed affair, the narrator thinks, "How easy it is to destroy the past and how difficult to forget it" (17). Destroying the evidence also suggests an unwillingness to analyze the situation. She/he begins to see the pattern of acting out these failures repetitively, and adopts a more confessional tone: "Did I say this happened to me again and again?" (17). She/he also seeks ways to step away from an identity defined by repetitive behavior fueled by trauma and the clichéd ideas and language of love. The narrator's critical engagement with the dilemmas of existence and love requires a critique of how language guides thought even as meanings are arbitrary and harmful constructions (e.g., love as possessive, too comfortable, or a trap). Completeness, whether in existence or in love, is unachievable and suspect, according to postmodernists, and Winterson expresses these doubts throughout the novel, but the protagonist's intense search for a real loving bond proceeds despite the taint of traumas of unfulfilling relationships, as well as skepticism about the possessive but tepid cultural ideals of love.

The narrator's focused contemplation of love after losing Louise is speculative, imaginative, and metaphorical, perhaps because the protagonist (and Winterson) tries to explore possibilities and specificities rather than settle on generalizations or clichés typical of socialized or fetishized views. This approach is consistent with the postmodernist questioning of essentialist, purposive views of existence. The narrator's actions suggest a deep swath of feeling under the surface, from which he or she seeks love obsessively but also ambivalently. This ambivalence or doubleness could indicate unresolved emotional issues, where there is a lack, something promised but denied or insufficiently fulfilled. N recognizes the problems with the repeated risky romances she/he has sought, and her or his ideal love is one involving bonds without chains, passion and deeper intimacy; she/he looks for new metaphors for love that go deeper, bone deep, involving the body as a repository of hurt but also of healing. In fact, the consequences of these destructive impulses provoke the narrator's intelligent philosophical and linguistic examinations of love that, if adopted, could be healing, and could aid in making healthy connections. The "facts" of the narrator's abandoning Louise, supposedly the narrator's great love, are insufficiently explanatory. Readers are left to look for an emotional connection or to fill in the gap of what the narrator does not or cannot explain about leaving Louise.

Love and Trauma

Love appears to have a strong causal relationship to trauma in *Written*, as something overwhelming and life-changing, at times ecstatic, but sending the narrator-protagonist running, as it seems to provoke every emotion except well-being. Several clues suggest the possibility of traumatic effects. The narrator does not discuss his or her upbringing except to say that she/he rejects the familiar plodding ideas of love the birth family practiced. However, N seems desperately to need love and obsessively pursues it, but repeatedly in situations that are unstable, hurtful, or nonexclusive, with married or emotionally unavailable lovers who objectify the narrator, all of which suggests that N has a fear of intimacy. Love is traumatic in this text because it frequently and violently alters the protagonist's life, and its obsessive pursuit is the measure of this character's life, and the central focus of his or her life and consciousness. This is also reflected in the focus of the narrative, which discusses numerous lovers before and including Louise. Winterson contemplates the impulsive nature of passion and wonders what relation it bears to love, and its destructiveness if focused on the wrong person.

The narrow focalization of the storytelling mirrors the narrowness of the narrator's viewpoint, which deemphasizes normal life details and denies her (or his) lovers full realization. Objectifying and fetishizing the people she/he has supposedly loved may be a self-protective defense, since there is evidence of the protagonist's wounds after being dumped numerous times. The narrator creates emotional distance from disastrous past relationships by stitching together pastiches of literary genres, such as the use of the picaresque mode to depict events as escapades. The humorous aspects of these "romantic follies" of love disguise the pain inflicted on or by the narrator and the narrator's lovers. Use of these genres is also appropriately depicted as defensive and dishonest structures of thought.

N seems to feel unaccountable to anyone in fulfillment of the ruthless pursuit of sensation (Vickroy, "Reading the Other" 13); and if the narrator's lovers have held back emotionally, then nothing is owed them either. The protagonist repeatedly shows an indifference to, or denial of, lovers' and their partners' feelings ("I've been through a lot of marriages": *Written* 13), inferred as N's lovers seek cruel retributions, which she/he initially depicts as comical, unwarranted, or surprising before becoming more introspective. The emergence of introspection marks the narrator's attempts to get beyond acting out, and during much of the book the narrator vacillates between avoidance and insight in moving toward understanding, a hesitation typical of the dialectical nature of trauma survivors' experience.

The central love attachment of the book, the narrator's with Louise, is the first to bring the protagonist mutual happiness and depth of feeling. Louise willingly leaves her husband (whom she no longer loves) for N. However, this love story also becomes traumatic; the narrator recounts first winning Louise, then losing her to illness and the jealous husband's demands, but mostly the narrator loses Louise because of his or her own fears and avoidance. The first line of the novel, "Why is the measure of love loss?," establishes the elegiac tone. Writing in retrospect, the protagonist's larger purpose is to chronicle her or his love life, particularly with Louise, but perhaps a more important purpose is to embark on a discovery of Louise, to recover the other that she/he must understand to further explore the nature of love, critiquing its well-worn and clichéd forms, and to figure out new, more personal ways to experience and express it. Leigh Gilmore attributes the narrator's trauma solely to losing Louise (134). I see many contexts of trauma, but the central trauma guiding the overall narrative seems to be the narrator's total encounter with love and death through Louise.

Loss Leads to Death

In order to give love and loss the import of other traumas, Winterson puts her protagonist through many of the same encounters with death, the death imprint, and death imagery that haunt survivors of mass death. The protagonist recreates Louise's suffering and the threat of death in safer imaginative contexts, but clearly is also haunted by this and tries to master fear and guilt through repeated death imagery scenarios that connect her (or him) to Louise. This capacity to symbolize is an adaptive defense and helps the narrator mourn Louise. Contexts of trauma overlap in *Written on the Body* with the narrator's loss of lovers, then loss of Louise as a lover, and then (apparently) loss of Louise to death. "The death encounter reopens questions about prior experiences of separation, breakdown, and stasis, as well as countervailing struggles toward vitality; it reopens questions, in fact, around all of life's beginnings and endings. So bound to the image can the survivor be that one can speak of a thralldom to death or a "death spell" (Lifton 19). However, since Louise's likely death precedes the narration of these events, the ultimate loss of death is perhaps the dominant traumatic lens through which all else is viewed. Initially, the narrator is convinced she/he can do nothing to help Louise, and, like many survivors who when confronted with death tend to see a threat to their own existence, feels guilt over a "limited capacity to respond to the threat and the self-blame for that inadequate response" (Lifton 20).

Relational loss is related emotionally to death, particularly if it is a life-changing loss. This can be seen in the commonly held fear of death that habitually preoccupies the thoughts and expressions of the traumatized when there is a diminishment of self, which the narrator-protagonist illustrates repeatedly. Moreover, in traumatic contexts particularly, the loss of connections that foster identity becomes existentially and emotionally tied to fear of death. A kind of death imprint permeates the book and the narrator's viewpoint, realizing Lifton's observations of survivors' "vulnerability to death imagery—not only to direct life threat but also to separation, stasis, and disintegration—on the basis of prior conflictual experience" (18).

The narrator-protagonist's thoughts and linguistic palette are loaded with safe versions of love and life as a kind of death. She/he seeks intensity, a vital life, and unstructured lovemaking as a taunt to settled life. For N, even bad love is resistance to a living death, to a life of "cocoa and hot water bottles" (*Written* 21), exemplified by motionless people in their homes; as the narrator observes voyeuristically about a girlfriend, "She must be dead . . . rigor mortis has set in" (60). One relationship is compared to a coffin (16) because it must be kept secret. Similarly, for the narrator, loss of love is a kind of death as well. Reassessing the damage of pre-Louise relationships, she/he formulates betrayal as the "death of love" through jealousy. Possessive love can be the death of one, the narrator implies, as she/he links the image of adjustable love knots to that of men tied to one another in a fight to the death. And when she (or he) hurts Louise: "As a lover I was lethal" (53). These death references reveal that the narrator's anxieties continue to underlie this character's hopes and correctives regarding relationships.

Fear of death becomes more immediate and unmediated when the protagonist learns Louise's life is threatened by leukemia. She/he is initially told the news by Louise's husband, Elgin, an eminent cancer researcher who jealously insists on separating the couple in exchange for his treating Louise. Faced with the potential loss of love and beloved, the narrator's shock, terror, and relative (compared to Elgin's) inability to cope with Louise's situation make him her or retreat, according to Elgin's wishes but not Louise's. A reader might quickly judge the narrator's panic as mere cowardice and immaturity. The character responds very much like a child to the threat of death, with feelings of helplessness and faulty cognition. She/he does not consult Louise before leaving, and treats Louise's condition as if it were a done deal and the loss already complete. Flight makes sense defensively, though: it makes the narrator immediately feel more in control of the situation than actually seeing

Louise's deterioration. However, N's avoidant isolation makes it impossible for this character to confirm the extent of the illness or the results of Louise's treatments, and reduces the character to fearful imaginings. The narrator's avoidant response could indicate the toll of recurrent patterns of emotional devastation in several ways. His or her tainted sense of self from a history of failed love affairs may convince N that she/he is unprepared to face this crisis or to take care of Louise. She/he needs to rationalize, and suppress, the fear of facing Louise, and so sends Louise a letter making the narrator's leaving seem a self-sacrifice, undertaken to aid Louise's recovery under Elgin's care: "Our love was not meant to cost you your life" (105).

Winterson depicts her protagonist's immediate reaction to Elgin's initial news about Louise's condition and prognosis as a poetically rendered fear of Louise's death, but also the narrator's fear, through Elgin's news:

> Two hundred miles from the surface of the earth there is no gravity. The laws of motion are suspended. . . . You are stretching slowly slowly, getting longer, your joints are slipping away from their usual places. . . . You will break up bone by bone, fractured from who you are, you are drifting away now, the center cannot hold. . . . Where am I? There is nothing here I recognize. . . . Who is this man with the revolving eyes, his mouth opening like a gas chamber, his words acrid, vile, in my throat and nostrils?. . . . He's poisoning me and I can't get away. My feet don't obey me. Where is the familiar ballast of my life? I am fighting helplessly without hope. I grapple but my body slithers away. I want to brace myself against something solid but there's nothing solid here. (100–1)

In this passage the narrator has clearly lost the sense of groundedness and wholeness that she/he thought Louise's love could bestow on a hitherto ungrounded and risk-prone personality. The narrator creates a necessary distance from terror by trying to understand through conceptualizing the effects on Louise's body. But in doing so, she/he ignores Louise's stated desire that they face the illness together.

The narrator's pattern of helplessness reoccurs before any treatment has been tried. She/he cannot fend off Elgin's words or his position as he authoritatively enumerates what Louise will endure as a cancer patient: enlarged organs, bleeding, bruising, nausea, and other ill effects. The narrator willingly seeks out his opinion again, and Elgin reiterates that the she/he needs to leave in order to save Louise. Though Louise wants to fight the disease and obtain other opinions, the narrator seems defeated by Elgin's scientific, expert, and dominating patriarchal knowledge, despite Elgin's admitted uncertainty as to whether he can cure Louise (104). The narrator is rendered valueless, ineffectual, by Elgin's skills and claims. Why does N believe him? She/he does not trust Louise's skepticism about Elgin or question his self-assertion as her only hope but gives up Louise, sending her the previously mentioned letter. N's departure is dramatic and sudden, compelled by events, but also, as in Atwood's work, Winterson suggests that patriarchal, gender, and class norms may exacerbate trauma by punishing deviations from the norms and by depriving individuals of meaningful action and valued identities. It's been demonstrated that Elgin is rich and knowledgeable, and that Louise is a status symbol for him.

Winterson creates the three conditions for her protagonist that trauma researchers indicate make bereavement most difficult: "the suddenness and unexpectedness of the loss, ambivalence toward the lost relationship, and over-dependence on the relationship suggesting an underlying insecurity about attachments" (Nader 20). The narrator is seemingly unambivalent about Louise, who is more devoted, reliable, and ethical than previous lovers, but she/he may have some doubts because Louise had not initially mentioned the illness. This omission too may prompt readers to wonder whether Louise may be protecting the emotionally vulnerable narrator (or may distrust Elgin because she is asymptomatic at this point). The ambivalence more likely originates in the protagonist's history of failed relationships. She/he idealizes Louise, hoping she will undo or make up for the mistakes of the past: "Louise's face. Under her fierce gaze my past is burned away. . . . Am I hoping for a savior in Louise? An almighty scouring of deed and misdeed, leaving the slab clean and white" (*Written* 77). Where the narrator had counted on Louise's promised "I will never let you go" (76), perhaps there is unconscious disappointment that this will not be fulfilled because of her illness. However, the narrator must deal with Louise's loss on his or her own defensive terms, minimizing feelings of helplessness by leaving. Facing trauma alters a survivor's ability to understand others' perspectives (Root 247), and though the narrator's escape may be a necessary survival strategy from the viewpoint of the traumatized, from Louise's standpoint, it is a betrayal, an abandonment—and will be articulated as such by Louise's family, the narrator's friend, Gail, and eventually the narrator as well.

Trauma, Love, and Death

In the second section of *Written*, the narrator-protagonist's account takes on an accumulation of death imagery around Louise and the narrator's own dread, through which she/he experiences Louise after they are separated. Now dislocated, the narrator becomes unmoored in a depressive emotional exile in the country. Death and physical destruction continue to permeate her or his imagination in an obsessive focus on the destructive effects of illness. N imagines rejoining the suffering Louise in the "Cells, Tissues . . . Cavities of the Body" section of the book:

> If I could not put Louise out of my mind I would drown myself in her. Within the clinical language, through the dispassionate view of the sucking, sweating, greedy, defecating self, I found a love-poem to Louise. I would go on knowing her, more intimately than the skin, hair and voice that I craved. I would have her plasma, her spleen, her synovial fluid. I would recognize her even when her body had long since fallen away. (111)

The suffering here is displaced, however, saving the narrator from real contact with Louise's suffering. N attempts to know and empathize with Louise's experience of her illness in manageable doses of reading, rumination, and (re)enactments and imaginings of death. This seems to be the place from which she/he can tolerate the situation; it's a path toward overcoming fear.

Thoughts of the body move from memories of Louise's eroticized body to images of the body that threaten and injure (e.g., sharp, cutting bones). Attempting to deal with paralyzing fear, the narrator mentally reconstructs the violence illness will do to Louise's body. This need for mediation exemplifies the dialectical experience of trauma that is characterized by compulsions to know and to not know what drives our fears. The narrator imagines sharing with Louise what would not be possible through actual contact: "I will embalm you in my memory" (119). N grieves through imagined "thoughts of disfigurement" to Louise's body, the possibility of the destruction of the beloved's sexual body, a source of intimacy and life for the narrator. Utilizing anatomy texts, the narrator produces a textual hybrid of science and poetry in which distance-producing, fact-based elements meet memorial or emotion-based poetic imaginings. Winterson has placed her protagonist in the realm of the artist who can "rediscover the intensity of the physical world" through the imagination and for whom "reality is continuous, multiple, simultaneous, complex, abundant and partly invisible. The imagination alone can fathom this and it reveals its fathomings through art" (Winterson, "Imagination and Reality" 151). The narrator and the author seem to share a similar quality of mind. The narrator goes through a grieving process by way of imagining, as if Louise's death has occurred. The reader must assume the fact of the death, though there is no direct confirmation of it in the novel. The nature of the narrative makes it difficult to interpret because the struggles with pain and loss are meant to affect readers but seem to exist in their own imaginative realm apart from what might transpire with Louise. "As I embalm you in my memory, the first thing I shall do is to hook out your brain through your accommodating orifices. Now that I have lost you I cannot allow you to develop. . . . You must be rid of life as I am rid of life. We shall sink together you and I, down, down into the dark voids where once the vital organs were" (*Written* 119). Here the narrator wants Louise to remain as she is as they come together in death: "I dropped into the mass of you and I cannot find the way out. Sometimes I think I'm free, coughed up like Jonah from the whale, but then I turn a corner and recognize myself again. Myself in your skin, myself lodged in your bones, myself floating in the cavities that decorate every surgeon's wall. That is how I know you. You are what I know" (120). Thus, to the narrator, Louise has become part of who she/he is, and yet this Louise is a figment of the narrator's mind.

The protagonist assumes Louise will die but cannot verify this expectation except through Elgin. This assumption suggests that N's mind is ruled by fear and by faulty cognition, which precludes any skeptical analysis of the situation. Though Elgin's prognosis is death, Elgin is neither certain nor reliable himself. He has his own agenda, to convince himself that only he can conquer Louise's illness. And he wants to separate the lovers (which the narrator should know). Readers can assume that at the time this is narrated, Louise has died, even though the final scene in the novel leaves open the possibility they have had some time together before that happens.[2] Is the room, the world in which the narrator imagines they are together at the end, in the narrator's own mind? Critics have pointed out that there is also a refusal of death in this account, manifested as a need for remastery of this helpless situation through the narrator's evoking Louise as alive (Ellam 112) and in her or his attempt to make the absent beloved "present" (Preston 224).

Imagining the possible, living, even if it is created, a version of life with increased vision and awareness, is Winterson's goal ("Imagination and Reality" 151). She aims more for emotional than for factual truth. The emotional truth that is her object is neither a delusion nor a truth divorced from reality but an exploration of possibilities for living that involves an imaginative leap. The novel is more concerned with the narrator's contemplating how one loves well, and with exploring desires and pain, than with whether Louise is alive. This overt concern emerges out of the defended aspects of the narrator's personality; however, N also wants to break free of his or her defenses. Though the narrator-protagonist cannot directly confront Louise's disease and death in Louise's presence, she/he tries to stage such a confrontation by imagining the disease and its effects on Louise. N can face death only by symbolizing and ritualizing traumatic events (Nader 24). As readers, we are confronted with the question of how much of the narrator's imagining represents avoidance and how much is the real work of empathizing with another's suffering. Though Winterson privileges the imagination for her theme, readers could see this as unethical in that the narrator's imagining does not bring comfort to the suffering Louise; the relational aspect of love is missing.

To deal with fear, "traumatized people construct their lives" (J. Herman 46). The narrator-protagonist needs to employ substitutes to explore death, to approach the deterioration of Louise's body. She/he engages in magical thinking, common to the bereaved, and in cognition based on defenses, whereby she/he transforms Louise's possible or imminent death into manageable thoughts on death, and imagines that they are suffering together. This narrative can be viewed as an act of postponing death (Ellam 117). As the narrator confronts and identifies with Louise's failing life, she/he must face her or his own annihilation. This is why distance is required. This identification is a gesture of love, but it may also set off the narrator's own fears of death and inability to cope. N's primary defensive reaction, avoidance of pain, becomes a key component of his or her or personality, of avoiding the ways she/he has wronged others. She/he seemed to be working through this with Louise, but with this new crisis she/he falls back on old patterns. The narrator's self-imposed isolation indicates both a traumatic detachment and an avoidance of familiar contexts, activities, or locations that would remind her or him of Louise. The narrator thus engages in the typical types of evasion sought out by trauma victims (Nader 25).

Despite the mediated and self-conscious qualities of the narration, Winterson takes readers through the lived, sensual, and visceral qualities, or qualia, of this experience of love and death so that readers might feel the illusion of entering her narrator's experience and consciousness (D. Herman, "Nexus" 140). Experience is "written on the body," as the title indicates, etched into one's flesh and physical responses. Winterson has chosen the body as the place of the most intimate and deeply felt emotions, of knowing the other: "the recognition of another person that is deeper than consciousness, lodged in the body more than held in the mind" (*Written* 82). "Written on the body is a secret code only visible in certain lights," the narrator says; "the accumulations of a lifetime gather there. In places the palimpsest is so heavily worked that the letters feel like Braille. I like to keep my body rolled up away from prying eyes. Never unfold too much, tell the whole story. I didn't know that Louise would have reading hands. She has translated me into her own book" (89). The narrator tries to recreate Louise's explorations by examining Louise's powerfully evoked, imagined body.

The body can also function as a repository of traumatic memory and experience, more so than the mind, which can refuse or bury memory. Traumas are often most felt and expressed through their impact on the body. In *Written on the Body*, the body itself becomes a vehicle for love, and the emotions attending love's loss are felt physically. Further, Louise's physical suffering becomes her lover's emotional anguish.

Through visceral (i.e., bodily) details, Winterson renders the bittersweet paradox of the living body undergoing the process of death. The body becomes the place where life/love and death/loss meet. For example, the narrator evokes memories of Louise's skin, which is also biologically dead: her "sepulchral body, offered to me in the past tense" (123). The narrator has largely focused on Louise's body as an aesthetically beautiful vehicle for sexual passion in the novel's first section. In the second section the narrator's emotional landscape has absorbed death, which is now provides the lens through which to read Louise's body, along with life and their love: "You were milk white and fresh to drink. Will your skin discolor, its brightness blurring? Will your neck and spleen distend?" (125). The beautiful body is blasted by cancer. In another rendering of death and the body, the narrator cuts an image of Louise's face in ice: "When I put my lips to your frozen cheek you burned me. . . . I held you as death will hold you" (132). N inserts her- or himself into the death process, which becomes an integral part of the narrator's imaginative life while she/he is separated from Louise. The narrator imagines jumping into "the fiery furnace and be[ing] burned up in you. . . . Do you see me in my blood-soaked world?" (138–39). She/he wants a blood connection, but it's not possible. She/he also admits to seeking shelter in words about the body, bones, and living flesh: "those are my shields . . . those words don't remind me of your face" (132). Again, the narrator is acting out a way to simultaneously approach and avoid trauma.

Survivors' self-protection makes them refuse help. As Robert Lifton writes, "One fends off not only new threats of annihilation but gestures of love or help. Part of this resistance to human relationships has to do with a sense of being tainted by death, of carrying what might be called the psychic stigma of the annihilated" (25). The narrator's physical distaste for Louise's middle-aged friend Gail indicates a discomfort with the ravages of age, additional evidence of her or his fear of the suggestion of mortality, and can only tolerate Louise's deterioration in the relatively safer place of the mind. Gail, however, is also depicted as vital and nurturing, not aggrieved and buried in death as the narrator is. The text (or author) seems to condemn the narrator's judgment of Gail, who helps N gain perspective by pointing out he or she never consulted Louise. The protagonist is unable to fully assess the situation until she/he eventually confides in someone else, and with Gail's help, the narrator begins to doubt Elgin's veracity and to face how she/he abandoned Louise. Before this point, the narrator's isolated viewpoint, oscillating between insight and short-sightedness, has crowded out others' feelings and prevented the development of a broader perspective. The protagonist then returns to London and is able to reconnect with memories of Louise in familiar places. Neither Louise's family nor Elgin knows Louise's whereabouts, and the narrator begins to doubt again whether Louise has survived (but has no evidence except her absence). The narrator symbolically engages in a mourning process: attending a graveyard burial, she/he ponders the grave hole and imagines the rituals of washing the dead, thus enacting what might be done if it was Louise's burial. This comes closer to a real encounter with death, but a real body is still missing.

Not finding Louise, the narrator returns to the isolated cottage with the realization that "I should have trusted you but I lost my nerve" (*Written* 187). Gail's presence gives an air of realism that provides a corrective to the narrator's blindness and denial, and possible evidence for Louise's reappearance at the end that could be taken as fantastical and yet is belied by the physical presence of Louise bearing scars she did not have before. The presence of Gail seems to point to the reality of this scene and to the possibility of the narrator's rejoining Louise, even temporarily. Gail observes that the narrator tried to invent Louise rather than accept her as a separate person. Just before Louise is scheduled to appear, Gail asks questions that Louise might reasonably want to know the answers to—for example, does the narrator still love her? Mary E. Preston argues that the ending could be reasonably interpreted in one of two ways. The text is not clear about where Louise's appearance "occurs ontologically: in the real world or in the world of the imagination" (229–30). Though the book ends with the narrator and Louise together in the small room they will share, a small universe, one can surmise from the novel's elegiac tone that the life they possibly share post-separation is a short one. It is formulated as a beginning because this attempt at togetherness is, the narrator asserts, missing the baggage of the narrator's past, the defenses and denial, and the fear of death. The emotional development of the protagonist, now ready to love, is highlighted above all.

Trauma and Ethics

Traumatized individuals are often ethically impaired as a result of the emotional damage they have endured. Trauma texts often focus on the unreliability of narrators as manifested in failures of judgment or ethics that are tied to symptoms such as helplessness, faulty cognition, shame, repression, or dissociation. This protagonist must try to overcome these symptoms by confronting and working through the fallout from unethical behavior, which the protagonist has suppressed, rationalized, aestheticized, or intellectualized. Initially she/he is unrepentant about pursuing married lovers, recognizing her (or his) own hurt only when lovers proclaim their allegiance to their partners even as they describe their lust for the protagonist. Part of the narrator's defensive attitude shows up in his or her critique of marriage as the antithesis of love and passion. Though legitimate philosophical arguments are made about the institutionalization of emotions, of concern here is how the narrator is affected by a devastating emotional history. The narrator chronicles the "follies" of past relationships with an array of lovers and the inflicted wounds, but almost never seems able to comprehend how her (or his) lovers feel. The narrator's making these romantic episodes seem comical and often expressing surprise at the vindictiveness lovers feel suggests the activation of defensive coping strategies, accompanied by an unwillingness or inability to feel for or with others and a narcissistic belief that only he or she bears emotional scars. Since this happens with more than one lover, the reader, even if sympathetic, is led to question the "Why me?" nature of the protagonist's attitude. As the narrator rails against being fated, of being condemned to repeat others' notions of love, she/he slowly becomes aware of personal repetitive patterns that drive these fruitless love quests.

This reassessment is brought on by the wounding the narrator endures in these relationships and by the effects of a real love that she/he seems to have discovered with Louise. To sympathize or understand, readers must be convinced of how much the protagonist fears and yet wants to confront his or her own destructive qualities. One key example of the protagonist engaging in this confrontation is when memories of past lovers are no longer expressed in entertaining stories of disastrous love affairs but rather in a haunting dream sequence in Louise's company:

> In the hours that followed waking and sleeping with a light fever that bore on me out of passion and distress it seemed as if the small room was full of ghosts. . . . The figures assumed shapes I recognized: Inge, Catherine, Bathsheba, Jacqueline. Others of whom Louise knew nothing. They came too close, put their fingers in my mouth, in my nostrils, drew back the hoods of my eyes. They accused me of lies and betrayal. I opened my mouth to speak but I had no tongue only a gutted space. I must have cried out then because I was in Louise's arms and she was bending over me, fingers on my forehead, soothing me, whispering to me. "I will never let you go." (68–69)

These ghosts of past loves haunt the narrator's conscience in a terrifying reexperiencing and realization of the pain he or she inflicted. Before meeting Louise, the narrator remained closed off from the lovers' feelings; this episode indicates an emotional opening that facilitates self-critical regret over the anguish of past lovers. As Lifton writes,

> The traumatized person seems to have to endure the additional internal trauma of self-blame. This is why there is a "paradoxical guilt" experience by victimized survivors. This guilt seems to subsume the individual victim-survivor rather harshly to the evolutionary function of guilt in rendering us accountable for

our relationship to others' physical and psychological existences. This experience of guilt around one's own trauma suggests the moral dimension inherent in all conflict and suffering. We have no choice but to make judgments about trauma and our relationship to it. (21)

To be with Louise, the narrator-protagonist must disappoint one final lover, Jacqueline, who was seen as a healing presence after all the risks and painful experiences with other lovers. However, because this relationship had the qualities of the staid relations the protagonist finds so revolting, readers can surmise it goes against the narrator's emotional nature. Jacqueline becomes the narrator's victim when she/he looks to her for shelter. Jacqueline was perhaps like the narrator's family, following a familiar pattern, but because the narrator has already tried to seek ways out of prescribed patterns, and because she/he has not loved Jacqueline sexually or passionately, the protagonist's involvement is unethical, though comprehensible because she/he is emotionally damaged. Though the narrator knows she/he is hurting Jacqueline in falling for Louise, she/he begins to defensively degrade the relationship with Jacqueline, comparing it to "container gardening."

The protagonist's involvement with Jacqueline compromises his or her own values and raises the ethical question of whether individuals have the right to pursue what they need no matter the emotional cost to others. The protagonist at least begins to see his (or her) own unfairness, at first unconsciously, in a guilt-ridden castration dream, and tries to resist feelings for Louise and the bad pattern of falling for married women. Eventually the narrator is able to consciously analyze how she/he weasels out of the relationship with Jacqueline with half-truths and ruthless retaliatory violence after Jacqueline has trashed the narrator's apartment.

These changes in the narrator seem to be influenced by Louise, who is established in the narrative as a model of ethical openness who rejects violence and reminds her lover not to impulsively declare love and who is willing to leave her marriage because she cannot sustain a life of infidelity or subterfuge. Louise's declaration stuns and grounds her lover: "I'm going to leave him because my love for you makes any other life a lie" (*Written* 98). Though Louise models a passionate, ethical, and open approach to love, it is undermined by Jacqueline's vindictive response to the narrator's callous abandonment of her, giving readers a view of love as savage as much as it is electrically sexual and healing. The narrator's later abandonment of Louise demonstrates that she/he is still working toward Louise's ethical example.

Throughout the novel, the narrator's discourse on love and engagement with it on so many levels is coupled ironically with a fundamental inability to connect deeply. She/he indulges in a romanticized, idealized discourse about Louise's beauty, describing her appearance and actions in aesthetic images and scenarios recalling the Pre-Raphaelites and the Gothic. The protagonist also expresses ambivalence and doubt about whether this union can last, fighting the propensity to move on after the thrill is gone (every twenty-four weeks), and seeking shelter with Louise: "I put my arms around her, not sure whether I was a lover or a child" (80), implying that Louise may open up the narrator's need for nurturance missed early in life. The narrator considers what risk love involves, thinking of early Christian figures that personify devotion by risking life and limb for love of faith, wanting to experience "recognition of another person that is deeper than consciousness, lodged in the body more than held in the mind" (82).

The narrator tries for a new formulation of the importance of the body. While before it denoted sex and discovery, the narrator wonders whether the body could not be the seat of less conflicted and more direct feeling, offering deeper intimacy because the mind can play tricks, be inhibitory, and is influenced by myriad social rules and memories. The protagonist begins to see the body as a medium of identification, of similarities, rather than the odd cliché that opposites attract: "You are my blood" (99). Or the protagonist begins thinking about how love affects the body: Louise "marks" the protagonist's back, and Louise has been able to "read" the protagonist's body with her hands. Though Louise's hands draw blood, the action is open to multiple levels of interpretation and some common understanding with her "reading hands" rather than merely leaving scars.

What are readers meant to conclude about the narrator's search for love? What ethical questions are raised about this kind of quest for anyone, let alone the psychically damaged? Initially, with her or his early relationships, using the oversized rhetoric of love, coming out of a literary and cultural sensibility (quoting Shakespeare's "love is not love/which alters when it alteration finds": *Written* 162), brings a kind of control or definition of a situation that Louise notes is possibly not sincere. Louise provokes the narrator into acknowledging a propensity for immediate romantic idealization and moving too quickly, anticipating plenitude and safety:

> I could have held her for a thousand years until the skeleton itself rubbed away to dust. What are you that makes me feel thus? Who are you for whom time has no meaning?
> In the heat of her hands I thought, "This is the campfire that mocks the sun. This place will warm me, feed me and care for me. I will hold onto this pulse against other rhythms." (51)

If one considers these words in light of the narrator's leaving the ill Louise, they come across as an excessively elaborated compensatory gesture after the fact. After the narrator declares love to Louise when they have first had sex, Louise replies that it's too soon for such declarations, and points out "so you try and regain control by telling me you love me. That's a territory you know, isn't it? That's romance and courtship and whirlwind" (53). Louise is depicted as ethically superior to the narrator, for she points out the destruction wrought by compulsive behavior patterns and how the narrator's amusing stories of former lovers make Louise believe she's another in a long line of callous encounters. Because the protagonist's use of the language of love has led to suffering and down roads of self-delusion, and because Louise has made the protagonist self-conscious about this, the protagonist spends much of the text rethinking the language and conceptions of love. Louise's accusations appear to be the catalysts for his or her inquiries about love, leading to questions like "Will I cherish you, adore you, make way for you, make myself better for you, look at you and always see you, tell you the truth? And if love is not those things then what things?" (11–12).

Winterson has stacked the emotional deck for readers in favor of the couple's love affair by making Louise's husband unfaithful, perverse, and vindictive. Elgin is described in more prosaic realistic detail than the other characters, probably because he is not seen from the protagonist's viewpoint as having an emotional life, while Louise is described in a passionate poetic language.

The central ethical failure of the narrator lies in not resisting Elgin's ultimatum, allowing his insistence to provide a reason for the narrator to leave Louise to him. The narrator leaves Louise, declaring love and a willingness to sacrifice their relationship to save her life. Given the protagonist's history of failed commitments and my contention that she/he may yet be subject to traumatic repetitions, the reader might question whether the narrator might be unaware of other motives besides love. The narrator and Louise discuss Louise's condition, and Louise wants them to deal with it together. But after hearing about the potential physical effects of the cancer and the treatments, readers can imagine the fears (largely unacknowledged by the narrator) that might underlie the narrator's decision to flee: fears of Louise's physical deterioration, fear of not being able to help her, and, above all—significant for trauma survivors—a fear of death and abandonment. The narrator's later rage at Elgin while looking for Louise helps the narrator deal with his or her guilt for not trying to find Louise sooner. Little attention is paid to the misery the protagonist has visited on Louise; readers do not get Louise's point of view, only the condemnation of the narrator by Louise's family.

For readers to sympathize with the protagonist, we must be convinced of this character's love for Louise, whether his or her pain is real, and how this proceeds from self-destructiveness tied to the narrator's traumatic fears of intimacy. Do readers believe ultimately that the protagonist has learned what is involved in ethical responsibility to a loved one? Winterson tallies the cost of objectification and self-absorption.

Winterson revisits many of these key themes and motivations in her own life in her recent autobiography, *Why Be Happy When You Could Be Normal?* It is not my intention to diminish Winterson's attempts to write seriously about love and death, or to draw an equivalence between Winterson and her protagonist or to undermine her challenges to heterocentrist and heterosexist identity and sexuality, which have been the subject of much critical work on the novel.[3] However, the writer's own experience with abandonment punctuates her sense of trauma-inducing situations that underlie the reckless love and sense of a split self that develops in crisis. In *Why Be Happy*, Winterson links her own failed relationships to a series of abandonments, physical and emotional, in her own life: abandonment by her birth mother, her adopted mother, and lovers. The end of an important relationship forces the author to turn inward, and a pronounced split in personality emerges as she is caught between the creative and productive part of herself, on the one hand, and on the other the self-destructive part that denigrates her as her adoptive mother did (174–75). Eventually she is compelled to learn the truth of why her birth mother gave her up for adoption. This search brings painful inner conflict, along with some knowledge and reconciliation, but also the realization that they cannot recreate the broken bond or the lost years. However, Winterson was then able to accept that she is really the product of her relationship with her adoptive, religiously fanatical mother. She concludes that wounding is "key to being human" (221). *Written on the Body* is one of Winterson's earlier attempts to reproduce in fiction this process of becoming aware of destructive life patterns and their origins. This novel recreates a process of healing whereby the imagination makes possible the empathic reconnection to a loved one.

FIVE

Trauma, Gender, and Commodification in Chuck Palahniuk's *Fight Club* and *Invisible Monsters*

With a postmodern sensibility and in a uniquely black humorous tone, Chuck Palahniuk tackles multiple familial and cultural contexts of trauma. He unveils stories of contemporary life through characters with chaotic lives and topical symptom formations of self-mutilation, self-medication, and support-group participation. Postmodernly irreverent and entertaining, his emotionally numb characters provide readers some emotional distance from traumatic material. And yet his absurdist contexts are expressions of genuine social criticism. Palahniuk walks a fine line in combining painful loss with the absurd ways his characters try to cope. Similar to the postmodernists Kurt Vonnegut and Joseph Heller, he creates tensions between tragic realism and fictionalization, and between trauma and absurdity, in the service of social satire. Readers must piece together the emotional subtexts of characters' behaviors because of the narrators' dissociated responses to the wounds they bear as a result of parental indifference, lack of social regard, and their objectification in late capitalist society. Palahniuk's narrators go through long processes of acting out, followed by gradual self-realization as they discover the violent and gender-specific coping mechanisms they have adopted to defend themselves against their traumas.

The protagonists of *Fight Club* and *Invisible Monsters* suffer failed recognition and nurturance in their families, making them vulnerable to seeking comfort in their own commodification. Palahniuk suggests this dynamic is typical of contemporary life. In *Fight Club*, the protagonist's life has been reduced to that of a numbed, emotionally arrested corporate drone and passive consumer. He describes himself as a thirty-year-old boy. The heroine of *Invisible Monsters*, feeling emotionally abandoned, objectifies her body as a model in a fetishistic culture of fashion, consumerism, and celebrity in which she receives attention but not caring. As *Fight Club* deals with disrespect experienced by men, *Invisible Monsters* does the same for women, as well as attempting some redefinitions of gender norms and identity, as Winterson has done. In postmodern fashion, Palahniuk demystifies contemporary culture in hilarious descriptions of cosmetic surgery, junkyard fashion shoots, and body-torturing clothes. His stories reveal the emptiness of a world that externalizes desire so that people purchase objects or create images they think will fulfill it. He demonstrates how this consumer existence deprives everyone of any kind of internalized identity, leaving people feeling empty and angry. As one of his characters observes, "[You are] trapped inside your culture . . . [it's] your cradle and your trap" (*Invisible* 219).

In these two novels, Palahniuk portrays prototypically male and female traumas in common societal contexts, with gendered forms of objectification and psychic and physical diminution. Historically, the usual gendered situations of trauma have been war for men and rape or incest for women. Palahniuk suggests, though, that the more common denials of human recognition, though not as horrifying, are also capable of serious wounding. Like many postmodern writers, he exposes how social and cultural forces can determine people's lives. Yet he humanistically tries to find ways for his characters to exit these traps through building connections, achieving self-awareness, promoting authenticity, and breaking the social conventions of gender, class, and sexuality.

Interpreting these novels through the lens of trauma illuminates many elements of Palahniuk's work for readers. His use of trauma intensifies the stakes and the action. It accounts for his characters' misrecognitions, self-deceptions, and defenses, as well as their alienation from people and society (they act out against both). The framework of trauma helps readers conceptualize characters' behaviors as symptomatic: their repetitions, dissociations, defenses, and acting out are the emotional consequence of destructive social and sexual designations and human objectification. His characters do not possess as many dimensions as those of the other writers in this study. Though they are amalgams of symptoms, they still are given enough spirit, wit, and rebelliousness to entertain, if not compel, readers.

Like Winterson, Palahniuk exhibits a postmodern sense of narrative and identity. He specializes in nonlinear narratives with shifting time frames (each change in *Invisible Monsters* begins with "Jump to") from the present to various times in the past. These shifts are more frequent, if less seamless, than in Morrison's writing, but as in her work, they help reveal his characters' pasts, correct misperceptions, and provide contexts for the scenes of violent, movieworthy mayhem that begin both his novels (and *Paradise*). His characters' performances of gender (male in *Fight Club* and female in *Invisible Monsters*) foster both a postmodern sense of identity as fragmented and subject to immediate environmental influences and the exhibition of trauma-based defenses that allow these protagonists an illusion of control. He maintains an ironic distance from them, chancing less emotional investment for readers, though the upside is that readers may feel less threatened by the traumatic material in Palahniuk's fiction. Winterson's protagonist makes a clear shift from comedic to serious qualities, but Palahniuk alternates between them, producing an abstracted, constructed quality to the characters that fits his theme of wounded people with superficial identities who act unreflectively and ease emotional pain with drugs and self-wounding. Palahniuk's protagonists narrate retrospectively, withholding crucial information from readers; Palahniuk uses this technique to pique interest, create suspense, and convey his characters' misconceptions, which are not fully sorted out until the conclusions. The gaps and fragmented storytelling mimic the chaotic emotional and conceptual states of mind of trauma victims, even if his work is more self-consciously plot-driven than the other fiction narratives I discuss in this book.

Palahniuk has Shannon, his narrator-protagonist of *Invisible Monsters*, tell her story in the chaotic form of a fashion magazine. Her frequent repetitions of the phrase "flash . . . flash," interspersed with insights, illustrate a process of discovering and resisting knowledge of her traumas. The "flash . . . flash" passages connote photographs, films, or flashbacks, as well as messages that would seem to contradict a quick consideration. This narrative strategy is a humorous and self-referential depiction of mass media consciousness that is begging to be infiltrated by unmediated emotional insights. As in a movie or photo shoot, the "flashes" provide quick, unexamined spaces for emotions. For example:

> Give me amnesia.
> Flash.
> Give me new parents.
> Flash. (90)

In both novels Palahniuk makes the narrators self-consciously voice knowledge of traumatic processes even as they act out, suggesting that they have not yet worked through their trauma. This narrative strategy incorporates survivors' typical struggles with knowing and not knowing the past. What they have repressed may also be revealed in repetitive and self-defeating actions and thoughts, or in resisting memories or recovering partial awareness with memory fragments (Laub and Auerhahn 288). Survivors may be partially aware, but that experience could still dominate their lives and provoke repetitions. For example, Shannon says, "Give me violent revenge fantasies as a coping mechanism" (*Invisible* 181), maintaining irrational patterns of coping even when she knows that the object of her anger wants her love. Her statement parodies media-driven knowledge of trauma, but unfortunately, her cognitive awareness of the concept does not guarantee emotional recovery. As in *Fight Club*, revenge scenarios give the characters a measure of control over what has hurt them and deprived them of identities. Shannon cannot imagine others' feelings because she is locked in her own world of hurt. This self-conscious acknowledgment of traumatic processes could also be a way to guide the broad reading audience that Palahniuk targets.

Both postmodernism and trauma theory share a view of self as fragmented and discontinuous. Postmodernists posit multiple, conflicting social forces that influence us and undermine notions of a stable and consistent identity. However, in traumatic situations fragmentation can be debilitating. Survivors feel out of control, disconnected from the past, and they adopt destructive or avoidant personality traits and cognition. They may also impose on themselves constricting structures that bring temporary relief but limit the individual's ability to live, connect, and feel fully. Trauma writers often depict traumatized characters creating a provisional identity as a way of adapting to adversity (Lifton 30; Vickroy, *Trauma and Survival* 125; Langer 121–61). For instance, Palahniuk's protagonists embrace narcissism to avoid painful emotions, and to fill in the gaps characteristic of an ungrounded, underrecognized identity that is driven by a seemingly unfillable emptiness that they fear and avoid.

Characters traumatized by neglect or lack of recognition suffer symptoms that include altered personality and extreme defenses. Prominent defenses in both novels analyzed here are splitting and dissociation. In *Fight Club* the nameless protagonist splits into two separate personalities. In *Invisible Monsters* Shannon is clearly disconnected from herself and others, and from any emotion save rage. In focusing on their own wounds exclusively, such characters experience a reduced capacity for feeling and caring about others. They both possess a tainted sense of self and the world and show alterations of their perceptual, decisional, and relational processes typical of the traumatized personality in survival mode (Root 247–51). Also, many of Palahniuk's characters exhibit borderline personality disorder traits, often associated with childhood abuse and trauma. This disorder, according to Ronnie Janoff-Bulman, is

> characterized by disturbances in self-concept, affect regulation, interpersonal relationships, and impulse control. Borderlines have an unstable, diffuse sense of self, and under certain types of stress they experience a disintegration of the self and "annihilation panic." They have poor affect tolerance, report feeling empty and bored, and overreact to relatively mild stimuli. Borderlines also have difficulty with interpersonal relationships; although they cannot tolerate being alone and actively seek involvement with others, their relationships are intensely conflictual and unstable. They manifest very poor impulse control and often engage in behaviors that are harmful to themselves or others. Suicide attempts and self-mutilation, particularly wrist-cutting, are extremely common among borderline patients. (86–87)

Borderline personalities are a staple of contemporary celebrity-obsessed, reality TV culture. Palahniuk picks up on these pathologies to help define his characters, who have fragile, easily mutable identities, frequently act out violently and sexually, and have volatile and dependent relationships. Both narrators are unreliable, perpetually misreading other characters, and are unaware of their own actions. They act out from narrow, wounded perspectives and are unable to give to or empathize with others. Both report their resistance to knowing the truth of their situations (by dissociating from or repressing events) even as they reveal numerous clues to readers. The "invisibility" or nonidentity of the two protagonists links them as well: he is submerged in his alter ego, Tyler Durden; Shannon's hideous facial scars make her invisible to others and herself. Both engage in physical self-wounding, representing an attempt to liberate themselves from social forces. Palahniuk seems to suggest that physical trauma might have an evasive or a liberating effect on psychological trauma and stasis. It moves the characters away from dominating norms, even if they must acquire physical wounds to make it possible.

Palahniuk depicts his protagonists' actions as outlandish and humorous, with a completely different tone than the other trauma writers. Pain is evident, but evaded. Seriousness is undermined because of the tension Palahniuk maintains between realism and black humor, harnessing a gay sensibility focused on homosocial relations and unstable sexuality. He also uses trauma to amp up the intensity and action, as opposed to the more internalized portrayals of Atwood and Faulkner. He aims for a different group of readers from those sought by the other authors: media-savvy, unsentimental, and masculine.

Fight Club: Acting Out Is the Best Defense

The unnamed narrator-protagonist of *Fight Club* embodies the depersonalizing effects of a world virtually devoid of human caring and meaning. As in many contemporary trauma narratives, Palahniuk depicts socially induced traumas originating in powerful ideologies, in this case a capitalism that fuels inequalities and alienates people from themselves and each other. The protagonist, who also mentions issues of childhood neglect and shame, seeks comfort from his pain-filled isolation in cancer support groups, but when his pain threatens to become conscious, it precipitates a dissociative psychic split. Out of this split emerges Tyler Durden, an alter or split-off aspect of himself that incarnates the narrator's psychic defenses and allows him illusions of control but also leads him away from potentially healing connections. Palahniuk complicates healing from trauma, particularly for men, because clinically speaking, healing necessitates acknowledging helplessness, which contradicts the masculine identity formed in bodies acting out. The protagonist's attraction to cancer support groups and his own repetitive behavior convey a sense of profound struggle to understand a typically empty existence in a social context that ignores psychological and existential pain. This narrator seems dissociated from his memory or his own feelings, which emerge in mediated form, through others, or as the narrator acts out in the guise of a split-off part of his psyche. He observes his "wet mask crying on Big Bob's shirt" (*Fight* 22), but he does not report feeling anything except relief. He can approach his own pain only vicariously, through others' pain. By examining the protagonist's gender-inflected shame and the unraveling of his "unknowing knowing" of his psychic split, I hope to show how Palahniuk uses traumatic symptoms to articulate a crisis of ungrounded identity in contemporary society.

Fight Club resembles other trauma narratives in raising questions about victims' identities and the possibilities of successful human connection. The novel shows how a dissociated world, blind to the consequences of its destructive actions, produces a deeply isolated protagonist who longs for attachments but has few means to achieve them. The narrator's irreverent tone reflects his discomfort with feeling, but it also re-creates an environment that limits individuals' ability to act and construct a cohesive identity. Palahniuk's approach to characterization is postmodern, entailing the fabrication of multiple functional and shifting identities, but his characters' behaviors could also indicate traumatic psychic splitting and fragmentation. The narrator's seemingly traumatic breakup with his father cuts him off from the past: "I knew my dad for about six years, but I don't remember anything" (*Fight* 50). He also compares his father's paternal negligence to his own capitalistic environment in the way his father had set up his new families like "franchises" (Kavadlo 13). Like many men in the novel, he indulges in rage-filled acting out that seems overdetermined—that is, having suppressed and multiple causes—and yet also seems an understandable response to a belittling world. The fights, eventually revealed to be the protagonist's self-mutilation, are symptoms of trauma that relieve his emotional numbness and make him feel alive and in control. The history of his father's abandonment and his conclusion that his mother raised a "thirty-year-old boy" is acted out rather than remembered, as he tries to reconstruct his nurturance by replacing his father with Tyler.

The narrator also exhibits symptoms of failure and shame. He feels ashamed of being emasculated, of not living up to or knowing male models of adulthood. This process begins with his relationship with his parents and his ongoing feminization by consumer culture (e.g., his obsession with his IKEA-furnished home). Marla, a fellow support-group junkie, also shames him, making him so self-conscious about attending support groups that they can no longer function as part of his defenses, and consequently he must resort to other defenses, and so creates Tyler. The narrator feels almost disembodied, effaced on many levels, and this is why recapturing his body's power in episodes of violent physical contact is so vital to him. Thomas J. Scheff and Suzanne M. Retizinger establish that "shame leads to violence . . . [when] . . . it is hidden to the point that it is not acknowledged or resolved" (3). This certainly is true of the protagonist, who tries to redeem himself by enacting violence that initially seems to have no purpose other than as an outlet for anger provoked by Tyler. These defenses continue to mask his shame and rage and fend off self-consciousness.

In recent years, American men's place in the social and economic hierarchy has declined, and some critics interpret Palahniuk's novel as part of a backlash against women's partial gains. However, other critics have noted that the novel addresses men's sense of diminishment in the new service economy. In *Fight Club* the narrator begins to recognize that moneymaking activities and the "scripted interactions of the service economy" deindividualize the employees (Lizardo 236). He first worries about fulfilling his role as the good consumer, but this does not satisfy his need for male companionship particularly. Worn down by relentless travel and work as a corporate recall campaign coordinator, the narrator is exposed to potentially traumatic information, as the reader surmises from his description of seeing photographs of people's legs cut off by exploding turbo chargers that the negligent company will not replace (*Fight* 99). He does not discuss his feelings about this incident, but a normal ethical reaction to being complicit in such malfeasance would be shame. When he becomes empowered as a man by the fight club and rebels against his superiors, he can see the photographs as something he can hold over the company and perhaps use to undo it.

The narrator's self-portrait reveals a bundle of possible consequences of trauma on personality, as noted in Bessel Van der Kolk's studies, including impaired trust, inability to attribute responsibility appropriately (he is unaware of his own actions), and identifying with the aggressor (his father, then Tyler) rather than accepting his own vulnerability (and Marla's). The narrator tries to escape helplessness through violent action and avoids emotional intimacy with Marla, to whom he is attracted.

The narrator records his first noticeable symptom of trauma as a relentless insomnia, which he describes as an "out of body experience" (19). He observes that with the "insomnia distance of everything, you can't touch anything and nothing can touch you" (21). This is also true of a dissociated state (Gold 16; Van der Kolk, "Complexity" 189). Insomnia is the first of many living death metaphors in the novel; another is his zombielike existence of monotonous travel and regulated environments (workplaces, hotels). He is initially cured of his insomnia, "resurrected," through participation in a cancer support group, where the threat of death to other members, but not him, makes him feel more alive (*Fight* 22). He can respond well to men like Bob who try to comfort him, but he does not respond as well to women. He cannot sexually comfort the dying Chloe as she wishes. Though he would like to help, she is terrifyingly too near death. His response to her may indicate his shame about not feeling manly, which makes him shy away from women generally. However, the support groups' focus on bodily suffering does allow the narrator to consider the idea of death as a release from his own emotional pain.

When Marla appears at the support groups, she recognizes a fellow "faker" and makes him feel self-conscious and ashamed of his fraudulent participation. As his dissociated emotions have been partially recovered in the safe context of the group, and as Marla's recognition of his motives shuts down this outlet, his psyche seeks relief elsewhere. Because she is an object of potential intimacy, Marla also makes him feel more vulnerable and defensive. She has enormous influence on him, though he denies it throughout most of the novel.

After Marla appears, the narrator "meets" his alter, Tyler, a decisive father substitute and a bolder provisional self who, unlike the protagonist, is unafraid to aggressively resist forces that oppress average men: humiliating and morally compromising jobs, the false promises of the American Dream, and their fathers' failures to provide them with a clear path to male identity. Tyler also persuades the narrator to join him in challenging his superiors at work through blackmail and violence. Though their jobs certainly add to their misery, these confrontations do not address the protagonist's deepest unresolved fears of living with the knowledge of mortality and his failure to form intimate connections to others. Tyler is a product of the narrator's trauma and consequent fragmented identity (George 71), and fulfills the narrator's need for a more cohesive identity. Despite the provisional sense of control he gains through Tyler, the narrator merely repeats earlier dysfunctional family relations by acting out his anger and hostility toward his parents, replaying how they ignored one another in his treatment of Marla. He then engages in self-mutilation, another kind of acting out, which is reactive, symptomatic behavior; the self-mutilation brings temporary relief but no healing or connection. These are all typical defensive strategies of the traumatized. Tyler helps the narrator-protagonist escape from an identity shaped by consumerism and family (George 73) but becomes the vehicle for the defensive manoeuvers listed above. The narrator becomes overly reliant on Tyler, feeling inferior to him until he realizes that his alter's violent proclivities (really his own suppressed rage) must be stopped.

The beatings administered in the fight club Tyler creates provide (as do the cancer support groups) displaced confrontations with the men's fears of the real world. They can create new, untarnished identities and find temporary relief as self-inflicted bodily pain trumps psychological pain in the short term. The popularity of fight clubs and reenactments in the book, film, and by audience members demonstrate that many others share the narrator's own fears: "Most guys are at fight club because of something they're too scared to fight," he says (*Fight* 54). As a symptom of trauma, his self-mutilation functions as a means of self-soothing or a release from mental anguish; it's often a means for victims to break away from experiencing a "sense of complete disconnection from others and disintegration of the self" (J. Herman 108). Self-harm can also "be a way of expressing the anger that has been carried for so long [and] . . . that has to be repressed over the years as a means of survival" (Bray Haddock 22). It also feels less dangerous than expressing anger to others directly (Favazza 273). The narrator's wounds are emblematic of life and action, but they are also self-punishment for his previous passivity and his doubts about his manhood.

The protagonist/Tyler split replicates the workings of dissociative identity disorder (formerly called multiple personality disorder), a rare and extreme manifestation of trauma. A person with dissociative identity disorder is typically split between a "primary passive identity and alternate identities with contrasting names and characteristics. In at least a third of cases, self-mutilation may be inflicted as a punishment by one alternate personality or another" (Favazza 247). This seems to be the case with the self-wounding protagonist's symptoms as he succumbs to the alter Tyler's stronger personality. Tyler beats and burns him with lye and rationalizes this punishment as providing the protagonist with essential knowledge of pain and death. However, the narrator is punishing himself for what he sees as his cowardice, helplessness, and failure to act, and he develops a hero worship of Tyler, who is the wish fulfillment replacement of the father who has abandoned the narrator.

Palahniuk's use of dissociative identity disorder may be overdetermined in the sense of realistic depictions. It raises speculation regarding this character's deep conflicts, but the text does not provide direct causal evidence, focusing instead on the severity of his symptoms. There could be several reasons why the narrator does not provide this information. The unreliability of his reporting is depicted to be part of his pathology, proof of his unawareness and defensiveness. Palahniuk's depictions are consistent with trauma defenses such as mistrust and fear of vulnerability; he has said his characters regularly "sabotage any chance of bonding with another person" (Kavanagh 184). The protagonist's deficient judgments help readers understand the effects of trauma on the quality of his mind. Forgetting important personal history is also a typical symptom of dissociative identity disorder (Bray Haddock 9) and relevant to the protagonist's forgotten but crucially reenacted relationship with his father. His silence about causes means readers must infer more with this text than with the other novels I have considered here because the author provides fewer cognitive guideposts. Besides extreme characterization, psychic splitting also functions as part of Palahniuk's plot strategy. The protagonist must hide what he already knows about Tyler until the end of the novel so that Palahniuk can build suspense as well as reconstruct the disorientations and conflicts of trauma that let readers into the narrator's experience.

If readers are led to see the emotional and cognitive limitations of survival mode, they may be able to consider to what degree the traumatized are capable (or not) of being able to bear responsibility for others and themselves, or to treat others fairly and compassionately. The symptoms of survival mode that this narrator exhibits include a split self, constricted emotion, distrust, altered perceptual, decisional, and relational processes, and a reduced capacity to love (Root 247–51). Trauma texts depict behaviors that are "externalizations of an internal state" (Hartman, "On Traumatic Knowledge" 541), and fittingly, *Fight Club*'s narrator focuses on externals and physical acting out because he is disconnected from his internal life.

Palahniuk demonstrates the traumatic effects on his narrator-protagonist's personality, with his callousness toward others also extending to himself in his self-punishment. The narrator's mind works in an indirect and defensive mode; he describes traces of emotional events that indicate experience but never feelings themselves, as with the mask of his tears on Bob's shirt or the masklike remnants of blood on the floor after a beating at fight club. Through much of the novel Marla is an indicator of his emotional distance; she is disgusted, for example, that he will not acknowledge they've made love. However, she also helps him recognize and act on his situation. Readers are taken through his gradual process of becoming aware of his split self, and how he takes responsibility and tries to atone for his own cruelty and violence.

The narrator's dissociative state, his primary traumatic symptom, is seen in both his behavior and storytelling. His reports of Marla's and

Tyler's behavior show the narrator's defensive disconnection and avoidance of the truth. For example, his silent hostility toward Marla and her frustration suggest that he is unaware of his sexual intimacy with her except as Tyler. His overdetermined admiration for Tyler reflects his own need for such a figure, prevents him from recognizing Tyler's (i.e., his own) sadomasochism, and slows the discovery of his own violent deeds as Tyler. The narrator presents himself as having few memories of the past, wanting to jettison his upbringing along with other controlling forces that Tyler demands as part of his philosophy. The protagonist occasionally expresses anxiety, for instance acknowledging his father's rejection of him, and fear that Marla will take Tyler from him, but humorously (defensively) glosses over it, feigning ironic detachment. His disconnection from his feelings is evidenced by his need to displace his unconscious, unfiltered, and unsocialized rage through Tyler: "These are Tyler's words coming out of my mouth. I am Tyler's mouth" (155). He draws the reader's attention primarily to immediate events, and remains more focused on Tyler than on Marla because Tyler is the angry, destructive part of himself that gives him a sense of control. By holding off Marla, a fellow isolated victim who tries to connect with her own and others' suffering, he avoids feeling and vulnerability, and forecloses a potential relationship.

Until he can confront Tyler's existence, he is consigned to repetitively seek reinforcement in bodily action. His identification with Tyler and the fight club appears to be an antidote to the narrator's sense of shame for failure to fulfill a masculine and adult self-image, which he tries to create through bodily strength, sexual prowess, and aggressive action. He can join other men in rejecting the limitations the world places on them. The fight club members seem to experience their devaluation by the culture as a communal trauma. Tyler articulates their anger at the false promises of the society and leads the others in collective resistance. However, Tyler is depicted as a fantasy figure, physically perfect, whose dangerous, callous masculinity is featured in advertising that offers men an illusion of control and women glamorized threats of violence. The rough sex he has with Marla as Tyler underscores this dissociated, mediated intimacy that seems to transcend inhibition and shame but does not accomplish the real emotional intimacy and friendship that the narrator needs but fears. He seeks refuge in media-driven images of masculinity that shun vulnerability and full humanity and mask why he has difficulty accepting Marla's love: she is like him, and he hates himself.

The narrator's focus on his own body becomes the concrete manifestation of his identity, an externalization of his psychological issues, and a platform for agency and control for his defensive personality. It becomes emblematic of living life fully: "I just don't want to die without scars" (47–48). It may also demonstrate the narcissism (but not vanity) of the provisional self in being so male-identified, following from the protagonist's notion that becoming a man is his sole salvation. The focus on the male body in the novel illustrates the work's concerns with masculinity, the likelihood that men are expected to prove themselves in violent situations, and their propensity to externalize their responses to traumatic, often violent events with action. Palahniuk is observing masculine responses to stress that tend to be acted out physically, while women more often internalize theirs. These gendered responses are borne out in psychological and literary accounts of trauma. The vulnerability of women's bodies and the ill are contrasted with the toughness of the fight clubbers' bodies.

Many writers of trauma narratives depict bodily humiliations as representing aspects of traumatic experience, making it more visceral for the reader. Palahniuk particularly links wounding and scars with the possibility of psychic pain reduction and with making connections with sympathetic others. *Fight Club*'s protagonist proudly alludes to the results of his fights—the unhealed hole in his cheek, his bleeding mouth and black eyes—and how these insignia horrify some but link him to hundreds of men seeking to challenge their lowly life status. He delights in terrifying his boss by beating himself and bleeding on him, describing himself from the perspective of the culture he wants to destroy: "the monster drags itself . . . hooks its bloody claw" (116). Palahniuk is creating analogies to war trauma and suggests men are more likely to act out their trauma issues than to seek therapy (Gold 18).

Embodiment provides a more revealing forum for trauma and anxiety with Marla. Her fears of illness and mortality are centered in her body's signals of illness and aging. Like the narrator, she punishes herself and tries to recover from fears of death and stasis through the body. However, she also invites his concern and friendship around her body as she asks him to feel her breasts for lumps. She offers connection and healing with her body by fulfilling the narrator sexually, though he can only acknowledge this in a displaced fashion. He rejects her attempts to seduce him when he's "himself" and not Tyler.

The protagonist's relationship with Marla is the most important actual one, stirring his feelings and defenses. Throughout much of the book his psychological defenses lead him to cut himself off from her (though as Tyler, he encourages her presence), perhaps associating her with his devalued mother: "I'm a thirty-year-old boy, and I'm wondering if another woman is really the answer I need" (51). However, Marla persists and confides in him, and he eventually wants to protect her from Tyler's violence. Marla's first appearance disconcerts him because she sees through his pretense of being a true cancer victim. Self-loathing and self-mutilating like him, she nevertheless has a relatively more integrated personality than he does and more directly faces her fear of death, at times amusingly, by saving her mother's liposuctioned fat for collagen antiaging treatments. She and the protagonist take the existentialist path of recognizing death as a way to appreciate life, though at times they wish for it as an escape or punishment. Marla persists with the narrator despite his constant resistance. He seems to love and then ignore her, making her feel, she says, like a "discarded Christmas tree." She becomes his reality base and conscience, and eventually helps bring him to greater self-awareness. He's loathe to recognize this, and critics have pointed out that because of the male focus of the novel, readers (especially the fight club imitators) often do not recognize her as the life impulse that sustains the protagonist because they take Tyler and his charming and dangerous ways at face value (Kavadlo 9–10). The narrator has to get past the "allure of Tyler" to discover Marla, who saves him (8).

For traumatic memory to be integrated with normal memory, a patient must undergo a therapeutic "controlled reliving experience" of traumatic events (J. Herman 182). Palahniuk does not make his protagonist undergo this type of remembering, but he does gradually become aware through others that Tyler is a destructive, dissociated part of himself. Palahniuk signals the narrator's growing awareness through his ambivalent relation to Marla. This begins with disguised memory: the narrator-protagonist thinks he dreams of sex with Marla (which he has actually had), but convinces himself that Tyler is doing it because he cannot yet succumb to this kind of intimacy. "Marla looks at me as if I'm the one humping her" (68). In calling him out on the black eye "Tyler" gave her, Marla will make him confront his struggle with memory. He slowly comprehends that for Marla, he and Tyler are the same person and that he is responsible for Tyler's actions.

He defends himself against this knowledge through most of the novel, keeping himself and Tyler separate through the secrecy rules of fight club. Thus he can avoid others' opinions of Tyler, his destructiveness, or the illusion of connection he provides. Tyler's existence depends on the protagonist's unawareness; Marla represents consciousness, though, and Tyler disappears when she appears to help save the suicidal protagonist toward the end of the novel. This reverses the order of their appearances at the beginning of the story. The narrator's treatment of her demonstrates his emotional split, the impulse toward her versus his tainted sense of self, his inability to envision a woman as part of his healing or future. If we read his symptoms, we can elicit clues to the real and destructive effects of Tyler on him, though he cannot recognize this until very late in the novel. For instance, his insomnia returns once he joins Tyler and stops going to support groups. He recognizes the paramilitaristic regimentation of Tyler's anticorporate Project Mayhem, referring to his recruits as "space monkeys." However, he still buys into some of their activities until his friend Bob is killed. At this point in the narrative Tyler is unavailable to him, circumventing his conscience and doubts. Noting evidence of murder in the back yard, he tries to protect Marla. Other critics have pointed out that Tyler and the men engage in conformist repetitions of "institutionalized violence and disregard for human life" (Gold 26), which the protagonist eventually recognizes he must stop.

The protagonist's psychological resistance persists as Tyler eludes and seemingly abandons him once the narrator begins to doubt Tyler, but he nevertheless repeatedly reassures himself with Tyler's mantras and feels he needs Tyler as this (in Tyler's words) "model for god" for whom he keeps searching. "I am nothing in the world compared to Tyler. I am helpless" (146). This dependency persists even though the satisfaction he experiences from fighting is diminished (123), and his participation in Tyler's project to sabotage the rich and powerful does not provide resolution of his trauma. Though the protagonist has the impulse to return to the origins of the trauma in hoping to repeat the father-son relation with Tyler, Tyler, enacting the protagonist's defenses, wants to liberate the men from social identity ("You're not your family . . . you're not your problems . . . you're not your age" (143). Though all these have their limitations, they are also things the narrator, or any survivor, needs to confront. Personal history matters and must be worked through, not merely denied.

He's slow on the uptake, but Marla and the recruits (who recognize him as Tyler) force him to become aware that he has done the things he's attributed to Tyler. He eventually has to fight for his own identity against Tyler, who wants to take over: "There isn't a me and a you anymore" (164). Tyler admits to all he's done that the narrator has remained unaware of, and refuses to leave. "I wouldn't be here in the first place if you didn't want me" (168). Comically personifying the narrator's pathological split, his desire to know and yet not to know, Tyler asserts his dominance despite the protagonist's identification of him as his own "dream . . . projection. . . . He's a dissociative personality disorder. A psychogenic fugue state" (168). However, the narrator's ability to diagnose his condition does not preclude his need to continue to enact and not resolve his pathology. This absurd, ironic use of scientific terminology illustrates the uselessness of rational discourse in the face of dire psychological need.

Once Marla has witnessed the protagonist murdering someone as Tyler, he knows he has to confront this part of himself and protect her. He must take responsibility for all of Project Mayhem and the deaths it has caused. In the climactic scene, he holds a gun to his own head to get rid of Tyler, even if it costs his life. Tyler disappears when Marla and the support-group members approach to help him, and now that he's assured Marla loves him, not Tyler, he makes sure Tyler "dies" by shooting himself.

He survives the gunshot. The final chapter situates him in a mental hospital, a refuge where he can rely on others to take care of him. However, some of the orderlies remind him they still admire his actions as Tyler Durden. At least some of his traumatic patterns remain. He sees his therapist as God, again searching for an all-knowing figure to lead him. In the end, he is given time to reflect, and he is still ambivalent regarding his life dilemmas: is the solution manly action or his growing connection to Marla? The brief but profound satisfactions of answering masculine shame with violent physical conflict and the provisional identity he creates in the form of Tyler do not heal the narrator; in fact, they almost destroy him, but they still seem as appealing to him as the potentially healing compassion and forgiveness he gets from Marla and the support group.

Clearly, violence and revenge represent being stuck in trauma. Steven Gold attributes this emotional stasis to being unable to change the soul-destroying social context in which "the characters are so hopelessly mired that even their attempts to transcend it are ultimately doomed to replicate or even compound its flaws" (26). Palahniuk does not try to sentimentalize his wounded characters. He visits the consequences of people's rage taken to the extreme, but his focus on the temporary relief fight club brings to the characters is what many in the film's viewing audience attended to, creating their own fight clubs. In his afterword to *Fight Club*, Palahniuk points out that for centuries, men (and women) have been able to cope with their oppression and frustrations through fighting, knowing they cannot affect the larger forces controlling them (218). The urge to action is compelling even if it does not alter the sources of trauma in the long run. From the standpoint of healing psychological trauma it is perhaps a step forward in confronting fears, but it is less complete than engaging in the emotionally painful work of braving the deeper fears of one's existence that cannot be confronted alone because we seem to be wired to bury them if left to our own devices.

So why, unlike many trauma writers, does Palahniuk avoid an emotional healing process? His postmodernist perspective seems to reject healing scenarios. There are no comforting cures. The protagonist does become more aware and extricates himself from unconscious patterns and a difficult situation, but he is ripe to land in another. The conclusion of *Fight Club* is less conclusive and potentially healing than that of *Invisible Monsters*.

Invisible Monsters: Beauty Objects and Creating a New Story

Invisible Monsters begins with a catastrophic scene of a burning house, Evie's ruined wedding, and Brandy lying shot on the ground. The rest of the novel intermittently revisits the past that leads us back to this scene, which will be a turning point in the characters' lives, with many things not what they seem. The narrator-protagonist, Shannon McFarland, once a model, has been shot in the face and horribly mutilated. She is estranged from her family—still jealous of her brother, Shane, who has apparently died of AIDS (though this is unconfirmed)—because her parents still pay more attention to his memory than to her. Shannon quickly befriends a beautiful, glamorous would-be transsexual, Brandy Alexander, in a rehabilitation hospital. After their release, Brandy takes Shannon and her boyfriend, Manus, on a road trip from one town and real estate property to the next, stealing drugs from medicine cabinets, taking and selling the drugs, and buying and returning expensive clothes. They are headed to Texas, where Shannon's once-close friend Evie is getting married. The point of their journey is ostensibly to confront Evie about her affair with Manus and the possibility that one of them shot Shannon. Shannon wants revenge on them all: she holds Manus hostage, twice sets fire to Evie's house, blackmails Evie, and wants to kill Brandy to achieve notoriety, imagining the headline "Monster Girl Slays Secret Brother Gal Pal" (182). Brandy gradually makes Shannon realize she (or he) is actually Shannon's brother, Shane. This realization helps Shannon remember she shot herself. Several mysteries veiled by trauma unravel: who Brandy is (Shane), why he's becoming a woman, Manus's history with both Shane and Shannon, who shot Shannon and why, and why Shannon is so angry with her brother. Mental and physical traumas, presented with a black humorous and camp sensibility, drive the obsessive characters to run from their pasts, which must eventually be confronted.

Brandy, Shannon, and Manus spend much of the novel "renouncing their own identities to escape the trap of having a static identity" (Viskovic and Summers Bremner 109). Their new identities offer no substantive changes but are merely repetitions of rejection and self-loathing that keep them mired in the past. "Rather than . . . transcending the events that trouble them, the characters are acting as a direct result of them and thus giving the events power over their lives" (109). Their repetitions are grounded in the trauma of being denied the intersubjective recognition that builds the foundation of a sense of self (Honneth, "Personal Identity"). All the central characters are alienated from their parents, who cannot accept children who are not sexually normative. These rejections create lingering pain and conflict for Shane, Manus, and Evie (and indirectly for Shannon). Similarly, the societies they inhabit, and the available jobs, objectify and alienate them from themselves. Palahniuk's social critique here is of the social devaluation of gay identity and pansexuality. These are examples of Honneth's contention that disregard damages individuals' relations to themselves and the "fulfillment . . . of the subject's own identity" ("Recognition" 24). In *Invisible Monsters*, consumerism also disregards human dignity, turning characters inward and making them narcissistic attention-seekers. This further alienates them, reinforcing the distrust formed by familial traumas and shaping their behavior and personalities. Because, as Shannon points out, "we're so totally trapped in ourselves" (266), most of the characters unjustly misconceive others.

Shannon's narration is unreliable, shaped by traumas; she reports but often cannot explain or integrate the information from past and present. She sometimes reaches insights about the influence of the past but cannot often act on this revelation. Viskovic and Summers Bremner point out that she has been given the task of narrating Brandy's story as Brandy lies shot, but it is questionable whether Shannon can identify with anyone else enough to testify for them (102). She seems to suffer from dissociated memory, just as the narrator of *Fight Club* does. Also, because she must tell a story with traumatic elements which she is trying to avoid, she can report acting out but offers few explanations, leaving readers to interpret her defended focalizations and to fill in emotional gaps. At first she may not seem up to the task. Palahniuk establishes Shannon's emotional detachment from others and defensive state of mind in her reaction to this traumatic scenario:

> What I tell myself is the gush of red pumping out of Brandy's bullet hole is less like blood than it's some sociopolitical tool. The thing about being cloned from all those shampoo commercials, well, that goes for me and Brandy Alexander, too. Shotgunning anybody in this room would be the moral equivalent of killing a car, a vacuum cleaner, a Barbie doll. Erasing a computer disk. Burning a book. Probably that goes for killing anybody in the world. We're all such products. (12)

This passage portrays the workings of a traumatized mind that assumes a tainted world that focuses on appearances to the detriment of deeper, more disturbing issues and that leaves no room for compassion because she can be attentive only to her own needs. Only later in the novel, as the connections and similarities between Shannon and Brandy/Shane stack up, can Shannon "recognize in Brandy her own tendency toward self-destruction. Healing comes through recognizing their bond and reclaiming their past, which provides both with a link to a world outside their present identities" (Viskovic and Summers Bremner 103). Shannon will in the end express a desire to reach outside herself and love another.

Before revealing (sparingly) earlier traumatic contexts, the narrative focuses on how each character lacks an identity or clear sense of an inner life beyond others' recognition that is reminiscent of the borderline personality characteristics in *Fight Club*. Others do not seek true knowledge of them; their attentions are based on superficialities encouraged by consumer culture: looks and indicators of status (clothes, real estate, jewelry, cars) or sexuality (young flesh, breast augmentation). The characters unthinkingly seek the control and attention that commodify them but never make them feel loved. Their dissatisfaction is evident in their compulsive consumption of beauty-enhancing products and drugs. As Shannon admits, "Evie, Brandy and me, all this is just a power struggle for the spotlight. Just each of us being me, me, me first. The murderer, the victim, the witness, each of us thinks our role is the lead" (16). They struggle for the kind of attention most given to women, for their looks, though interestingly, two of the three are or were men: "It's all mirror, mirror on the wall because beauty is power the same way money is power the same way a gun is power" (16). Shannon and Evie have spent their youth objectifying themselves and fantasizing about a glamorous life. Their photo shoots hilariously evoke their humiliation and commodified bodies. More self-aware, Brandy will later sum up these women's motivations to be models: "Love me, love me, love me, love me, love me, love me, love me, I'll be anybody you want me to be. Use me. Change me. I can be thin with big breasts and big hair. Take me apart. Make me into anything, but just love me" (266).

Shannon also selfishly focuses on how her parents have always paid more attention to her dead brother. To her, their ways of mourning seem pathological, at best pathetically compensatory. Though they rejected his gay sexual activity, after his "death" they become obsessed with gay issues and active in an organization for parents of gays and lesbians. Shannon expresses the cold-hearted view that he does not seem dead, for all the attention he gets instead of her. She mocks her parents' Christmas gift of condoms; they fear she too will die of AIDS. This is one way the obsession with death is raised in the book: though presented with a comic veneer, Shane's death and loss are traumatic for both the parents and Shannon, though she defends herself against any but hateful feelings for him, while they mourn him.

However, Shannon's rejection of Shane is her originary trauma, which must be resolved so she can be released from her self-imprisoning shame and rage. Jealousy alone cannot fully explain Shannon's hatred of her brother, or her desire to kill Brandy to be free of her continued obsession with looks: "Brandy looks just like I used to" (255). Her past actions begin a series of soap-opera-level intertwined pathologies. Shannon eventually reveals that the night Shane was cast out, he went to her, and she refused to help him. Moreover, she made anonymous calls to the police to incriminate her parents about Shane's mutilation in a spray can explosion. This allows Manus to sexually coerce and blackmail Shane, who leaves home rather than implicate his father in abuse.

She carries this guilt and shame, but displaces these feelings into rage at him. He could equally resent her, but does not. As Brandy he offers her love and support. Palahniuk reveals the mechanisms that motivate Shannon, but she retains a two-dimensional identity, and remains a postmodern abstraction even more than the characterizations in *Fight Club*. She displays other symptoms of trauma and shame: dissociation, a narcissistic focus on what has been done to *her*, and seeking control through violence. Shannon begins to work through her own defenses as she observes Evie's familiarly shameless product-selling. She realizes she hates others because they resemble her: "vain and stupid and needy . . . What I really hate is me so I hate pretty much everybody" (266). Shannon particularly hates those who might recognize her shame.

Manus is a source of repetition and desire for the McFarlands, and his own desires have torn them apart: he gives Shane gonorrhea and essentially drives him from home; he has sexually abused Shane and coerced and betrayed Shannon. But because they need his attention too desperately, they dismiss his abuses until later. Manus's sexuality (his name says it all), like Shane's, is unacceptable to his parents, and he must work through this rejection to regain his suppressed desires. His sexual pathologies and denials, manifested in victimizing others and pretending heterosexuality, become part of this process. Manus says at one point, "Your parents . . . give you your life, but then they try to give you their life" (210). Shannon's loyalty to Manus may be another self-inflicted wound, since he constantly expresses sexual interest in men. She keeps him around because he's the last man who wanted her, yet she wants to stop her own objectification. He represents what she wants to transcend. Finally, her repressed anger toward him over his infidelities since her mutilation and her suspicion that he might have shot her emerge in violent rage. During the course of the novel, both Brandy/Shane and Shannon want to humiliate and punish Manus, not declaring so outright but acting on impulses to punish him for his violating and betraying them. They get revenge by slowly chemically turning him into a woman without his knowledge.

Brandy is initially presented as a powerful persona who embodies the kind of power through beauty that Shannon once envisioned. Brandy/Shane realizes that in their culture they are all "products," not in control of who they are—there is no "real you" (217–18). She/he has tried to find a path through becoming a woman physically and performatively, fetishizing and enhancing her body with haute couture clothes, surgical procedures and hormones. As Brandy, Shane has charisma, sex appeal, and a provisional identity that gives him the illusion of control, guiding the lives of his followers Manus and Shannon (his sister, though Shannon does not know it for a while). However, appearances are deceiving: Brandy offers clues to Shannon that she's her brother and admits to wanting to become a woman to scare himself out of complacency, out of the cycle of repetition: "What I wanted looked more and more like what I'd always been trained to want. What everybody wants" (220). He wants to escape the known sociosexual categories, chasing the "beauty of a depthless anarchical will," "the beauty of the act" (Mendieta 400). In the end, he puts off sexual reassignment surgery, to see if he can find one person who can love him as he is (with characteristics of both sexes). Shane and Shannon want out of the trap of substituting attention for love.

Generally, for the traumatized, self-mutilation is a defensive strategy to gain self-control because physical pain trumps psychological pain in the short term. It does not bring healing or connection (Bray Haddock 22; Favazza 273); it does provide a release from mental anguish. In *Fight Club*, self-wounding is treated as a sign of masculine power, endurance, and will, as well as bonding with others. However, it also becomes life-threatening to the protagonist. Shannon's self-mutilation comes from a need to release herself from the prison of looks, the pain of not being loved. Initially she cannot accept the horrible scars from the shooting. She misses being beautiful, but eventually realizes that self-acceptance will enable her to love. This is the necessary if painful transformation beyond the limits of physical beauty. For Shane, plastic surgery becomes his available vehicle to self-transformation.

Beyond self-mutilation, fire is a trope for trauma as a repetitive expression of rage and dissatisfaction linking brother and sister; it's another form of control through destruction. Shane's throwing a spray can in a fire is his first attempt to change his fate through self-injury, and he angrily burned his family's clothes before he left home at sixteen. Similarly, Shannon, enraged, wants to "cremate" everyone she knows before she sets fire to Evie's house. "That's what I love about fire, how it would kill me as quick as anybody else. . . . It's so beautiful and powerful and beyond feeling anything for anybody, that's what I love about fire" (273). Thus she expresses her wish to overcome pain and guilt. As the fire she starts in Evie's house rages, she feels "supreme and ultimate control over all" (274). These fires and shooting herself are echoes of

Shane's reactions to rejection, perhaps more so in that she adopts violent responses that are more typical of how males counter helplessness in traumatic contexts. Palahniuk here may be destabilizing gender categories, or appealing to male readers or a popular audience, with repeated control-seeking violence—a staple of popular culture.

Palahniuk provides some resolution of trauma, approaching and avoiding a "feel good" conclusion. Brandy and Evie have staged the whole scenario of Evie shooting Brandy, replaying Shane's "death" to make Shannon really confront it this time. They understand Shannon resists awareness and has to have things acted out so she can emotionally reexperience loss. The reader must infer this because Shannon does not report their motives, but this therapeutic interpretation makes sense. When she thinks Brandy/Shane might be dying, Shannon can finally recognize why she shot herself: much like Shane, "to force myself to grow again" (286). Here Palahniuk echoes Atwood's and Morrison's points that individuals should try to understand the forces that seek to mold them in a certain way and not participate in their own oppression. Shannon has been retraumatized by her shooting wounds; though she wants a new life free of trading on her looks, she is not prepared emotionally to take that step until the end of the novel. Brandy/Shane and Evie help her understand the costs of a sawn-off emotional life of neediness and appearances. Knowing she did not try to stop Evie from shooting Brandy, though she knew Brandy was Shane, Shannon realizes her shortcomings as a human being. She still lacks compassion and serious connection to anyone: "I'm tired of being me, hateful me" (291). In the end, she recognizes she must take steps to become emotionally functional: "I have to know I can love somebody. Completely and totally, permanently and without hope of reward" (295).

She starts on that path as she can now remove the veils that hide her face: "I need a new story" (296). As she sees Shane again in the hospital, as he was before becoming Brandy, she remembers how unhappy he had been at home. Her final act is to give Shane her identity, wanting the world to "embrace what it hates" in the form of a man/woman model. Her final words are a declaration of love for Brandy Alexander, who is her brother's attempt at a new life story. Here Palahniuk promotes an existentialist, ethical ideal of a more authentic self who can choose the nature of his or her existence. Shane embraces what most women are conditioned to emulate, but as a man he can break the gender rules while transforming away from what he does not want to be.

Implicit in these characters' escapism is Palahniuk's social critique of fashion culture and its obsession with the body and aging, and with self-alteration (and self-mutilation) for acceptance. Brandy undergoes several physical traumas: she/he has two ribs removed to attain a sixteen-inch waist and undergoes numerous surgeries to achieve a more feminine appearance. Brandy's clothes are so painfully tight she has to take painkillers (some of several instances of laughably excessive drug-taking). Palahniuk's examples indicate fashion and consumerism produce trauma. Brandy wears a kind of scarf that poor children go blind making. Brandy's clothes also bear signs of exploitation—of animals, of the earth's precious stones, and of human labor—all of which help create glamour.

Palahniuk's use of trauma is overstated in a realistic sense in that there is no evidence of the severe trauma that *Fight Club*'s narrator's symptoms would indicate. In *Invisible Monsters* he accumulates multiple symptoms to the point of excess and absurdity. Palahniuk has a somewhat different approach and agenda from the other writers I have considered. He uses trauma for dramatic effect and to further his social critiques: it highlights the multiple and fragmented nature of postmodern identity; it illustrates the severe effects of commodification and dehumanization of contemporary capitalistic and consumerist life; and it suggests existence itself can be a trauma to which we have little access. His satirical purpose gives readers a different tone and less hopeful sense of resolution. There is less emotional depth and less progress toward healing than for the protagonists in the other novels (save Faulkner's). He makes his characters' suffering less accessible to his readers. In this sense he denies readers some of the human aspects of trauma, but he does not pull any punches in terms of what he sees as the intransigence of social and personal patterns of trauma.

Trauma has additional thematic value for him. Acknowledging that traumatizing situations are usually an encounter with death, Palahniuk's work demonstrates how the culture both expresses and disguises human responses to this threat, for example in cartoon violence. Inherent to both is fear, and he suggests we measure the quality of our existence in the ways we try to face this. Palahniuk asserts that people must survive with their human qualities intact and resist becoming objects. For example, Shane's death imprints on Shannon unconsciously; she fears recognizing her failure to help him. She dissociates from her self-inflicted gunshot wounds and from how near she was to putting herself to death out of self-loathing. Trauma creates a kind of living death for Shannon, who refers to herself as an "already dead ghost" (158). Ugliness has made Shannon invisible, another kind of death without human recognition. The fashion youth culture that the characters (and readers) inhabit ultimately functions atop the fearful subtext of death, with its focus on selling everyone on young (or young-looking) bodies in a denial, and attempted obliteration, of aging and death. Trauma becomes a reminder of how much we fear death, of the necessity of confronting it and living in total awareness of that eventuality. Marla and the protagonist in *Fight Club* try this with the cancer groups, the men with fight club. For Palahniuk, that awareness is the measure of living fully, for without it, life becomes a living death.

CONCLUSION

Trauma as a Critical Juncture of Society, Culture, and Human Psychology

In this book, I have endeavored to offer readers a unique framework for unraveling the complexities of trauma fiction. I hope it may help readers absorb the many interconnected aspects of psychological and social life that trauma literature represents in ways that no other medium can. My theoretical approach combines interdisciplinary conceptions of trauma studies, narrative and cognitive studies, and new historicism. I believe this combination best shows how this genre makes accessible the interconnections of society, culture, and human psychology.

Literary works offer invaluable insights into trauma. First, they allegorize the therapeutic process of putting the traumatic experience into words. Second, they pinpoint the misuses of power that create the trauma-based, defended mentalities of survivors. And third, they bring to the surface social evasions of the psychological consequences of objectifying individuals. Literary works provide contemplative and experiential links to traumatic processes (Vickroy, *Trauma and Survival* 24). Readers are presented with analogous examples of a fraught, split, and at times dramatically overdetermined sense of being characteristic of the trauma personality. The divisions within individuals are particularly compelling, for affected persons appear to exist both inside and outside their experience, wanting both to remember and to forget. Such divisions complicate characterizations of personality and make it difficult to discern the circumstantial dynamics influencing personality shifts.

Most trauma literature aims to create reader empathy by testifying to the human experience of pain and locating the defensive mechanisms by which we survive it. It provides some of the deepest meditations on our humanity in our reactions to stress and adversity. Recent studies indicate that reading this type of thought-provoking fiction can help readers commiserate with survivors by challenging readers' thinking about human responses and engaging them in detailed explorations of the human mind (Comer Kidd and Costano 377).

Studying trauma is important because trauma is often connected to such basic life issues as fear of death, how we determine the meaning and quality of existence, psychological and physical survival, how we understand and cope with loss and self-diminishment, and the nature of bonds and disconnections among individuals. Because all these issues have bearing when we consider traumatic responses, trauma becomes a phenomenon that touches many more people than just the obviously traumatized.

Fictional narrative has a unique capacity to represent the interplay of environment and human emotions. Many fiction writers are able to re-create the lived experience and atmospheres surrounding the linkage of individual traumas with social oppression. This kind of fiction seems able to suggest connections between individual wounding and broader cultural pathologies that would be more difficult to see without the psychological and experiential framework of narrative. For example, fiction readily demonstrates the basis in fear of so much human behavior. Fear drives those who traumatize others so as to dominate them, and fear leads the aggressors to instill more fear in the traumatized so they will not challenge established power and norms.

Literature, particularly trauma literature, can shed light on human endurance of the painful dilemmas we face in our culture, past and present. Trauma is a common phenomenon because of the many stressors in the world, and its conceptualization helps us measure the costs of human diminishment, violence, and objectification. In their approaches to trauma from humanist, social, and political angles, trauma texts promote a progressive hope that situations might change. They portray change as beginning with the growing consciousness of one's situation. Trauma studies' and trauma fiction's examinations of this experience have the potential to expand our culturally inculcated views of human complexity beyond the simple binary thinking that divides the world into right or wrong, guilty or innocent, possessed of free will or predetermined in one's actions. Writers rely on readers having some cultural knowledge of trauma, and so present trauma with more depth and consequences than other media, which tend rather to exploit or simplify the experience.

Trauma fictions may also supplement historical knowledge by rendering historical experience through characters' consciousness and behaviors, highlighting relationships between individuals, their societies, and times. Hayden White speaks of literature's facility in presenting a range of historical and cultural discourses and using specific kinds of stories or genres to translate discursive meaning (43) (e.g., events as tragic or psychologically complex). Literature can also open up topics that other discourses may restrict. Through "patterns of meaning that any literal representation of them as facts could never produce," White writes, real events are given meaning in the way that "literature displays [them] to [readers'] consciousness through its fashioning of patterns of 'imaginary events'" (45).

Just as trauma can offer us historical insights, it can also be a barometer of social life and contemporary culture. Isolation, objectification, and disregard characterize the treatment of the majority of people in late capitalist society. Among the writers I have considered, Atwood, Morrison, and Faulkner show us that cultural values can be debilitating to individuals as those values are processed through families and communities. However, the diminishing and constantly shifting connections in contemporary society, as Winterson and Palahniuk observe, may precipitate an equally damaging sense of isolation and dissociation. Many people feel they have less and less control over their lives, yet they maintain a desire to play some role in their own decision making. People are objectified in capitalist cultures, where media daily try to mold us into images that make us unhappier the more we are exposed to them. Individuals from lower socioeconomic classes are exploited to fight wars that benefit a few. Many of us are increasingly deprived of self-respect and a meaningful place in the world by corporate and financial systems that focus on profit and money schemes at the expense of people, communities, and societies. The ethical philosopher Axel Honneth in "Recognition and Moral Obligation" makes a compelling argument that these types of circumstances create trauma; individuals deprived of recognition feel a deep sense of personal injury. Situations of inequality and injustice that deprive people of an ethical life are the most pressing causes of injury in the characters I have discussed, and preoccupy most of the writers.

Trauma literature highlights different levels of understanding of human experience: the psychological, humanistic, social, cultural, and historical. Consequently, it is important to bring together different disciplinary perspectives to examine not only these texts but also the many dimensions of human situations and experience. My approach to trauma studies includes contemporary psychological, cognitive, narrative, and ethical scholarship. Combining these theoretical lenses reveals the many levels of knowledge offered by these texts, and different methods of reader engagement.

Contemporary trauma theorists and fiction writers try to depathologize trauma symptoms and responses, to show that trauma victims' defenses can be adaptive responses to stress. They help us see how trauma and trauma fiction challenge established views of human personality, motivation, and free will. They do so by emphasizing the situational and dynamic qualities of behavior and discrediting stagnant and simplistic trait-driven conceptions of human nature.

Trauma and trauma narratives involve many ethical dimensions. Trauma texts raise ethical questions about both the treatment of the traumatized and how they in turn treat others. Readers' judgments of traumatized characters, and where we lay responsibility or blame for their behavior, forms another ethical site of action. If we carefully consider the psychological impact of characters' situations, our conceptions of human personality may gain greater depth, and once we are submerged in the traumatized mind-set, simplistic judgments are more difficult to make.

Many factors complicate traumatic responses and healing. One factor is that trauma affects people individually, and different people in similar situations can be damaged to a greater or lesser degree. Another factor is the role played by the social environment: are victims treated ethically by the community? Often the public blames victims, assuming a view of self as whole and self-sustaining. This view could change if symptoms were read as signs of wounding.

Narrative theorists remind us that there is an ethical dynamic to the reading process as well. During reading, the viewpoints and backgrounds of narrator, implied author, and reader all meet, and the reader must consider, among other things, what kind of case the author and narrator are making. Readers must also be sensitive to the narrative's guidance on ethical issues and behavior, effected through the use of such devices as voice, imagery, or repetition, for example. The implied author is the conscience and/or consciousness underlying the overall message of a work; in trauma narratives, this position can be inferred from how a text presents the causes and consequences of trauma. Readers may also ask whether the implied author offers an implicit value structure against which a character's or the narrator's behavior can be measured. Most of the works interpreted here provide detailed accounts

Conclusion

of lives in pain and disarray because of unyielding social standards and exploitation. Atwood's characters may do the best they can under the circumstances, even if they betray others and disappoint themselves (Iris) or lay the blame on victims (Grace), because social forces are too overwhelming to challenge. The odd outlier character may resist those forces, the implication being that such resistance is rare, but necessary.

And what more ethical, alternative behaviors does the writer or the text suggest? Toni Morrison's alternatives to Ruby's lifestyle lie with the more progressive views of the convent women and Reverend Misner, with some town members ready to embrace these new views even if others remain in set patterns. Faulkner offers a temporary alternative in the sorority of women working together but seems to accept that the old ways, the men's ways, should die out. He features the death of Sutpen's family and short-circuits others' bloodlines, too, which may be tragic in Quentin's case but will at least terminate the cycle of repetition. All the writers offer suggestions of more humane, inclusionary values and allowing victims to have a voice.

Most of the novels I have discussed in this book ask readers to identify with survivors in some way, often by channeling the reader's perspective through a survivor's, sometimes by more blatantly casting the harms social standards and circumstances inflict. The traumatized characters' subsequent destructive behavior, although a sign of trauma, can make them difficult to sympathize with. One key challenge to readers of trauma texts is to give up the powerful cultural ideal of personal responsibility as an absolute. Can these works of fiction help readers understand why traumatized individuals are not in a position to take responsibility easily, why even the concept of personal responsibility bears a thoroughgoing reexamination?

Another issue is how well readers are able to contend with narrators' unreliable or unstable viewpoints. Unreliability, narrative theory explains, can involve failure to inform, but more significant are failures of judgment or ethics, which in the case of trauma narratives could be tied to symptoms such as helplessness, faulty cognition, impaired memory, shame, repression, and dissociation. Readers must be able to assess the reasons for unreliability by evaluating in what direction, and how, the narrator or author draws readers' attention, and from what perspective contradictions or inner conflicts are presented in the narrative.

Are some depictions of trauma more rewarding or authentic than others? Each of the works I have discussed offers its own unique take on trauma, but all feature the objectification or commodification of individuals. The American writers especially condemn a rampant, dehumanizing materialism that has driven and haunted our culture from its beginnings. Morrison's, Atwood's, and Faulkner's works use narrative techniques to develop a detailed sense of what the human mind experiences under stress, an approach that is more satisfying for readers interested in close revelations of characters' states of mind and the complexity of human motivations. Winterson's narrator is somewhat less psychologically elaborated but has an inquiring mind that leads readers to many ethical considerations about human connections, love, and death. Palahniuk's narrators are the least elaborated and most pathologized. But if he does not confront readers as realistically with harrowing traumatic material, it may be in the service of reaching a broader audience and providing a caustic if humorous social critique. Though some of these works yield greater psychological insights into their characters, they all in their own fashion underscore the key role of trauma in questioning and understanding profound issues of human suffering and inequality.

Notes

Introduction

1. See discussions of qualia as part of consciousness in Alan Palmer's *Fictional Minds*, Antonio Damasio's *The Feeling of What Happens*, Joseph Levin's "Qualia," and David Herman's *Story Logic*.

2. The study of the creative imagination by developmental psychologist Marjorie Taylor and colleagues Sarah Hodges and Adele Kohanyi found that writers scored higher than the norm on dimensions of empathy, feeling empathic concern for others, and feeling distress at others' suffering. Women writers tended to score higher than men. Writers' relations with their characters can be analogous to children creating imaginary companions, and the pursuit of writing "may cultivate novelist's role-taking skills and make them more habitually empathetic" (Keen 127). Writers were found to display dissociation, or a separation of mental processes from conscious awareness, as with intense daydreaming. Thus they can lead readers to "readily adopt other people's perspectives, and . . . revel in the imaginative worlds of fictional characters, fantasy and daydreams" (Taylor, Hodges, and Kohanyi 377).

3. Numerous studies of readers' responsiveness indicate that it is based on readers' own experience and identity, including their age, historical period, location in culture, knowledge, and ability to negotiate literary genres and conventions. These responses could be indicators for the acceptance of or familiarity with trauma texts, as the general cultural knowledge of PTSD and other psychological issues is common. Factors limiting a reader's comprehension or absorption of texts include prejudice, bias, impatience with a style of writing, or feeling pressured to finish. Some readers have greater understanding and emotional resources to draw from as they read, says Suzanne Keen in *Empathy and the Novel* (72).

1. Re-creating the Split Self in Margaret Atwood's *The Blind Assassin* and *Alias Grace*

1. Staels argues plausibly that Grace was sexually abused by her father, on the basis of a recurrent terrifying image of a man on the stairs that haunts Grace (436).

3. Obsessions and Possessions in William Faulkner's *Absalom, Absalom!*

1. *Absalom, Absalom!* demonstrates how trauma is passed down over the generations. Sutpen's traumas and their consequences determine the lives and fates of all his children (and grandchildren). Faulkner, in the book's title, suggests a connection to ancient father-son conflicts. As John Irwin writes, "This archetype of the brother who must kill to protect or avenge the honor of his sister pervades *Absalom, Absalom!* In the Old Testament (2 Sam. 13), Absalom, one of David's sons, kills his brother Amnon for raping their sister Tamar" (47). Like Absalom, Henry rebels against his father and ends up destroyed by him. "David's cry—the novel's title—is prompted not by Absalom's murder of Amnon . . . but by the later death of Absalom, the son who has risen up in rebellion against his father" (Sundquist 144).

2. There are many other versions of Faulkner's traumatized men: Sartoris in *Flags in the Dust*, Quentin Compson in *The Sound and the Fury*, and Jim Hightower in *Light in August*. Similarly, Faulkner's work features many silenced women, including Eula Varner in *The Hamlet*, Narcissa Benbow in *Flags in the Dust*, and Lena Grove and Hightower's wife in *Light in August*.

3. Hysteria is now viewed as an incomplete diagnosis, a historical concept, its symptoms characterized by somatic disorders (physical reactions related to psychological stress) and dissociation. The historical diagnosis has been discredited by modern psychology because it involved such an array of symptoms and was almost exclusively associated with women. It is now called histrionic personality (Reber 351).

4. The Traumas of Love and Death in Jeanette Winterson's *Written on the Body*

1. Many critics, including Susana Onega, argue that in eliminating gender or sex specifics, Winterson tries to universalize the conflicts and complexities of love. Brian Finney argues that readers should respect Winterson's presentation of the narrator as exhibiting both male and female characteristics (Onega 25).

2. Brian Finney also thinks Louise is already dead and the novel is some sort of elegy. Some evidence in the narrative leaves the possibility of her living still open—her family's not acknowledging her death, Gail's comments in the final scene, and the warmth of Louise's body—though these telltales could all be fictional constructions to throw readers off.

3. Winterson's challenges to heterosexism and gendered identities and sexuality have been explored by Ute Kauer, Andrea L. Harris, Susana Onega, Brian Finney, Leigh Gilmore, Jane Haslett, and Jennifer Hansen.

Bibliography

Abbott, H. Porter. *The Cambridge Introduction to Narrative*. Cambridge: Cambridge UP, 2008.
Alexander, Jeffrey C., Ron Eyerman, Bernhard Giesen, Neil J. Smelser, and Piotr Szompka. *Cultural Trauma and Collective Identity*. Berkeley: U of California P, 2004.
Ashcroft, Bill, Gareth Griffiths, and Helen Tiffin. *Key Concepts of Postcolonial Studies*. London: Routledge, 2001.
Atwood, Margaret. *Alias Grace*. New York: Random House, 1996.
———. "Author's Afterward." *Alias Grace*. New York: Random House, 1996, 461–65.
———. *The Blind Assassin*. New York: Doubleday, 2000.
———. *Cat's Eye*. New York: Anchor Books, 1988.
———. "In Search of Alias Grace." *American Historical Review* 103.5 (1998): 1503–16.
———. "Notes on Power Politics." *Acta Victoriana* 97.2 (1973): 7.
———. "Spotty-Handed Villainesses: Problems of Female Bad Behavior in the Creation of Literature." *Writing With Intent: Essays, Reviews, Personal Prose, 1983–2005*. New York: Carroll and Graf, 2005. 125–38.
Belluck, Pam. "For Better Social Skills, Scientists Recommend a Little Chekov." *New York Times*, October 3, 2013.
Blackford, Holly. "Haunted Housekeeping: Fatal Attractions of Servant and Mistress in Twentieth-Century Female Gothic Literature." *Literature Interpretation Theory* 16 (2005): 233–61.
Bouson, J. Brooks. "A Commemoration of Wounds Endured and Resented: Margaret Atwood's *The Blind Assassin* as Feminist Memoir." *Critique* 44.3 (Spring 2003): 251–69.
———. *Quiet As It's Kept: Shame, Trauma, and Race in the Novels of Toni Morrison*. Albany: SUNY P, 2000.
Bray Haddock, Deborah. *Dissociative Identity Disorder Sourcebook*. Chicago: Contemporary Books, 2001.
Brooks, Peter. *Reading for the Plot: Design and Intention in Narrative*. Cambridge, MA: U of Harvard P, 1984.
Brown, Laura S. "Not Outside the Range: One Feminist Perspective on Psychic Trauma." *Trauma: Explorations in Memory*. Ed. Cathy Caruth. Baltimore, MD: Johns Hopkins UP, 1995. 100–12.

Cantiello, Jessica Wells. "From Pre-racial to Post-racial? Reading and Reviewing *A Mercy* in the Age of Obama." *MELUS* 36.2 (Summer 2011): 165–83.
Caruth, Cathy. *Unclaimed Experience: Trauma, Narrative, and History*. Baltimore, MD: Johns Hopkins UP, 1996.
Cobb Moore, Geneva. "A Demonic Parody: Toni Morrison's *A Mercy*." *Southern Literary Journal* 44.1 (Fall 2011): 1–18.
Collado-Rodriguez, Francisco. *Chuck Palahniuk: Fight Club, Invisible Monsters, Choke*. London: Bloomsbury, 2013.
Comer Kidd, David, and Emanuele Costano. "Reading Literary Fiction Improves Theory of Mind." *Science* 324.6156 (2013): 377–80.
Cooke, Natalie. "The Politics of Ventriloquism: Margaret Atwood's Fictive Confessions." *Various Atwoods: Essays on the Later Poems, Short Fiction, and Novels*. Ed. Lorraine M. York. Concord, ON: Anansi, 1995. 207–28.
Crockett, Norman L. *The Black Towns*. Lawrence: Regents P of Kansas, 1979.
Damasio, Antonio. *The Feeling of What Happens: Body and Emotion in the Making of Consciousness*. San Diego: Harcourt, 1999.
Darroch, Heidi. "Hysteria and Traumatic Testimony: Margaret Atwood's *Alias Grace*." *Essays on Canadian Writing* 81 (Winter 2004): 103–21.
de Vries, Marten W. "Trauma in Cultural Perspective." Van der Kolk, McFarlane, and Weisaeth 398–413.
Donaldson, Susan V. "Subverting History: Women, Narrative and Patriarchy in *Absalom, Absalom!*" *Southern Quarterly* 26.4 (1988): 19–32.
Edwards, Justin D. *Gothic Canada: Reading the Spectre of a National Literature*. Edmonton: U of Alberta P, 2005.
Ellam, Julie. *Love in Jeanette Winterson's Novels*. Amsterdam: Rodopi, 2010.
Emmott, Catherine. "'Split Selves' in Fiction and in 'Medical Life Stories': Cognitive Linguistic Theory and Narrative Practice." *Cognitive Stylistics: Language and Cognition in Text Analysis*. Ed. Jonathan Culpepper. Amsterdam: John Benjamins, 2002. 153–81.
Erikson, Kai. "Notes on Trauma and Community." *American Imago* 48.4 (1991): 455–71.
Evans, Dylan. *Emotion: A Very Short Introduction*. Oxford: Oxford UP, 2003.
Faulkner, William. *Absalom, Absalom!* New York: Vintage, 1990.
Favazza, Armando R. *Bodies under Siege: Self-Mutilation and Body Modification in Culture and Psychiatry*. Baltimore, MD: Johns Hopkins UP, 1996.
Felman, Shoshana, and Dori Laub. *Testimony: Crises of Witnessing in Literature, Psychoanalysis, and History*. New York: Routledge, 1991.
Finney, Brian. "Bonded by Language: Jeanette Winterson's *Written on the Body*. *Women and Language* 25.2 (Fall 2002): 23–31.
Fludernik, Monica. *Towards a "Natural" Narratology*. London: Routledge, 1996.
Foner, Eric. "Black Life during Reconstruction." *Major Problems in the History of the American South*. Vol. 1. *The Old South*. Ed. Paul D. Escott, David R. Goldfield, Sally G. McMillen, and Elizabeth Hayes Turner. 2nd rev. ed. Boston: Houghton Mifflin, 1999. 421–30.
George, Sean M. "The Phoenix Inverted: The Rebirth and Death of Masculinity and the Reemergence of Trauma in Contemporary American Literature." Diss. Texas A&M U, 2010.

Gerrig, Richard J. *Experiencing Narrative Worlds: On the Psychological Activities of Reading.* New Haven, CT: Yale UP, 1993.

Gilmore, Leigh. *The Limits of Autobiography: Trauma and Testimony.* Ithaca, NY: Cornell UP, 2001.

Gold, Steven N. "Fight Club: A Depiction of Contemporary Society as Dissociogenic." *Journal of Trauma and Dissociation* 5.2 (2003): 13–34.

Gwin, Minrose. *The Feminine and Faulkner.* Knoxville: U of Tennessee P, 1990.

———. "The Silencing of Rosa Coldfield." Hobson 151–87.

Hakemulder, Jemeljan. *The Moral Laboratory: Experiments Examining the Effects of Reading Literature on Social Perception and Moral Self-Concept.* Utrecht Publication in General and Comparative Literature 34. Amsterdam: John Benjamins, 2000.

Hansen, Jennifer. "*Written on the Body*, Written by the Senses." *Philosophy and Literature* 29 (2005): 365–78.

Harris, Andrea L. *Other Sexes: Rewriting Difference from Woolf to Winterson.* Albany: SUNY P, 2000.

Hartman, Geoffrey H. "On Traumatic Knowledge and Literary Studies." *New Literary History* 26 (1995): 537–63.

———. "Public Memory and Its Discontents." *Raritan: A Quarterly Review* 13.4 (Spring 1994): 24–40.

Haslett, Jane. "Winterson's Fantastic Bodies." *Jeanette Winterson: A Contemporary Critical Guide.* London: Continuum, 2007. 41–54.

Henke, Suzette. *Post-Traumatic Fiction: Gender and Mourning in Woolf, Joyce and Lawrence.* New York: Palgrave-Macmillan. Forthcoming.

———. *Shattered Subjects: Trauma and Testimony in Women's Life-Writing.* New York: St. Martin's P, 1998.

Herman, David. *Basic Elements of Narrative.* West Sussex, UK: Wiley-Blackwell, 2009.

———. "Cognition, Emotion and Consciousness." *Cambridge Companion to Narrative.* Ed. D. Herman. Cambridge: Cambridge UP, 2007. 245–59.

———. "The Nexus of Narrative and Mind." *Basic Elements of Narrative.* Ed. David Herman. West Sussex, UK: Wiley-Blackwell, 2009. 137–60.

———. "Stories as a Tool for Thinking." *Narrative Theory and the Cognitive Sciences.* Ed. David Herman. Stanford, CA: Center for the Study of Language and information Publications, 2003. 163–92.

———. *Story Logic: Problems and Possibilities of Narrative.* Lincoln: U of Nebraska P, 2002.

Herman, Judith. *Trauma and Recovery.* New York: Basic Books, 1992.

Hobson, Fred, ed. *William Faulkner's Absalom, Absalom! A Casebook.* Oxford: Oxford UP, 2003

Hoffmann, Gerhard. *From Modernism to Postmodernism: Concepts and Strategies of Postmodern American Fiction.* Amsterdam: Rodopi, 2005.

Honneth, Axel. "Personal Identity and Disrespect: The Violation of the Body, the Denial of Rights, and the Denigration of Ways of Life." *The Struggle for Recognition: The Moral Grammar of Social Conflicts.* Cambridge: Polity Press, 1995. 131–39.

———. "Recognition and Moral Obligation." *Social Research* 64.1 (Spring 1997): 16–35.

Irwin, John. "Repetition and Revenge." Hobson 47–67.
Jaffe Schreiber, Evelyn. *Race, Trauma and Home in the Novels of Toni Morrison.* Baton Rouge: Louisiana State UP, 2010.
Jahn, Manfred. "Focalization." *The Cambridge Companion to Narrative.* Ed. David Herman. Cambridge: Cambridge UP, 2007. 94–108.
Janoff-Bulman, Ronnie. *Shattered Assumptions: Toward a New Psychology of Trauma.* New York: Free Press, 1992.
Jordan, Don, and Michael Walsh. *White Cargo: The Forgotten History of Britain's White Slaves in America.* New York: New York UP, 2007.
Kauer, Ute. "Narration and Gender: The Role of the First-Person Narrator in Jeanette Winterson's *Written on the Body.*" *I'm Telling You Stories: Jeanette Winterson and the Politics of Reading.* Ed. Helena Crice and Tim Woods. Atlanta: Rodopi, 1998. 41–51.
Kavadlo, Jesse. "The Fiction of Self-Destruction: Chuck Palahniuk, Closet Moralist." *Stirrings Still: The International Journal of Existential Literature* 2.2 (Fall/Winter 2005): 3–24.
Kavanagh, Matt. "On Failed Romance, Writer's Malpractice, and Prose for the Nose: A Conversation with Chuck Palahniuk." *Sacred and Immoral: On the Writings of Chuck Palahniuk.* Ed. Jeffrey A. Sartain. Newcastle upon Tyne: Cambridge Scholars, 2009. 178–92.
Keane, Terence M., Brian P. Marx, and Denise M. Sloan. "Post-Traumatic Stress Disorder: Definition, Prevalence, and Risk Factors." *Post-Traumatic Stress Disorder: Basic Science and Clinical Practice.* Ed. Priyattam J. Shiromani, Terence M. Keane, and Joseph E. LeDoux. New York: Humana P, 2009. 1–19.
Keen, Suzanne. *Empathy and the Novel.* Oxford: Oxford UP, 2007.
Kinney, Arthur F. *Critical Essays on William Faulkner: The Sutpen Family.* New York: G. K. Hall, 1996.
Knelman, Judith. "Can We Believe What the Newspapers Tell Us? Missing Links in *Alias Grace.*" *University of Toronto Quarterly* 68.2 (Spring 1999): 677–86.
Krumholz, Linda J. "Reading and Insight in Toni Morrison's *Paradise. African American Review* 36.1 (Spring 2002): 21–34.
LaCapra, Dominick. *Writing History, Writing Trauma.* Baltimore, MD: Johns Hopkins UP, 2001.
Langer, Lawrence. *Holocaust Testimonies: The Ruins of Memory.* New Haven, CT: Yale UP, 1991.
Laub, Dori, and Nanette C. Auerhahn. "Knowing and Not Knowing Massive Psychic Trauma: Forms of Traumatic Memory." *International Journal of Psychoanalysis* 74.2 (1993): 287–302.
Lepore, Stephen J., and Joshua M. Smyth, eds. *The Writing Cure: How Expressive Writing Promotes Health and Emotional Well-Being.* Washington, DC: American Psychological Association, 2002.
Levin, J. "Qualia." *The MIT Encyclopedia of the Cognitive Sciences.* Ed. R. A. Wilson and F. C. Keil. Cambridge, MA: MIT P, 1999. 693–94.
Levy, Robert I. "Emotion, Knowing, and Culture." *Culture Theory: Essays on Mind, Self and Emotion.* Ed. Richard A. Shweder and Robert A. LeVine. London: Cambridge UP, 1984. 214–37.

Lifton, Robert J. "Understanding the Traumatized Self." *Human Adaptation to Extreme Trauma*. Ed. John P. Wilson, Zev Harel, and Boaz Kahana. New York: Plenum P, 1988.

Lizardo, Omar. "Fight Club, or the Cultural Contradictions of Late Capitalism." *Journal for Cultural Research* 11.3 (July 2007): 221–43.

Lodge, David. *Consciousness and the Novel*. Cambridge, MA: Harvard UP, 2002.

MacCurdy, Marian M. *The Mind's Eye: Image and Memory in Writing About Trauma*. Amherst: U of Massachusetts P, 2007.

Marouan, Maha. "Candomblé, Christianity and Gnosticism in Toni Morrison's *Paradise*." *The African Diaspora and the Study of Religion*. Ed. Theodore Louis Trost. New York: Palgrave Macmillan, 2007, 111–30.

Mathews, John T. *William Faulkner: Seeing through the South*. Malden, MA: Wiley-Blackwell, 2009.

McNally, Richard J. *Remembering Trauma*. Cambridge, MA: Belknap P of Harvard UP, 2005.

McFarlane, Alexander C., and Bessel A. Van der Kolk. "Trauma and Its Challenge to Society." *Traumatic Stress*. Ed. Bessel A. Van der Kolk, Alexander C. McFarlane, and Lars Weisaeth. New York: Guilford P, 2007. 24–46.

Mendieta, Eduardo. "Surviving American Culture: On Chuck Palahniuk." *Philosophy and Literature* 29.2 (Oct. 2005): 394–408.

Michael, Magali Cornier. "Rethinking History as Patchwork: The Case of Atwood's *Alias Grace*." *Modern Fiction Studies* 47.2 (Summer 2001): 421–47.

Mischel, Walter. "Toward a Cognitive Social Learning Reconceptualization Personality." *Psychological Review* 80.4 (1973): 252–83.

Morrison, Toni. *The Bluest Eye*. New York: Washington Square, 1970.

———. "The 'Foreigner's Home': Introduction." Lecture. Paris, November 6, 2006.

———. *A Mercy*. New York: Knopf, 2008.

———. *Paradise*. New York: Knopf, 1998.

Nader, Kathleen O. "Childhood Trauma: The Deeper Wound." *The Posttraumatic Self: Restoring Meaning and Wholeness to Personality*. Ed. John P. Wilson. London: Routledge, 2006. 117–56.

Nunning, Ansgar F. "Reconceptualizing Unreliable Narration: Synthesizing Cognitive and Rhetorical Approaches." *A Companion to Narrative Theory*. Ed. James Phelan and Peter J. Rabinowitz. Malden, MA: Blackwell, 2005. 89–107.

Oatley, Keith, and Jennifer M. Jenkins. *Understanding Emotions*. Malden, MA: Blackwell, 1996.

Onega, Susana. *Jeanette Winterson*. Manchester: Manchester UP, 2006.

Palahniuk, Chuck. "Afterword." *Fight Club*. By Chuck Palahniuk. New York: Norton, 1996. 209–18.

———. *Fight Club*. New York: Norton, 1996.

———. Interview with Matt Kavanagh. *Sacred and Immoral: On the Writings of Chuck Palahniuk*. Ed. Jeffrey A. Sartain. Newcastle upon Tyne: Cambridge Scholars, 2009. 179–92.

———. *Invisible Monsters*. New York: Norton, 1999.

Palmer, Alan. *Fictional Minds*. Lincoln: U of Nebraska P, 2004.

Phelan, James. *Living to Tell about It: A Rhetoric and Ethics of Character Narration*. Ithaca, NY: Cornell UP, 2005.

Porter, Carolyn. "The Significance of Thomas Sutpen." Kinney 151–55.
Preston, Mary Elizabeth. "Homodiegetic Narration: Reliability, Self-consciousness, Ideology, and Ethics." Diss. Ohio State U, 1997.
Read, Andrew. "As if word magic had anything to do with the courage it took to be a man": Black Masculinity in Toni Morrison's *Paradise*." *African-American Review* 39.4 (Winter 2005): 527–40.
Reber, Arthur S., ed. *Dictionary of Psychology*. London: Penguin, 1995.
Roberts, Diane. *Faulkner and Southern Womanhood*. Athens: U of Georgia P, 1994.
Rogeron, Margaret. "Reading the Patchworks in *Alias Grace*." *Journal of Commonwealth Literature* 33.5 (1998): 5–22.
Romero, Channette. "Creating the Beloved Community: Religion, Race, and Nation in Toni Morrison's *Paradise*. *African American Review* 39.3 (Fall 2005): 415–30.
Root, Maria P. P. "Reconstructing the Impact of Trauma on Personality." *Personality and Psychopathology: Feminist Reappraisals*. Ed. Laura S. Brown and Mary Ballou. New York: Guilford P, 1992. 229–65.
Rosenblatt, Louise. "The Transactional Theory of Reading and Writing." *Making Meaning with Texts: Selected Essays*. Portsmouth, NH: Heinemann, 2005. 1–37.
Searle, John. *The Rediscovery of the Mind*. Cambridge, MA: MIT P, 1992.
Scheff, Thomas J., and Suzanne M. Retzinger. *Emotions and Violence: Shame and Rage in Destructive Conflicts*. Lexington, MA: Lexington Books, 1991.
Shweder, Richard A. "Cultural Psychology." *The MIT Encyclopedia of the Cognitive Sciences (MITECS)*. Ed. Robert A. Wilson and Frank C. Keil. Cambridge, MA: MIT P, 1999. 211–13.
Smiley, Jane. *A Thousand Acres*. New York: Anchor Books, 1991.
Smith, B. C. "Situatedness." *MITECS* 769.
Stannard, David E. *American Holocaust*. New York: Oxford UP, 1992.
Staels, Hilde. "Intertexts of Margaret Atwood's *Alias Grace*. *Modern Fiction Studies* 46.2 (Summer 2000): 427–50.
Strehle, Susan. "I Am a Thing Apart": Tony Morrison, *A Mercy*, and American Exceptionalism." *Critique: Studies in Contemporary Fiction* 54.2 (2013): 109–23.
Strobel, Woodrow. "A Brief for Thomas Sutpen." Kinney 162–69.
Strongman, K. T. *The Psychology of Emotion: Theories of Emotion in Perspective*. Chichester: John Wiley and Sons, 1996.
Sundquist, Eric. "*Absalom, Absalom!* and the House Divided." Hobson 107–49.
Tal, Kali. *Worlds of Hurt: Reading the Literatures of Trauma*. Cambridge: Cambridge UP, 1996.
Taylor, Marjorie, Sara D. Hodges, and Adele Kohanyi. "The Illusion of Independent Agency: Do Adult Fiction Writers Experience Their Characters As Having Minds of Their Own?" *Imagination, Cognition and Personality* 22.4 (2002–2003): 361–80.
Urgo, Joseph R., and Noel Polk. *Reading Faulkner: Absalom, Absalom! Glossary and Commentary*. Jackson: UP of Mississippi, 2010.
Van der Kolk, Bessel A. "Complexity of Adaptation to Trauma." *Traumatic Stress*. Ed. Bessel A. Van der Kolk, Alexander C. McFarlane, and Lars Weisaeth. New York: Guilford P, 2007. 182–213.

Van der Kolk, Bessel A., and C. R. Ducey. "The Psychological Processing of Traumatic Experience: Rorschach Patterns in PTSD." *Journal of Traumatic Stress* 2 (1989): 259–74.

Van der Kolk, Bessel A., and Alexander C. McFarlane. "The Black Hole of Trauma." Van der Kolk, McFarlane, and Weisaeth 3–23.

Van der Kolk, Bessel A., Alexander C. McFarlane, and Lars Weisaeth. *Traumatic Stress: The Effects of Overwhelming Experience on Mind, Body, and Society.* New York: Guilford P, 2007.

Van der Kolk, Bessel A., and Onno Van der Hart. "The Intrusive Past: The Flexibility of Memory and the Engraving of Trauma." *American Imago* 48.4 (1991): 425–54.

Varsava, Jerry A. *Contingent Meanings: Postmodern Fiction, Mimesis, and the Reader.* Tallahassee: Florida State UP, 1990.

Vickroy, Laurie. "Reading the Other: Love and Imagination in *Written on the Body*." *CEA Critic* 71.1 (Fall 2008): 12–26.

———. "Sexual Trauma, Ethics, and the Reader in the Works of Margaret Atwood." *Critical Insights: Margaret Atwood.* Ed. J. Brooks Bouson. Ipswich, MA: Salem P, 2012. 254–75.

———. *Trauma and Survival in Contemporary Fiction.* Charlottesville, VA: UP of Virginia, 2002.

———. "Voices of Survivors in Trauma Fiction." *Contemporary Approaches in Literary Trauma Theory.* Ed. Michelle Balaev, New York: Palgrave Macmillan, 2014. 130–50.

Viskovic, Richard, and Eluned Summers-Bremner. "The Opposite of a Miracle: Trauma in *Invisible Monsters*." *Chuck Palahniuk: Fight Club, Invisible Monsters, Choke.* Ed. Francisco Collado-Rodriguez. London: Bloomsbury, 2013. 97–115.

Wagner-Martin, Linda. "Rosa Coldfield as Daughter: Another of Faulkner's Lost Children." Kinney 227–38.

White, Hayden. *The Content of the Form: Narrative Discourse and Historical Representation.* Baltimore, MD: Johns Hopkins UP, 1987.

Widdowson, Peter. "The American Dream Refashioned: History, Politics and Gender in Toni Morrison's *Paradise. Journal of American Studies* 35.2 (2001): 313–35.

Winterson, Jeanette. "Imagination and Reality." *Art Objects: Essays on Ecstasy and Effrontery.* New York: Vintage, 1995. 133–51.

———. *Why Be Happy When You Could Be Normal?* New York: Grove P, 2011.

———. *Written on the Body.* New York: Vintage International, 1992.

Woodward, C. Vann. *The Burden of Southern History.* Baton Rouge: Louisiana State UP, 1960.

Wyatt, Jean. "Failed Messages, Maternal Loss, and Narrative Form in Toni Morrison's *A Mercy*." *Modern Fiction Studies* 58.1 (Spring 2012): 128–51.

Index

Absalom, Absalom! (Faulkner), 22–23, 24–25, 100–131
African American history, 67, 75
Alexander, Jeffrey, 77
Alias Grace (Atwood), 10, 13, 22, 37–38, 49–60, 62–63; and ethics, 59–60, 62–63, 64; and quilting, 58–59
Ashcroft, Bill, 17
Atwood, Margaret, 33–34; *Alias Grace*, 10, 13, 22, 37–38, 49–60, 62–63; *The Blind Assassin*, 19–20, 21–22, 25, 31, 38–39, 40–49; Canadian history, 36–40; *Cat's Eye*, 25; "In Search of *Alias Grace*," 39; "Notes on Power Politics," 38, 48–49; and power, 33, 48–49; "Spotty-Handed Villianesses," 64

Beloved (Morrison), 63–64, 86
Blackford, Holly, 57–58
Blind Assassin, The (Atwood), 19–20, 21–22, 25, 31, 38–39, 40–49, 60–61; and ethics, 46–48, 60–61;
borderline personality, 158, 172–73
Bouson, J. Brooks, 42, 68, 73, 75, 76
Bray Haddock, Deborah, 52–53, 163, 164, 175
Brooks, Peter, 105, 127
Brown, Laura S., 7

Cantiello, Jessica Wells, 69
Caruth, Cathy, 7

Cobb-Moore, Geneva, 70
cognitive psychology, and narrative, 21, 22
Comer-Kidd, David, and Emanuele Costano, 2, 32, 179–80
commodification, 100, 101
Cooke, Natalie, 54
Crockett, Norman L., 68
cultural carriers of trauma, 77
culture and behavior, 17, 18

Damasio, Antonio, 6, 21
Darroch, Heidi, 56
denigration, and effects on personality, 12
de Vries, Marten, trauma and culture, 9
dissociative identity disorder, 163–64
Donaldson, Susan V., 129
dreams as depictions of trauma, 25, 44, 53–55

Edwards, Justin D., 51, 63
Ellam, Julie, 143, 144
Emmott, Catherine, 33
Erikson, Kai, 7
ethics: and narrative, 26–27, 29, 34; and trauma, 27–28
Evans, Dylan, 18

Faulkner, William: *Absalom, Absalom!*, 22–23, 24–25, 100–131; *Flags in the Dust*, 186; *The Hamlet*, 186;

Faulkner, William (continued)
    Light in August, 186; narrative strategies, 105–7; *The Sound and the Fury*, 106, 186
Favazza, Armando R., 52, 163, 175
Felman, Shoshana, and Dori Laub, 106
Fight Club (Palahnuik), xiii–xiv, 13, 154–55, 156, 157, 158, 159–70, 172, 177, 178
Finney, Brian, 186
Fludernik, Monica, 24
Foner, Eric, 69

gender and misrecognition, 72–73, 105, 114–15, 116–18, 123
George, Sean M., 162
Gerrig, Richard J., 16–17, 28, 34
Gilmore, Leigh, 138, 186
Gold, Steven N., 161, 166, 168
gothic novel, and *Alias Grace*, 57
Gwin, Minrose, 105, 111, 116–17, 122, 123, 124, 125, 128

Hakemulder, Jemeljan, 31
Hansen, Jennifer, 186
Harris, Andrea L., 186
Hartman, Geoffrey H., 14, 36, 164
Haslett, Jane, 186
Henke, Suzette, 16, 102
Herman, David: on framing, 31; on narrative and readers, 26, 34, 145; on stories as mental models, 26
Herman, Judith, 6, 8, 16, 41, 53, 135, 144, 163, 167
Hoffmann, Gerhard, 4–5
Honneth, Axel: on denial of recognition as traumatic, 11–12, 70, 101, 171, 181; on forms of denigration, 12, 88; on recognition and the relation to self and society, 12

Invisible Monsters (Palahnuik), xiii–xiv, 154, 155, 156–57, 158, 170–78
Irwin, John, 108, 109, 111, 186

Jaffe Schreiber, Evelyn, 87, 90, 93
Jahn, Manfred, 35

Janoff-Bulman, Ronnie, 5–6, 10, 158
Jazz (Morrison), 87
Jordan, Don, and Michael Walsh, 70

Kauer, Ute, 186
Kavadlo, Jesse, 160, 167
Kavanagh, Matt, 164
Keane, Terence M., 7
Keen, Suzanne, on reader empathy, 17, 18, 30, 31, 32, 34
Knelman, Judith, 37
Krumholz, Linda J., 68, 81, 86–87

LaCapra, Dominick, 19
Langer, Lawrence, 134, 157
Laub, Dori, and Nanette C. Auerhahn, on trauma and memory, 41, 72, 157
Lepore, Stephen J., and Joshua M. Smyth, on writing and self-perceptions, 14
Levy, Robert I., 17
Lifton, Robert J., 134, 138, 146, 148–49, 157
literature, historical and memorial value of, 36–37, 68
Lizardo, Omar, 161
Lodge, David, 23

MacCurdy, Marian M., on writing and therapeutic effects, 9, 14
Marks, Grace (basis for *Alias Grace*), 39
Marouan, Maha, 81
masculinity, 97, 101, 103, 125
Mathews, John T., 100, 103, 114, 123, 126, 128, 129
McNally, Richard J., on trauma and memory, 8
McFarlane, Alexander C.: on trauma and culture, 9; on trauma and defenses, 41; on trauma and shame, 45–47
Mendieta, Eduardo, 175
Mercy, A (Morrison), 66, 69–70, 87–99
Michael, Magali Cornier, 58–59
Mischel, Walter, on learning theory, 9, 18–19

modernist texts, psychology and trauma in, 2–3, 102
Morrison, Toni, 66–72; *Beloved*, 63–64, 95–96; *The Bluest Eye*, 69, 71; commodification, 88; European domination, 88; "The 'Foreigner's Home,'" 87; *Jazz*, 87; *A Mercy*, 66, 69–70, 87–99; narrative techniques, 71–72; *Paradise*, 2–3, 20, 22, 23–24, 72–87, 126; and religious intolerance, 88–89, 97–98; and slavery, 87, 88, 89–90, 95, 96

Nader, Kathleen O., 141, 144
narcissism and failed recognition, 12–13
narrative theory, x, 20–21, 22, 24; and ethics, 26–32; narrative and readers' emotions, 16, 34; narrative strategies and trauma, x, xi, 1–6, 35
narrative techniques: duration, 103–4; focalization, 3, 23, 26, 41, 104; frequency, 103–4; narrator perspectives, 35–36, 41, 105–7, 127–28; qualia, 24–25, 55–56; thought reports, 51; unreliable narrators, 35–36, 47–48, 133, 183
novel, the, and individual psychology, 2–3
Nunning, Ansgar F., 21

Oatley, Keith, and Jennifer M. Jenkins, on storytelling and emotions, 14, 16
Onega, Susana, 186
Oranges Are Not the Only Fruit (Winterson), 133, 134

Palahniuk, Chuck: afterword to *Fight Club*, 13, 170; borderline personality and lack of identity, 172–73; capitalism, 159; and ethics, 176–78; existential questions, 177–78; *Fight Club*, xiii–xiv, 13, 154–55, 156, 157, 158, 159–70, 172, 177, 178; Kavanaugh interview, 298; *Invisible Monsters*, xiii–xiv, 154, 155, 156–57, 158, 170–78; male and female trauma, 155; masculine body, 165, 166; masculinity, 165, 166; as postmodern, 154, 155–56, 177–78; self-wounding, 163, 166, 175
Palmer, Alan, 22, 35, 51
Paradise (Morrison), 2–3, 20, 22, 23–24, 72–87, 126
Phelan, James, 27, 61–62, 126
Porter, Carolyn, 100
postcolonial views of culture and behavior, 17
postmodernism and trauma fiction, 3–5, 157–58
post-traumatic stress disorder (PTSD), and gender, 7, 15
Preston, Mary Elizabeth, 143, 147
psychoanalysis, x
psychological effects of coercion, 41
psychological research versus psychoanalysis, x, 15–16; culture and behavior, 17–18
psychology of fear, 66, 97–98

racism, psychological effects of, 73; internalized, 74–75, 83–84, 100–101, 113; racial trauma, 102, 113; and social class divisions, 108
Read, Andrew, 67, 69
readers: and empathy, 26–28; and ethics, 182; and narrative engagement, 26–32
Roberts, Diane, 112, 113, 114, 115
Rogeron, Margaret, 58
Root, Maria P. P.: community defenses against trauma, 10; coping with trauma, 9; dimensions of security, 11; effects of trauma on personality, 9–11, 80; insidious trauma, 9–10, 49, 109; and social disconnections, 74; victims' lack of empathy, 76, 141; survival state, 34, 48, 75, 79, 158, 164
Rosenblatt, Louise, 3, 28–30

Searle, John, 21
Scheff, Thomas J., and Suzanne M. Retzinger, 160

Shweder, Richard A., 18
Smiley, Jane, *A Thousand Acres*, 19, 31
Smith, B. C., 22
social class divisions, 108
Stannard, David E., 70
Staels, Hilde, 52, 54
Strehle, Susan, 68, 95, 99; on exceptionalist culture, 94
Strobel, Woodrow, 116, 123
Strongman, K. T., 17
Sundquist, Eric, 111–12, 186

Taylor, Marjorie, 30, 185
theory of mind, 23
Thousand Acres, A (Smiley), 19, 31
trauma, psychological: and cognition and emotion, 23; and commodification, 6; conflation of past and present, 56, 103–4; contexts of, ix, xi, 1–2, 6; cultural trauma, 102; and defenses, 24, 41, 81–82, 133, 139–40, 162, 164, 168; definition, 6–9; dialectical experience of, 33, 41, 135; dissociative identity disorder, 52–53, 163–64; dissociative state, 161; effects on personality, xii, 5–6, 26, 91–92, 101–2, 110–11, 135, 157–58, 165; and ethics, 26–28, 71–72, 147–53; and gender, 118, 155; generational, 112–13; interdisciplinary inquiries of, 15; and memory, 121–22; normalizing ideologies and, 15; and oppression, 96; post-traumatic stress disorder, and gender, 7, 15; and shame, 84, 110–11, 160–61; and silence, 106, 128; social effects, 101, 109, 123; survival state, 34, 48, 75, 79, 158, 164; symptoms, 6–7, 9–11
trauma fiction: definition, 1–2; depiction of traumatic experience, 25–26; depiction of traumatic processes and personality, 14, 25, 26, 33–34, 41, 81–82, 84; dissociative state, 55–56, 57; ethics, x, xi–xii, 29–31, 80, 86–87, 126–31, 176–78, 179–80; ethics and reading, 182, 183; fear, 120; reader engagement and effects, 5–6, 18, 19, 66–67, 73–74, 78; split consciousness, 50; visual imagery and trauma, 54–56; working through trauma, 81; social injustice, ix, xi, 7, 9–10, 181; value of trauma-based interpretation, 1–2

Urgo, Joseph R., and Noel Polk, 116

Van der Kolk, Bessel A., 8, 161; on trauma and culture, 9; on trauma and defenses, 41; on trauma and repetition, 7, 44; on trauma and shame, 45–47
Van der Hart, Onno, on trauma and repetition, 7, 44
Varsava, Jerry A., 4
Vickroy, Laurie, xi, 1, 67, 69, 106, 130, 137, 157, 179
Viskovic, Richard, and Eluned Summers-Bremner, 172

Wagner Martin, Linda, 118, 123
White, Hayden, 36–37, 68, 181
Widdowson, Peter, 67, 69
Winterson, Jeanette: death as trauma, 138–41; illness, the body, and death, 142–47; "Imagination and Reality," 143, 144; love as trauma, 136–38; *Oranges Are Not the Only Fruit*, 133, 134; as postmodern writer, 133–34, 136; *Why Be Happy When You Could Be Normal*, 135, 152–53; *Written on the Body*, 13, 25, 132–53
Woodward, C. Vann, 101
writing and therapeutic effects, 14
Written on the Body (Winterson), 13, 25, 132–53
Wyatt, Jean, 92, 94

www.ingramcontent.com/pod-product-compliance
Lightning Source LLC
Chambersburg PA
CBHW021809220426
43662CB00006B/246